WORKING

WISDOM

WORKING

The Ultimate Value in the New Economy

WISDOM

JOHN DALLA COSTA

Published in 1995 by
Stoddart Publishing Co. Limited
34 Lesmill Road
Toronto, Canada
M3B 2T6

Tel. (416) 445-3333
Fax (416) 445-5967

Stoddart Books are available for bulk purchase for sales
promotions, premiums, fundraising, and seminars. For
details, contact the Special Sales Department
at the above address.

Canadian Cataloguing in Publication Data

Dalla Costa, John

Working wisdom

ISBN 0-7737-2918-6

1. Success in business.   2. Wisdom.   I. Title.
HF5386.D35 1995   650.1   C95-931329-X

Cover Design: Bill Douglas at The Bang
Typesetting: Tony Gordon/Image One Productions Ltd.
Printed and bound in Canada

*Stoddart Publishing gratefully acknowledges the support of
the Canada Council, the Ontario Ministry of Citizenship, Culture
and Recreation, Ontario Arts Council, and Ontario
Publishing Centre in the development of writing and
publishing in Canada.*

To my mother, Gemma, who taught me to believe.
To my father, Arturo, who taught me to drive.

We trained hard — but it seemed that every time we were beginning to form into teams, we would be reorganized. I was to learn later in life that we tend to meet any new situation by reorganizing. And, what a wonderful method it can be for creating the illusion of progress while producing inefficiency, confusion and demoralization.

— Gaius Petronius Arbiter
1st Century AD

Contents

Preface

Out of this world of rapid and incessant change, we have come to expect instant insight and immediate reward from those offering advice or solutions. Even though business affects the very fabric of society, and extracts the largest commitment of our time and energy, many of us have become somewhat facile consumers of the latest management dictum. We want answers, results, and action. Yet change has its own rhythm. And ideas borrowed from others rarely have the efficacy of our own. Most business people are realizing the limited applicability of borrowing concepts, and are now anxious to seek solutions that are less disposable and more enduring.

My quest for a deeper insight — for wisdom — has taken place primarily in my consulting work. I have applied, tested, and stretched the precepts of this book through my recent involvement with such companies as Molson Breweries, Bell Canada, General Mills, Ontario Hydro, the Canadian Imperial Bank of Commerce, Procter & Gamble, Mediacom, Alberta Government Telephone, and Midland Walwyn.

Because it is a notion that values something companies and individuals already have within themselves, this concept of wisdom has touched a nerve — and it receives more momentum, more validation, with each new wave of business learning. I am convinced that the appreciation of what is wise will only grow, particularly as issues become more complicated, as companies exhaust the outside supply of relevant, transforming ideas, and as individuals seek meaning and motivation in an economy that often makes them disposable and vulnerable.

The examination of wisdom is not an abstraction for me. I have run my own company, not once but twice. The first was a mid-sized advertising agency that, along with three other partners, I built up to include fifty employees. As CEO, I struggled with maintaining quality during a period of aggressive growth, and then with trying to resurrect momentum after a period of stagnation. The many mistakes along with the achievements have contributed to the lessons imbedded in this material.

My current enterprise is the single-person operation that is believed to be the prototype of the networked economy now emerging. Working one day from home and the next from within the boardrooms of some of the largest corporations in North America has sensitized me to the vagaries of serving as a virtual employee of a virtual company. The lessons, confusion, and hope from my exposure to both the changing world of the corporation and the trying world of the entrepreneur are distilled in the chapters that follow.

John Dalla Costa
Toronto, 1995

Acknowledgments

Many people have had a hand in creating *Working Wisdom*. My agents, Bruce Westwood and Carolyn Brunton, provided encouragement and enthusiasm throughout the process. The friendship they each extended beyond professional counsel helped give scope to the project when it was only an outline.

Jack Stoddart recognized the potential in this material, and gave it his full support. Having the commitment of such a publisher made it easier to take the risks that this topic required.

From Stoddart Publishing I received advice, suggestions, and a deep belief in the concept. Don Bastian, Angel Guerra, and Lynne Missen confirmed to me in every exchange that *Working Wisdom* had indeed found the right home.

Several people provided important input to the manuscript in progress. Alan Middleton took time away from his Ph.D. thesis to offer thoughtful counsel about the book's key concepts. Greg Ioannou provided helpful feedback on the first draft. And Marty Myers provided page-by-page suggestions for simplifying the writing and improving its clarity.

Two friends also volunteered to be a test market for the manuscript. With their perspective and comments, Darcia Joseph and James MacKinnon provided the voices of practicality, applicability, and bottom-line accountability.

The research for this book involved a series of interviews. Many very busy men and women whose comments appear in this text took the time to see me and provide their perspective on business. Roxanne Carmanico organized the letters, schedules, and follow-up that made the interviewing possible. And Sue Fenwick, in addition to providing transcripts, offered the questions and observations that emerged from her growing familiarity with the research material.

Domenic Santini shot my photo for the cover, although he did not know when he took the picture in Tuscany that it would be used for this. And Gerald Rich thoughtfully and patiently provided a fresh set of eyes to help with proofreading.

Lucinda Vardey, my wife, continuously gave her insight, understanding, and questioning to this project. Her faith provided assurance in times of uncertainty. Her business sense even provided the title for the book. And her own wisdom provided inspiration as well as comfort.

To each of these individuals I offer my deep gratitude.

Introduction

Getting Smarter
Without Getting Wiser

What would you do? At Air Canada, customer service representatives were recently given a seminar on empowerment. Each individual was encouraged to take full responsibility for the complete satisfaction of customers. Rather than process requests, representatives were invited to exercise discretion, to use their judgment to make each and every contact an opportunity for extending care and service. Here was that elusive win-win situation. Customers came first. Employees were more fulfilled. The juices of renewal began to flow.

But then Air Canada embarked on another renewal initiative.

Shortly after being told to put the customer first, sales representatives were introduced to new performance measures based on principles of reengineering. Against the new priorities of efficiency, sales representatives would henceforth be monitored on such dimensions as the time spent on each call, and the ratio of sales-to-calls. Self-conscious employees served customers while vigilant consultants stood by with stopwatches. The duty to serve the customer was not reversed, but that responsibility was now in a direct struggle with the productivity demands of a ticking clock.

What had happened? Well-meaning and indeed legitimate initiatives had collided. The empowered became the stressed. The served became a statistic. The goals became confusing. How comfortable can the representatives be investing the time to listen and respond intelligently to

1

customers when they are being evaluated by timelines, turnover, and a tally-sheet?

Air Canada may have stepped knee-deep into this contradiction, but it is obviously not alone. The question I am most often asked to resolve in my consulting practice is "Where do we go from here?" Despite adopting the concepts for "excellence," "quality," and "empowerment," despite buying into the principles for "teamwork," "learning," and "reengineering," many business people remain frustrated by the complexity of the issues they face, and many of their companies remain mired in unfulfilled potential.

Rather than look at the next "where," I have tried to understand the "why." From my vantage point, as I drop into offices big and small, the men and women involved in the drama of day-to-day decision-making are for the most part smart and sincere. They often have an appreciation and understanding for the need to change. And they have numerous models, processes, and case histories that are valid and current, for instance, Total Quality Management (TQM) and Just-In-Time (JIT) delivery. Still, many have experienced change as more traumatic than productive, more destructive than renewing.

Why? Why are so many business people at so many different career points both scared and cynical? Why are so many companies simultaneously smart and stupid? Why is the activity that preoccupies the major portion of our time and energy so devoid of meaning and joy?

In building my own business, and in my consulting work with numerous other companies, I have struggled personally and professionally with the gap between need and will. The issue of change — and genuine regeneration — requires going beyond the obvious logic of business analysis. A deeper insight must be found, a more generative motivation must be activated, to guide business in this time of transition. From this experience I have come to believe that organizations trying to reinvent themselves ultimately need that integrative, balancing, and persistent intuition known as wisdom.

Wisdom represents a pinnacle of human achievement, yet it is so rarely experienced that most of us tend to know and appreciate it only by its absence. Cultures throughout history and across the modern world share both a search and a respect for wisdom. It is one of those inherent capacities that defines our spirit as human beings. Yet we spend surprisingly little time or attention trying to understand and master it, so wisdom remains elusive in our personal lives and mostly irrelevant in our work.

Indeed, for a society and a global economy that worship at the altar of technology, wisdom is almost an anachronism. It reverts value to a distinctly human capability in a time when society ascribes the most value to the productivity and growth potential of hardware and software.

Wisdom is a combination of knowledge and experience, but it is more than just the sum of these parts. Wisdom involves the mind and the heart, logic and intuition, left brain and right brain, but it is more than either reason, or creativity, or even both. Wisdom involves a sense of balance, an equilibrium derived from a strong, pervasive *moral* conviction. This morality is not necessarily religious, although it may embrace spiritual practice and religion. Rather, it is the conviction and guidance provided by the obligations that flow from a profound sense of *interdependence*. In essence, wisdom grows through the learning of more knowledge, and the practical experience of day-to-day life — both filtered through a code of moral conviction.

The need for wisdom is painfully clear. As befits a high-tech and wired society, information is assumed to be power. With all the bits and bytes of data swirling on our planet, the collective view is that with enough brainpower, solutions to virtually any problem can be found. However, the complexity of our modern world and its disorienting pace of change are finally exhausting the limitations of this logic. The contradiction between service and efficiency, the displacement of a conventional career path, and the growing intrusion of work into personal life are some of the pressures unwinding faith in the supreme power of logic. As the messiness of modern life overpowers the rational capacity to manage it, there is a renewed, if indirect, appreciation of the gifts and perspective of the wise.

Despite the daunting complexity of modern life, business people are nevertheless impatient for the "bottom line." If wisdom is an asset, what is its return? In fact, why would wisdom necessarily have any value in the hyper-competitive world of products and services, and profit and loss?

To answer these questions I have had to ask some others.

- If companies are already so oriented to their customers, then how can one as smart, hip, and plugged-in as Intel still so severely underestimate the angst and angry reaction of the savvy buyers of its marginally flawed Pentium microchip?
- If quality is so ingrained as an imperative for global competitiveness, then how can Ford, one of quality's most dedicated advocates,

find itself having to recall almost a whole year's production of its exhaustively tested Windstar mini-van?

- If synergy is so strategically important, how can such patient and insightful companies as Sony and Matsushita ensnare themselves in the ego-trap of Hollywood studios?

And there are more questions.

- Most business people understand that value is increasingly created by knowledge, so why has it remained so difficult to create the already well-modeled and well-understood "learning" organization?
- If innovation is so important to renewal, why do so many companies struggle with creativity?
- Why are so many managers confused and dispirited?
- Why are so many employees discouraged, overworked, and fearful?
- Why do companies keep mortgaging the future for the short term?
- Why are consultants like me so busy?

What is often misinterpreted to be a reluctance to change is actually an exhaustion with change that is reactionary, superficial, and disconnected from the broader needs of human belonging, achievement, and growth. Within organizations, we keep trying to get smarter without taking the time to get wiser. We collect more facts, train more advanced skills, and organize around new titles, without fostering the inner clarity, conviction, and confidence that make the new processes practicable and fulfilling. The bottom line is that business today is inherently unpredictable, so much so that conventions no longer apply. In the chaos and confusion, the only real values we can rely on are our own good judgment, the compass of our inner beliefs, and the confidence that comes from a deep understanding of self.

Working Wisdom explores the need for wisdom and its application in business. Any inquiry into such a topic necessarily requires philosophical reflection. However, the test and real value of wisdom is only derived from its practice. Throughout the material, I have sought to balance the essence with the implementation, and the ideal with the reality. This means that for insight and perspective I have often drawn from the wisdom writings of Jewish, Buddhist, Christian, and Confucian sources — not the typical business bibliography. I have also included questions and suggestions to help individuals and organizations personalize and customize the lessons in the book. This two-sided exploration is important. Wisdom affords a context that brings both meaning and fulfillment. But it is also a capacity that can only be realized in the practice.

There are no shortcuts in this process. The inspiration and implementation are both critical. While often taxing, this very effort provides wisdom with its enduring value. This very effort deepens our capacity to deal with the accelerating changes in business.

I

WHY WISDOM NOW?

ONE

THE REHUMANIZING AFTER THE REENGINEERING

It used to be only the future that was unpredictable. Today even the present is uncertain. Opportunities are more fleeting, customers tend to be more fickle, and innovation realizes an ever shorter shelf life.

Dealing with this unpredictability has become a global problem. Large and small companies in North America, Japan, Korea, Italy, and the United Kingdom have lost their way — and their confidence. Old and proven approaches have become frayed and unproductive. Where competitiveness once required inventiveness in product design and production, it now requires inventing new ways of managing and motivating. Companies have valiantly tried to "think global and act local," or to "empower," "reengineer," and "innovate," but the prescriptions for these and other business goals have often created more ambiguity than they have resolved. The net result has been that a majority of companies have realized only a fraction of the benefits they sought.

James Champy, co-author of *Reengineering the Corporation*, admitted that the "revolution we started has gone, at best, only halfway." He has authored a sequel, *Reengineering Management*, advancing appreciation for the importance of shared beliefs and values. While representing some progress, the whole concept is basically flawed because the very metaphor of engineering for renewal is inappropriate. Organizations that derive their models for change from machinery, computers, and systems will inevitably miss the importance of human comprehension, self-reflection, and insight. Revitalization hinges on rehumanizing the practice of business, not reengineering it.

Change-Fatigue

I have spent the last four years doing strategic and organizational consulting for a variety of companies. Several had been through at least three restructurings in the last five years. As part of my preparation for these assignments, I usually audit a small group of employees from a cross-section of disciplines and departments. In the course of this work I found that one of my most basic assumptions about corporate change was wrong.

Like many people involved in planning or managing change, I had assumed that the principal barrier to effective change was resistance. Creatures of habit resort to familiar patterns, especially when change is of a threatening variety. Or so goes the orthodoxy of change management. In fact, the problem in many instances is not *change-resistance* but *change-fatigue*.

Most people have already survived several waves of cutbacks, so they know from harsh experience that old ways of operating are no longer viable. Habits have been broken. Attitudes have perhaps taken longer to shift, but the majority of workers now understand that change is imperative. However, understanding that change is necessary does not mean that people actually have the energy and personal resources to act upon it.

As I met more people and did work for other companies, I began to recognize the more obvious symptoms of change-fatigue. These include:

- Employees read the new corporate mission, attend its launch meeting, or see the explanatory video, and still walk away lethargic, uninspired, or even ashen. In subsequent meetings they will say things like: "We need to wait until the mission is worked out."
- Throughout the company individuals use the language of change like real pros, with the facility of the consultant who introduced it into the corporate culture, but without meaning a word of it. It is not for lack of trying. They have mastered the vocabulary because they know it is important, but no one was there to help them through the mess of implementation, so for the sake of getting things done they resort to old practices.

- People are convinced that there is another "shoe to drop." While committed to making the new practices work, they quite naturally deflect a lot of attention and hallway discussion to speculation about what will come next. Beneath the anxiety of change is the greater anxiety of dispensability.
- Senior management and employees come to value the opinion of an outside change specialist more than any opinion generated internally. This continuous seeking of a second opinion is perhaps the most telling symptom of change-fatigue because it suggests an exhaustion of judgment.

Change-fatigue is more than the organizational equivalent of yuppie flu. It occurs when employees are expected to absorb new stimulus and direction before they have fully understood a previous wave of change. Many companies have rushed through implementation of programs for total quality, and then moved to actualize empowerment, and then reconfigured again for reengineering. Each initiative was seen as a total solution, yet the benefits were harder to realize and more elusive than management had planned. Rather than sort out why quality programs failed at a majority of companies, or why empowerment never delivered the impassioned performance it promised, companies simply moved on to the next model for renewal and regeneration. Change-fatigue is not the result of too much change, but of too much mismanagement of change.

Bill Etherington, until recently the CEO of IBM Canada, and now promoted as one of Louis Gerstner's executives running IBM North America, explained in an interview: "Change is not an option . . . accelerating change is the harsh reality affecting all businesses and all employees." What used to be the exception is now the norm.

And this is exactly the point: when change was an infrequent aberration, everyone accepted the temporary suspension of obligation that was needed to accommodate fixing a problem or averting a crisis. Now that the norm is flux, obligations are in perpetual suspension. Employees in particular never have time to settle down, to recreate the needed networks of trust. Confidence is continuously shaken. It is not change itself that is so draining, but the fact that so much of it is proceeding without support, reciprocity, or context. The full human ramifications of change need to be acknowledged.

One year after a significant restructuring, a large multinational company asked me to help complete the implementation of new practices that had been introduced the previous year. On the surface, progress had been significant. Fewer people were, in fact, doing more work. But morale was low, and the momentum for change, the belief in the new way, seemed to be stalling. Here is what employees told me when I asked them for their view of where they were:

- "I don't know what I'm supposed to do anymore."
- "Obviously what I was good at is no longer good enough."
- "I am doing what I'm told to do, but I see all the empty offices in my section and wonder whether the people who are leading this company have any sense of where they're going."
- "In our group, this is the fourth restructuring in five years. Every one of those changes had a big rationale. So which one are we supposed to believe? Which is the one we should act on?"
- "A lot of people just don't know what they're doing. But everyone is too worried about being the next expendable one to ask for help."
- "I have been through training on teamwork, but with so few jobs left who can you really trust?"
- "We're supposed to reengineer and change, but who is seeing to the reengineering of the senior people?"

There were three basic lessons from this exercise that I think have application in the majority of change situations. First, the self-confidence of the individuals involved takes a severe battering in even the most methodical, well-planned change. Second, trust between employee and company, as well as between employee and employee, gets dangerously frayed or broken. Third, confidence in the whole company, but especially in senior management, is destroyed.

Between Four Rocks and a Hard Place

Business practice in this global, competitive, and information-driven economy indeed seems caught between a rock and a hard place. In fact, there are at least four equally confounding and heavy rocks. These avalanching pressures are creating the urgent need and rationale for those traits, insights, and practices that constitute wisdom. One potential crusher is the paralyzing effect of paradox; the second is the disappearance of boundaries; the third is information overload; and the fourth is the growing sense of powerlessness and despair.

Rock One: Paralyzed by Paradox

Most business people realize that change is both inevitable and necessary. Traditional structures and approaches have shown themselves to be too slow, too rigid, and too disconnected from the needs and expectations of the marketplace to be viable. However, for even the most ardent and flexible of change agents, the paradox between what *needs* to be done, and what *must* be done is perplexing. Most of us have suffered through the contradictory imperatives of:

"Do more with less."
"Do better with fewer."
"Improve quality and lower price."
"Reduce costs and increase innovation."
"Improve service and reduce employee count."
"Engage employees as partners and reduce benefits."
"Take more risks and do not make expensive mistakes."
"Nurture employee commitment and eliminate the costs of job security."

Such contrapositions have left managers and employees often chasing their own tails, endlessly restructuring and rationalizing themselves. In much of this frenetic change, purpose has been lost, vision obfuscated, and credibility compromised.

Rock Two: Naked Without Boundaries

At the same time that contradictions hinder change, the definitions of work, job, departments, companies, value, and competitiveness have lost their traditional form and integrity. Boundaries have become porous to accommodate the more ready transfer of information. Departments have been deconstructed. Systems have been disassembled. Roles have been redefined. But, in bashing through the barriers that kept workers apart and inefficient, many organizations have inadvertently destroyed employees' sense of purpose, value, belonging, and protection. Having battled through change, many individuals have yet to feel any pride in the achievement.

And it is not just individuals who are left vulnerable. Entire corporations and industries are caught in the undertow of ambiguity. There is no right way. There is no only way. There are pressures and choices, but little clarity. Coke used to compete with Pepsi. Apple used to compete with IBM. Banks used to compete with other banks. Companies earned their profits and reputations in the intense heat of competition. Now, it is not so easy. With so many shifting boundaries, Coke has had to change its once-global tactics and take on feisty regional independents like Cott one-on-one. The confluence of hardware and software forced Apple and IBM to put aside their bitter rivalry and collaborate on creating the Power PC chip. Banks now face the prospect of competing not just with other institutions in other locations, but also with Microsoft and the bits and bytes that flow on the information highway.

As the boundaries keep falling, the essential core of a company and its competencies become harder to focus. Airlines are competing with phone companies for the traffic of business meetings. Phone companies are competing with Hollywood studios for the programming to fill their information pipeline. And now that "box office" means a computer terminal or TV set, as well as a movie screen, studios are competing with teenage video game software writers for the next big hit.

Such real and far-reaching interdependence, while intellectually clear, remains unfamiliar and even antithetical to the majority of business people. Struggling to earn a place in this hazy business world, most ask:

- "How can I prove myself if I must advance the goals of a team?"
- "How can I gain permanent advantage if I am sharing information, ideas, and energy?"
- "What's in this for me?"

Without knowing how to contain the raging fires of competitiveness, managers and employees are now expected to administer the soothing balm of cooperation.

Rock Three: Overwhelmed by Information Overload

In a reversal of conventional thinking, it seems that the more we know, the more uncertain things become. Rather than enriching our possibilities, the plethora of data spewed out by technology has produced much more of what Robert Wurman calls "information pollution" than understanding. The insatiable appetite for new ideas within business is but one example.

Already, management practitioners have borrowed precepts like strategy from the military. They have also taken concepts about mission from theology, while using the insights of psychology and sociology to advance the effectiveness of marketing. Anthropology has become a source for models about organizational structure and for insight into group behavior and rituals. Management theorists have even drawn from architecture and literature for metaphors such as deconstruction. All of these inputs have added new dimensions to the understanding of management. But there are also several unfortunate side effects to this conceptual borrowing.

First, when people presume themselves to be informed, they assume that they are experts. This impedes deeper learning.

Second, the constant giving in to the seductive promise of new data tends to create an ethic of management-by-infomercial:

- "Do this new exercise for twenty minutes and achieve improved productivity."
- "Adopt this new program and enhance efficiency."
- "Use this system and sharpen competitiveness."

With so much data, in so many slick packages, supported by so much smart marketing, it is easy to mistake salesmanship for substance.

Third, after a while, the ideas and terminology co-opted by business inexorably lose their validity and worth. What is borrowed rarely has the value of something we create ourselves. New ideas, however promising, are quickly drained of their essential meaning.

The voracious appetite for new ideas to solve the quagmire has locked the modern practice of management into a type of dieter's nightmare. There is a burning desire to transform oneself. There are endless spurts of commitment and self-sacrifice. Sometimes the desired result is even quickly achieved. Then slowly, once the glow of starting something new wears thin, the old habits return, and the hard-fought-for progress recedes.

Nutritionists tell us that over 80 percent of dieters fail to achieve sustained weight loss — about the same ratio of failure to success that research estimates for quality and reengineering programs. Dieters often discover that the next diet is harder: pounds regained are tougher to lose, and more harmful to the organism than those originally lost. Companies are finding it harder and harder to motivate with confidence and sincerity in the next round of revitalization.

Rock Four: Drained by Despair, Disillusionment, and Corporate Disease

If companies have become more susceptible to the charms of the latest management fad, then the victims have been the people within them. Michael Hammer, one of the original proponents of reengineering, has

suggested that he regrets that his principles for renewal have given organizations yet another rationale for dislocating so many individuals.
Many will argue that the efficiency gained by disassembling old processes and constructing the "disintermediated" new ones was necessary
and clearly worth the price. This overlooks the fact that companies must
eventually move beyond productivity, and actually create the ideas, momentum, and sense of purpose that really increase value. Despair and
distrust are hardly the ideal ingredients for combusting such innovation.

Even as they adopt new structures and roles, many employees have
withdrawn their commitment and barely conceal their skepticism. Others, threatened by the possibility of further rationalization, put up with
the often unrealistic pressure of trying to master all the skills, attitudes,
and cultural attunements the legion of how-to specialists have been prom-
ulgating. Imagine a composite of this current worker of the future:

> These super-managers would be visionary, seeing the liberating po-
> tential through the fog of chaos. They would define a mission that
> would inspire followers, and they would coach them with both firm-
> ness and sensitivity on how to get there. "Walking the talk," these
> non-egotistical team builders would visit customers, visit employees
> in the plant, build consensus through communication, and help peo-
> ple resolve conflict in win-win ways. They would be entrepreneurs
> who know when to let go, and tightfisted spendthrifts who would
> recognize when to innovate. They would take risks, recover from falls,
> learn from mistakes, and give to the community. Calm under pres-
> sure, they would have the aplomb to be opportunistic, the curiosity
> to continuously learn, and the humility to give up their corner office.

However, companies are made up of real people and not caricatures. They
have flaws as well as strengths, limitations as well as capacities.

Few of the prescriptions for management or organizational renewal
start with an appreciation of the real human value within a company.
Since restructuring is usually in response to a problem or threat, most
programs for improvement focus on "what's wrong" and "what's weak"
and "who's got to go." Obviously such critical analyses are important,
but without a counterbalancing appreciation for capabilities, organizations tend to destroy some of the very aspects of themselves that are needed
for recovery.

The Unifying Power of Wisdom

Companies feeling the squeeze under the weight of these four rocks usually have a fragmented and segmented approach to renewal. They tend to focus on individual initiatives, such as enhancing customer service, improving productivity, aligning culture with strategy, and coaching and fostering participation of workers, yet fail to generate a unified renewal. There are a couple of reasons for this. One, the priorities of a particular initiative, such as those for customer service, often reverse those of other programs, such as efficiency. Two, in simultaneously attempting to change so many things at the same time, companies have often sacrificed the character and qualities that make them distinct. The inconsistency of objectives, along with the splintering of identity, have created the need for a context that brings the pieces of regeneration back into unity.

An essential dynamic of wisdom is exactly the quality of integration missing in so many organizations. Wisdom brings together knowledge and experience. It makes the systems for continuous learning seamless, harmonizing even the most diverse initiatives within the meaning of the guiding mission. Wisdom is the sensibility that allows the needs of the company, the needs of employees, and the needs of customers to operate in fulfilling interaction.

Sounds like a panacea. It is not. Wisdom unifies by introducing reciprocity and constructive compromise into the complex workings of an organization. Corporations have been very good at setting objectives that reflect the goals for market share, growth, and profitability. Wisdom includes these important goals, but it also transcends them. Wisdom creates a coherence that, in the case of business, combines results with conscience.

Understanding Wisdom

Wisdom is one of those concepts like quality. It implies something positive, something everyone agrees is desirable. But it is also sufficiently intangible that it easily slips into the vernacular of business without meaning anything in particular. This is how business concepts become both grandiose and empty. To avoid such potential depreciation, I have defined specific attributes of wisdom that have direct application in business. (These dimensions will be explored in depth in subsequent chapters.)

I have clustered these ten attributes into four categories.

- In all cultures the wise person is one who is able to make the right decision in circumstances in which reason alone is inadequate. This

17

ability to see a beneficial order within chaos and ambiguity I call *perspective*.

• The wise have the ability to balance seemingly opposing agendas because they recognize the obligations that flow from interdependence. These dimensions have been clustered into a second category called *values*.

• Wisdom is not some transcendent, theoretical ideal, but an immanently practical, practicable skill. This is a third category I call *action*.

• Wisdom is not so much a goal as a life journey, and so needs nurturing and development. I call this category of attributes *support*.

What follows is a highly condensed application of wisdom in business.

WORKING WISDOM	IMPLICATION FOR BUSINESS
PERSPECTIVE	
Timelessness	• Responsibility for the past, and present, as well as future
Clarity and Focus	• Consistency and accessibility of direction to all involved
Compassionate Detachment	• Evaluation of opportunity and weakness without ego to see interconnections
VALUES	
Truth and Honesty	• The prerequisites for earning trust and credibility
Justice	• The broader accountabilities required by interdependence that increasingly connect profit to values
ACTION	
Unity and Integration	• Fulfillment of interdependencies, within and outside the company
Intellectual and Emotional Harmony	• Motivation to engage and reward the whole human being, to unleash the talent of employees, and to serve the fuller needs of customers
Equanimity	• The inner balance during periods of both sacrifice and success
SUPPORT	
Substantial Subjectivity	• Personal judgment to "stand on the shoulders" of facts
Mentorship	• The human talent to develop the enterprise

Not Just Another Management Theory

As a society, we are distracted by the amount of new knowledge to learn. As a result, we have failed to develop the understanding and insight to bring the possibilities of this often wonderful knowledge to its fullest completion. The proof of this is easy to see. Often brilliant breakthroughs are really only old lessons not fully learned and integrated. In fact, most of the current concepts and recommendations for management renewal, including this one, really only recycle knowledge that failed to become wisdom.

For example, since antiquity people have known that quality requires the pride of craftsmanship and the attention to detail. Yet somehow this most basic appreciation of the mastery of quality was mislaid, and business people (particularly in North America) had to scramble to learn Total Quality Management as if it were a mysterious revelation. Similarly, history has provided innumerable examples of a motivated group that produced outcomes far in excess of the potential of its individual contributors. From the Manhattan Project of the early 1940s to the 1969 New York Jets, teams have shown their mettle. Nevertheless, the respect and accountability needed for teamwork has had to be relearned by an entire generation of management and labor. Even obvious knowledge in the hands of smart people is not enough to achieve growth and completion. That "finishing" requires the insight and mutuality that we characterize as wise.

Given the amnesia brought on by information-overload, it is perhaps inevitable that any definition of what it means to be wise requires reverting to the advice and teachings of the great spiritual masters. It is in these traditions that our contemporary (if hazy) notion of wisdom is indeed grounded.

Throughout the world, in Jewish, Christian, Buddhist, Islamic, Native, and Confucian traditions, wisdom is accorded the highest honors of human achievement. And in each of these traditions wisdom is predicated on compassion. King Solomon describes wisdom as "a spirit devoted to mankind's good." This biblical perspective stresses that wisdom is not an "abstract speculation," but a practical, pragmatic ability to see beyond the narrow confines of self-interest. Similarly, the Buddhist "awakening to wisdom" involves, in the words of Sogyal Rinpoche, a Tibetan monk, "seeing things as they are as impermanent and radically interdependent." Learning that accumulates in an individual is knowledge. Knowledge that is applied for the good of many is wisdom.

In Eastern tradition, wisdom and compassion are sometimes called the two wheels without which a cart cannot function. Compassion arises as a generous response to the other party with whom we are in interdependence. Such compassion is not a denial of an individual's self-interest, but a realization that self-interest is also served, sometimes best served, in the context of a broader good.

This suppression, or sacrifice, or obligation of the individual to serve the collective is an institutionalized feature of Confucian societies, and has been used by some analysts, including Harvard's Samuel Huntington, to explain part of the unprecedented economic growth achieved in Japan, China, and the Asian rim. Yet this notion of responsibility beyond the individual is not uniquely Eastern. In all traditions, wisdom is only realized or effective in action. And the wise action is inevitably of benefit to others. Aristotle concluded that knowledge which is only beneficial to oneself, no matter how advanced, no matter how learned, is not wisdom.

While interdependence may foster compassion, the question remains: what is the benefit or meaning of all this extended responsibility for business? Reporting on a six-year research project at the Stanford University Graduate School of Business, professors James C. Collins and Jerry I. Porras explain: "Visionary companies pursue a cluster of objectives of which making money is only one — and not necessarily the primary one. Yes, they seek profits, but they are equally guided by a core ideology — core values and a sense of purpose beyond making money. Yet, paradoxically, the visionary companies make more money than the more purely profit-driven comparison companies."

Collins and Porras are not talking about Ben & Jerry's, nor about The Body Shop. They are explaining why companies like Motorola, Merck, Sony, Procter & Gamble, General Electric, and Boeing, among others, have lasted a long time, thriving even in times of great adversity. The "core values and sense of purpose" they note are not the fluff of recently composed mission statements, but expressions of a deep-seated, genuinely pursued sense of responsibility for employees, customers, the environment, and the communities they affect. The genuine mutuality and reciprocity with which these companies operate reflect the respect and empathy that defines compassion.

Wisdom is not so much a skill of prediction as it is a form of heightened self-knowledge. This human value in part drew me to this topic at a time when so many people are being depreciated and displaced. Any person who is self-aware, in touch with their greater capacities for wisdom, will enjoy the self-confidence to handle even the most disruptive eventuality. The more defined and secure the inner being, the more adaptable that individual will be in changing and trying circumstances. A wise perspective is therefore both a value and an insurance policy.

The same holds true for companies. The sense of self, the consciousness of identity, including both self-appreciation and self-criticism, are fundamental for managing healthy organizational change and overcoming the unpredictable challenges of the new economy.

There is a danger in treating wisdom like a cookie recipe in that it will seem to be the rational sum of its parts. If it were that easy and obvious, wisdom would be in abundance. It clearly is not. Among the reasons why is that even when the moral conviction is in place, and even when the knowledge and experience accumulate, wisdom happens not as a result of these properties but in the interactions between them.

This likely raises new questions. If companies are struggling to master something as logical and relatively simple as quality, how can they possibly develop the higher consciousness for something as complicated and unselfish as wisdom?

While the descriptions I have used for this inner intelligence involve aspirations of the spirit, wisdom is fundamentally a practical quality that earns specific recognition and appreciation in day-to-day practice. Wisdom that is not of use (or that is not used) is not, in fact, wisdom. Basic pragmatism — creating trust with customers, building reciprocity with suppliers, developing mutuality with employees, sharpening strategies with insight, balancing implementation with generous compromise — makes a wise business a smart business.

Wisdom is not a quick fix. Many companies have given up on quality programs because management lack "the constancy of purpose" that W. Edwards Deming, the father of the statistical quality movement in postwar Japan, defined as a prerequisite for continuous improvement. Such constancy — the desire to persevere and the patience to find meaning and growth in each experience — is also fundamental to growing wise. Not taking the time to do it right or to learn the full meaning of each lesson usually only means redoing or relearning later. We all know this from personal experience. Yet, our (my) impatience is such that each new shortcut in our frenetic work schedule seems seductively viable. This is folly, the antithesis of wisdom. It is more damning than stupidity because folly involves doing what we already know will ultimately damage our own self-interest.

There is unfortunately a profusion of folly in our current, highly scrambled economic situation. Not unrelated, there is also considerable pain as companies struggle through waves of dislocation. These suggest that the need for a wise, sagacious perspective is indeed genuine and substantial. But in addition to this obvious need there is also evidence of a heartening desire for just such a new context. People in business are looking within, seeking meaning as well as competence. After several years of stooping to the pressures of productivity, they are again looking up, seeking the big picture. This desire, also genuine, seems to be growing as more and more companies and individuals wear out their enthusiasm for practicing what others preach.

Two

Character
Through Crisis

The 1990s are a time of economic transition and organizational upheaval. Imposed and unrelenting change is causing structural displacement and personal suffering — many companies career from restructuring to crisis. While uncomfortable, this "crisis" actually provides the source of the reflection and growth that contribute to the development of wisdom. However, instead of grasping this opportunity, people and companies are often gripped with fear. Rather than using the situation to learn the deeper lessons of cause and effect, many individuals deny its causes and many managers resort to dictate. Only the empathy of compassion and the insights of wisdom can break the stifling atmosphere of fear and anxiety.

Crisis as a Catalyst of Wisdom

Wisdom is an achievement born of suffering. That alone is reason enough for most of us to avoid seeking it. Still, to evade learning from suffering may be possible, but to avoid suffering is not. In this current economy, organizations and individuals cannot escape the trauma of transformation. As in any major societal change, virtually everyone will be impacted, but only relatively few will consciously seek to learn the deeper lessons from their distress. Others may well be forced ultimately to accept these lessons. Yet, if history is any judge, the majority will try so hard just to get by that they will miss the opportunity to extract the meaning from this difficult but potentially enriching passage.

Adversity is an inextricable aspect of our human experience. Often displacement, pain, or challenge involves a suffering that crystallizes our personal character. Artists suffer for their craft, breaking the comfortable bonds of the conventional in order to create something new. Soldiers suffer for their duty. Athletes endure often grueling physical and psychological suffering for the chance to win.

As a human construct with human foibles, it is inevitable that the practice of business will also include the experience of suffering. However, while other political, religious, and arts institutions see the need for suffering, valuing it as the price for the transformation to a new level of human experience, business organizations still regard suffering through that adolescent perspective of avoidance and presumed immunity.

One reason for this institutional immaturity is that the profits of business are often based on serving a need that eliminates pain, discomfort, or unhappiness. Suffering and sorrow are words that for fifty years have been squeezed out of our consumer culture by the endless stream of products and services promising relief, convenience, self-fulfillment, and instant gratification. Business in many ways provides the antidote to suffering, so it naturally tends to devalue that which it seeks to profitably eliminate.

The image of success, which so motivates business people, is also incongruous with the image of suffering. People seek advancement to escape the potential deprivations of poverty and to have the resources to "buy the best," minimizing pain, risk, or inconvenience. This has fixed the impression in the corporate mind that suffering, with its sticky questions and stigma of failure, is to be shunned. Rather than explore the dread that exists in their own organizations, rather than reflect on the lessons in their own suffering, most business people seem content to follow their public relations instincts, and put a distancing spin on anything that hurts.

Since business behavior is so conditioned to avoid pain or to rationalize its reality, it is difficult to imagine willingly undergoing pain for its potential insights. It is especially difficult to find the calm willingness to seek understanding in those threatening, disturbing circumstances that cause the most turmoil. Yet this very suffering reveals wisdom. Sirach, the Jewish prophet whose writings precede Solomon's in the Bible, exhorted his fellow Israelites to "prepare for trials — for gold is tested in the fire." Adversity is the crucible for realizing our fullest consciousness as human beings, so the upheaval in our companies and the discontinuity overtaking the larger economy are, in a sense, potential blessings. What we need is the courage to see beyond the trauma to the meaning.

Business and capitalism have always involved the dislocation that economist Joseph Schumpeter described as "creative destruction." Schumpeter observed that an innovation by one enterprise created opportunity, but always at the expense of rendering obsolete another system, industry, or company. This renewing cycle has happened innumerable times in innumerable sectors, such as when passenger planes displaced passenger trains, when personal computers displaced mainframes, and when fax machines displaced telegraphs and telexes.

Now, for the first time since the industrial revolution, the whole structure of the economy is undergoing this "creative destruction." And in this universal turmoil, individuals in all countries, in all the social, educational, and managerial strata, are facing radical and distressing change. (It is one of the ironies of the global village that, while ancient political, ethnic, and ideological divisions persist, human beings are now finally united by their encountering of the uncertainty and suffering caused by this massive economic dislocation. Workers in Germany, Korea, and China and managers in the United States, Japan, and Britain all face similar pressures and worries.)

Companies That Renew

Too often, the suffering must build to a crisis before we open our hearts to the possibility of its wisdom. Abba Eban, the Israeli foreign minister who helped Menachem Begin negotiate the historic 1977 peace treaty with Egypt's Anwar Sadat, said that "nations and people become wise — once they have exhausted all other possibilities." Corporations, as human institutions, are prone to this same pattern. Ford adopted its now central commitment to quality when its very survival was at stake. The improved styling, quality, and employee relations the company now enjoys flowed directly from its crisis.

The renewal underway at IBM also reflects wisdom as the painful achievement of last resort. For years the company persisted in pushing mainframes even though its customers wanted faster and less expensive alternatives. IBM sabotaged its own relationships with customers because its internal profitability patterns did not align with the external demands of the market. After several high-profile restructurings during the last half decade, IBM was finally forced by an $8 billion loss to radically redefine its operations, culture, and customer service systems. Motivated by its brush with catastrophic failure, change has now been realized more quickly than most anticipated. In an act that galvanized its commitment to customers, IBM reacted quickly to the problem with Pentium chips, and immediately stopped shipment of products based on this processor to customers. Some would say that this was but a smart PR move; however, IBM earned back some of the trust it had lost. And not incidentally, the company has returned to assuring profitability.

Arguably, Chrysler is now among the wisest of the North American car producers. It has made the most revolutionary changes to its processes and is the most aggressive in new styling and engineering. In fact, Nissan and Toyota both took apart a Chrysler Neon to study and analyze the ideas, components, and system improvements that went into the nifty little car. Chrysler recently launched an in-house university to help employees develop the team skills and technological literacy needed for more flexible, more imaginative manufacturing.

Now a progressive and visionary company (with some pestering quality problems still to work on), Chrysler, too, is benefiting from its own hard-won wisdom. It faced bankruptcy not once but twice. In both cases, the downturns in the car buying cycle and the market share gains of its Japanese competitors exacerbated the quality, styling, and service mistakes that Chrysler (and the other North American car companies) made. But for Chrysler, the risk of being a heartbeat away from going out of business focused the mind, pumped the adrenaline, and stretched the willingness to innovate.

Avoiding Truth

Unfortunately, there are many examples of companies that even in great struggle are unable to discern the wisdom they need to see themselves through change. Instead, they allow arrogance, introvertedness, or fear to bury or fudge the truth of their situation.

Consider General Motors. Now finally profitable, GM still lags behind other car makers in productivity, quality, and for many consumers, even service. The company, like others, has faced harsh lessons. Yet, unlike Chrysler, GM has not so far been able to extract from its painful transformation the insight and perspicacity that makes change momentous instead of simply distressful. One of the most telling examples is GM's experience with the Fiero in the late 1980s.

The sporty car represented a revolution in design and materials, but in its haste to market the car, GM also left unresolved some of the riskier aspects of its engineering. The engine contained so little oil that it over-heated, occasionally bursting into flames. The plastic body panels turned engine fires into even more serious conflagrations. GM's PR machine denied the obvious, writing that the "actual risk to motor vehicle safety was minimal," even though by 1987, one in every 508 Fieros built caught fire. As Paul Ingrassia and Joseph White explain in *Comeback*, GM not only denied the problem of overheating, but also shifted the responsibility for any future fires to the consumer by using what the authors call "a lawyer's repair" — a sticker informing owners to check oil at every single fuel fill. Even when the Fiero was canceled, GM persisted in its absurd denial of the truth. The company claimed that the U.S. market had lost interest in two-seat sports cars: a delusion shattered only one year after the Fiero's demise by the arrival of the enduringly popular Mazda Miata.

Truth, as experienced by customers, as reported by dealers, and as expressed by employees failed to penetrate the consciousness of the people making GM's big decisions. As Ingrassia and White report, "the fires were overshadowed by a more pressing concern. The Fiero was becoming a money loser." So in the preoccupation of attending to corporate priorities, the validity of truth was lost, and the urgency of honesty was compromised. GM's suffering — caused by public embarrassment, discourtesy, inconvenience, and insensitivity toward customers, closed factories and lost jobs, and even ultimate financial cost — generated little of the potential insight latent in this experience.

Avoiding Risk

Avoiding risk is yet another way companies avoid pain. Underlying risk is the possibility of failure — one form of suffering abhorrent to buttoned-down, bottom-line managers. Most management behavior eschews the risk-taking required for creative renewal. By not taking the risk of licensing its operating system in the mid-1980s, Apple allowed Microsoft to develop an alternative, now dominant, interface with its Windows product. No risk. No gain.

But the loss of untaken risk goes further than missed opportunity. By avoiding indeterminacy, organizations are depriving themselves of the possibilities to exercise the skills, judgments, and stretching and recovery mechanisms that increase their overall capacity for effectively managing change and ambiguity.

A few companies like 3M break the mold and innovate incessantly. In fact, innovation is so institutionalized that 3M expects its divisional managers to achieve 30 percent of each year's revenue from new products that have been introduced only in the last four years. Although it has more practice than most companies at new product development, 3M is not immune to the law of averages. Many of its products fail. But those setbacks, always uncomfortable, demoralizing, and painful, are mined fully for their rich lessons. Former 3M CEO Lewis Lehr comments, "you can learn from success, but you have to work at it; it's a lot easier to learn from a failure."

3M is not inviting suffering. The employees are not casual about making mistakes. The company has simply realized that failure is often the pain through which gain is achieved. James Collins and Jerry Porras explain that, as innovators, management and workers at 3M "accept that mistakes will be made. Since you can't tell ahead of time which variations will prove favorable, you have to accept mistakes and failures as an integral part of the evolutionary process."

This is wisdom in action. The Tibetan monk Sogyal Rinpoche explains that "pain, grief, loss and ceaseless frustration are there for a real and dramatic purpose: to wake us up, to enable and almost force us to break out of our cycle of samsara [suffering], and so release our imprisoned splendour."

The risks of this volatile economy are pressing themselves on every organization and will extract from most a significant penalty of pain. Only the companies conscious of the value of what they are suffering through can hope to release the "splendour" of their own wisdom.

Fear as the Management of Last Resort

For a company to reflect on its own pain requires a sophisticated level of self-understanding. The spin-doctoring that characterizes this wave of renewal, with its "rationalization," "right-sizing," and "delayering," shows how hard it is for many to own up to the human reality of organizational change. However, in choosing to ignore or suppress the realization of organizational and individual suffering, companies have unleashed a great wave of fear. Many of the employees I interviewed for my consulting work, and for this book, are operating under a constant, threatening strain. In many situations, this fear is used as a substitute for vision, or as a replacement for purpose and motivation. Some fear, when it alerts us to danger, is natural, healthy, and even smart. But when it is created so unconsciously and so callously, the result tends to be a damaging distortion.

Of course, fear is a much broader issue than that of corporate culture. Societal worries about issues like crime, violence in the home, immigration, terrorism, pollution, and technology have altered the expectations and self-confidence of the general population. Fear is therefore an inescapable and important factor, affecting the attitudes and needs of consumers and employees.

Fear has made consumer confidence fragile even after four years of economic expansion. With their job security stripped away, and therefore their future buying power questionable, many people now purchase products more selectively, with greater deliberation, and with heightened expectations for performance, quality, value, and the fulfillment of social responsibilities. Companies selling to these less secure, more skittish consumers must respect these new influences and attitudes.

While job insecurity undermines the principles of consumption, other fears come into play that create more complex demands on the companies trying to serve customers. For example, fear of pollution, ozone depletion, and toxic waste have forced companies to engineer environmental practices into their products and services. Fear of growing street violence has prompted customers to retreat into what futurist Faith Popcorn now calls "armored cocoons," forcing companies to adopt new selling, distribution, and billing practices. As fear builds on fear, the relationships between customers and companies become harder to sustain, more cynical, and more distrustful.

Within companies themselves, the fear in the hallways, factories, and boardrooms is clearly present. As in the broader community, this fear has become endemic. Employees are afraid of the additional displacement caused by more technology. Middle managers distrust more restructuring and bureaucratic flattening. CEOs are frightened of the demands for quarterly results. Even many of the self-employed, supposedly on the vanguard of the new economy, fear the unpredictability and disconnection of their independent circumstances.

Yet there is an even more insidious dread to contend with. In some companies — more than would perhaps admit it — fear has been deployed as an intentional motivator, used to add urgency to restructuring, immediacy to role changes, and as leverage in compensation negotiation. Whatever the short-term results, motivation by fear can only be regarded as both the easiest and the lowest form of the art of management.

Fear at this intensity is ultimately crippling. It defeats hope, creates anger, and corrodes confidence. And such dread cannot be contained:

managers fearful of the CEO tend to create an even sharper angst among their own subordinates. Thus fear not only cascades down to the lower levels of a company, but it also inevitably leaks out to frustrate and contaminate relationships with customers and suppliers. Those who create fear disrespect those whom they control. This may not matter much to those so inclined, but the use of intimidation in management also devalues the individual, office, or culture creating that anxiety. Such authority, based only on power, does not create the trust and inspiration that companies so desperately need to reinvent themselves.

Airlines as an industry seem stuck in this quagmire of fear. And no manager used dread more destructively as a management tool than Frank Lorenzo at Eastern Airlines. Several generations of bad planning and pricing, poor service, and missed trends had left Eastern especially vulnerable to deregulation. In his zeal for renewal, Lorenzo cut costs and bashed the airline's unions. He proceeded with such disregard for employees, using threats and intimidation, that he finally earned the reputation as one of the worst bosses in business. Employees were more embittered than cowed, hardly creating the conditions for ensuring the safety of planes and the timeliness of operations, or for extending greater courtesy to customers. Proving that a "house divided against itself falls," Eastern crumbled, and Lorenzo lost the power he so brazenly wielded.

Organizations cannot graduate to the next level of renewal — that of continuous regeneration — without recognizing the fears that subvert them. So far, very little has been written about this in the business literature. Before proceeding to the positive development of wisdom, let us look at the full consequences of an even casual reliance on or acceptance of fear.

• *Fear defeats learning.* The creation of value depends more and more on managing knowledge and interconnecting new understanding. While companies are determined to become what MIT professor Peter Senge calls a "learning organization," — adding value by increasing knowledge — many have been unable to rid themselves of fear, blocking the flow of ideas. Management often understands that raising the importance of knowledge inside a company would help fashion greater value for customers. Such continuous learning would also foster continuous renewal. However, while subscribing to the precepts of learning, many companies have forgotten that it requires a general attitude of openness, as well as an enthusiasm for the unknown. Fear achieves the opposite — closing people to new stimulus, breeding caution, and cynicism.

Total Quality Management, a concept that most business people believe is valid and valuable, is more of a disciplined learning loop (input–application–feedback–improvement) than system of control. W. Edwards Deming, who revolutionized quality management, believed passionately that a precondition for quality was "to drive fear out and build trust." That the majority of companies undertaking quality improvement have stopped their programs suggests not that quality has become less important, but that fear is too prevalent, too obstructive, and too entrenched to extract.

• *Fear "disempowers" the accountable.* Like quality, empowerment has largely failed to realize its potential. Why do so many rational and important initiatives fail? Shoshana Zuboff, a professor at the Harvard Business School, explains: "Persuasion, influence and education — these are not easily compatible with the beliefs necessary to maintain imperative control." While preaching empowerment and delegating greater accountability, companies have frequently exercised the ultimate control of instituting restructuring after restructuring. Such disruptive change imposed from the top reinforces the ultimate power. As always, actions speak louder than words. Even when the restructuring has been essential, the forced nature of the change has made the promise of empowerment thereafter ring hollow.

• *Fear undermines cooperation.* Most organizations understand that this age requires skills of alliance and collaboration. Management and labor need one another; companies need both customers and suppliers; sometimes companies even need joint ventures with competitors. While the management of cooperation involves starkly different interactions from the management of control, the actions in restructuring often contradict the ethos of mutuality. Internal relationships are poisoned by these contradictions. Lee Smith, a business journalist, captures the paradox, explaining that productivity-obsessed companies force "mid-level bosses to face two incompatible assignments: Be a cold-blooded cost-cutter, and be liked."

• *Fear destroys creativity.* Creativity is usually thought of as a solitary process in which one exercises talent to make a new breakthrough. In fact, creativity is interactive. Mihaly Csikszentmihalyi, former chairman of psychology at the University of Chicago, suggests that creativity occurs in the interaction among three elements: the talent of the creative individual; the domain or discipline within which the creative individual operates; and the broader field of judges and institutions which react with that effort. Creativity is fully realized not in the isolated creation by the artist, but in the exchange among artist, craft, and audience.

As a product of an exchange, creativity requires a basic foundation of trust. Fear undermines this foundation, eroding the confidence of the "creator," as well as the openness and receptivity of the "audience." Virtually any act of creation involves a resolution of tension, a solution or clever interconnection of ideas. With fear, that tension is fixed and ominous. It is a constriction rather than inspiration, a threat rather than a motivator.

Successful innovators like Hewlett-Packard introduce challenge for their knowledge workers but eliminate fear. Bill Hewlett elaborates: "Engineers are creative people, so before we hired an engineer we made sure he would be operating in a stable and secure climate. We also made sure that each of our engineers had a long range opportunity with the company, and suitable projects to work on. Another thing, we made certain that we had adequate supervision so that our engineers would be happy and would be productive to the maximum extent."

• *Fear creates disease.* Many of the people I have interviewed for this book admit to a high level of stress. They feel overworked — having to do more with less — and in many cases underappreciated. In addition to this pressure, most people also fear the personal and organizational displacement of further change.

Many companies have forgotten that anxiety is healthy and manageable only in short bursts. Prolonged exposure to stress creates what Dr. Hans Selye, the pioneer in this field, calls "the diseases of adaptation." In physiological terms, the human body seeks homeostasis, and it will produce an imbalance to compensate for imbalance. Uninterrupted anxiety will therefore increase the likelihood for the ulcers, tumors, and other surprising disorders of the body, mind, and soul that we now understand to be the side effects of stress.

Individuals under such pressure pay a huge price, yet their companies are not the beneficiaries. In fact, organizations also suffer, breeding cynicism, defensiveness, and mistrust, along with consistent mediocrity.

Companies grow their own tumors and cancers. This is perhaps most evident in those organizations implementing the next new management model, without having addressed the problem that sapped the energy and health of previous restructurings.

• *Fear burns out even the successful.* I have studied several companies that have been very successful in transforming themselves. Yet even in the most positive situations, the change was still unsettling enough to provoke fear. This was sometimes expressed as a deep nostalgia for the old company that had been swept away. Even though employees readily admitted that the company's problems had been severe and required that old approaches be discarded, people still longed for the systems and rituals of that discredited model. With further discussion, I learned that what the employees really missed was more than the predictability and comfort of the familiar, but, more deeply, the confidence in themselves and faith in the system to perform.

The Balm of Compassion

Fear is created by a perceived threat to self-interest, so it is an emotion that fundamentally isolates. When nations fear the loss of jobs, they turn protectionist. When managers fear their bosses, they turn defensive. Fear therefore hardens boundaries between people, stifling the process of communication, exchange, and understanding. Dealing with fear, bridging the gaps it creates, requires creating a commonality.

In the book of Solomon, wisdom is described as "a counselor in times of prosperity, a comfort in anxiety." In situations of divisive dread, that comfort is provided by the empathy and compassion that the wise individual extends to others. Again, even the wisest manager may not be able to alleviate all the reasons for pain and anxiety, but, through compassion, wisdom breaks us free from the paralysis of fear. This is not a utopian ideal, but a pragmatic, proven reality. In the darkest moments of human experience it has been just such compassion that has brought meaning to suffering and hope to those afflicted by fear.

Viktor Frankl, a classically trained psychoanalyst and survivor of Auschwitz, realized in the harshest possible place, in circumstances of unrelieved despair, that human life seeks meaning as if it were the oxygen of the spirit. In *Man's Search for Meaning*, Frankl writes: "We must never forget that we may also find meaning in life even when confronted with a hopeless situation, when facing a fate that cannot be changed. For what matters then is to bear witness to the uniquely human potential at its best, which is to transform a personal tragedy into a triumph, to turn one's predicament into a human achievement. When we are no longer able to change a situation — we are challenged to change ourselves."

The meaning that many in Auschwitz derived from this most horrific of experiences was to give to others, to be unselfish in a situation in which the stakes for the individual were most dire. While fear destroyed dignity, compassion reasserted the value of the individual.

In business, the outcomes are obviously on a lower plane of importance than what Frankl experienced, but the fundamental lessons apply. The pain caused by fear is real and damaging: the isolation and despair are acute. Management that uses only the levers of control will push people into further self-interest just when cooperation is most needed. Breaking the cycle of fear requires the wisdom to see beyond self-interest, to "provide comfort in anxiety," and context in a time of confusion. This is why Buddhists state unequivocally that "compassion is the prerequisite of wisdom."

Compassion is not an instinct of weakness, but of great strength. It takes courage to extend comfort to others when the pressure and threats are common to all. Compassion is also an activist energy. It is as dynamic as the "radical interdependence" that governs our relationships with others. Those companies seeking to harness the energy of teams and interdisciplinary project work must necessarily create the reservoir of compassion from which people may derive a sense of belonging, security, and personal importance. Compassion is also essential for reciprocity. Extending empathy earns empathy in return. This is a fundamental skill to be mastered especially for those corporations aiming to develop more extensive, more rewarding relationships with customers.

Compassion may be the ultimate expression of human nobility, but how does it work precisely in business? To illustrate the progression I have created the following diagram. The attributes of fear, identified along the left side, are transformed by those on the right. Compassion can be seen as a prism that refracts the fear and helps us resolve its sources as well as its outcomes.

THE COMPASSION PRISM

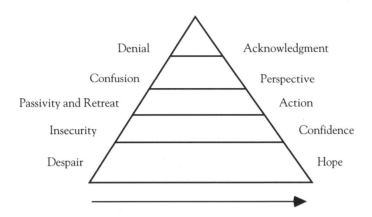

Denial — Acknowledgment
Confusion — Perspective
Passivity and Retreat — Action
Insecurity — Confidence
Despair — Hope

• **ACKNOWLEDGMENT:** When individuals are unaware or in denial of the fear consuming them, compassion provides acknowledgment. This sounds passive, but to know that fear exists and is understood is necessary for overcoming it. (Hence Franklin Roosevelt's admonition that "the greatest fear is fear itself.") In companies undergoing drastic change, employees are often hungry for management to acknowledge the scale of difficulty and the pain of dislocation. Such honest acknowledgment is often the first step in restoring confidence in the organization, and in evoking faith for a new mission.

• **PERSPECTIVE:** Harvard professor John P. Kotter, in his study of leadership, believes that managers "undercommunicate by a factor of ten" the needs, urgencies, and opportunities of a new vision. The uncertainty employees and organizations have about the future is creating confusion as well as angst. Providing honest perspective, even if it admits that direction is uncertain, is a way to extend respect to people. It also provides the understanding that helps bring down the boundaries of isolation.

• **ACTION:** The primary reaction to a great fear is retreat, yet the only way to break out of the bonds of this fear is to move into action. Compassion gives people the faith to try new things. It provides the support for the experimentation that is so vital when old systems and practices have become ineffectual. 3M does not assume to know all the actions to take to realize the greatest future opportunities, so it allows its R&D people to use up to 15 percent of their company time to explore projects of personal interest. This not only supports an ethic of innovation, but also honors the employee's capacity to solve problems management has even yet to articulate.

• **CONFIDENCE:** One of the inevitable consequences of radical change is that security and comfortable norms are harshly displaced. New standards for productivity and business performance are obviously essential, but most change models underestimate the importance of rebuilding and restoring human confidence. With compassion, the needs of the individual are appreciated in the broader scheme of the needs of the organization. Confidence is the essential characteristic for effectively managing uncertainty and ambiguity, so compassion for the individual ultimately serves the needs of the company.

• **HOPE:** As Frankl showed, compassion can create hopefulness even while encountering the most crushing despair. While people in many organizations are traumatized by the unceasing change, the basic instinct for most is to work it through, to find a way to persist through the adversity. Compassion extended to employees at this juncture begins the process of building reciprocity. As this empathy is exchanged, trust grows. And with this trust comes the faith in management, the hope in the vision, and a common commitment to face the future.

Compassion is an asset not only for companies in great stress, but also for those organizations that are growing and expanding into new potential. As we will see in later chapters, this expression of wisdom does indeed fulfill Solomon's description as a "counselor in times of prosperity." With compassion, the isolation of fear is broken. With compassion, the opportunity to extract understanding from strife is activated. With compassion, the empathy to see beyond the constriction of current difficulties is realized.

Those who become wise are not necessarily natural leaders. Nor are they necessarily highly intellectual or academic. What the wise have in common is an openness, a willingness to connect the day-to-day experiences of life with a larger meaning. Often, this involves using the setbacks, suffering, and discontinuities of life and work as the forge for a wider, more motivating meaning to be made.

AN INQUIRY AND A REFLECTION

The experience of suffering and pain at work is a highly personal one. The loss of a job, or of friends who have lost theirs, creates anxieties that are rarely acknowledged within the company going through transition. Elisabeth Kübler-Ross has explored the stages of dealing with loss — the process of shock, grief, anger, resignation, reconciliation, and finally growth and healing. Those who work in palliative care explain that this model is valid, but that every person approaches loss differently. Some do indeed follow the sequence. Others move randomly along the spectrum. Others experience only parts. Others experience none of what is detailed. The point is that pain, whether of the body, mind, or spirit, touches us at a deep place within our own identity. The lessons we take from this experience, like the process for recovery, are highly personal.

Respecting this, the following questions are not meant to be definitive or exclusive. Instead, they try to address the issues of dislocation and discontinuity that business, in its haste to discover productivity, generally has little patience to reveal.

• What has been your personal experience with disappointment, pressure, change, or setback?
- How have you handled the stress of uncertainty?
- Have you been aware during the dislocation of its wider causes?
- What have been the most salient lessons you have distilled from your own experience of pain?
- How can these lessons contribute perspective and resiliency when you encounter new difficulties?
• How frank has your company, department, or colleagues been about acknowledging the human difficulties of organizational transformation?
- What lessons have been learned? What steps have been taken?
- How have processes for change been adapted to deal with the human factors?
- What role has compassion played in managing disruptive change?
- What has your company learned from its most defining crisis?

- How can this learning be extended and applied to other change needs?
    - How is confidence for both individuals and the collective culture reestablished after periods of intense deconstruction and reorganization?
    - Which initiative are you most proud of from your latest experience with company change or renewal? Why?

Fear in such chaotic times is natural and understandable. However, the key is to distinguish between the healthy fear of self-protection and the debilitating fear of helplessness. Any fear that is unconscious, incessant, or oppressive will be damaging.

- Has fear emerged as a factor at work?
- How has it been used? Acknowledged?
- What has management done to either mitigate or compound the fear?
- How have you dealt with it as an individual?
- Have you personally added to the fear or worked consciously to dissipate it?
- Is fear even recognized within your company? How?
- In what ways has fear affected creativity and confidence?
    - How has it impacted peer interactions?
    - How has it affected suppliers and resources?
    - How has it affected the needs, attitudes, and expectations of customers?
- How is hope expressed in the strategy and interactions of the company?

THREE

CONSCIENCE AS A COMPETITIVE ASSET

Crisis may activate wisdom, but not all people who suffer emerge from the experience as wise. What then is missing from the equation? Why do some people achieve a thoughtful broadening when most only suffer a draining diminution from painful change? The absent factor is a highly developed sense of moral purpose.

Morality is central to wisdom because it is impossible to be wise without being of service to others. As the context and commitment for obligation, morality is like a filter through which our knowledge and experience are refined into a higher consciousness. The interactions among what we learn, what we do, and what we believe form the basis of our individual wisdom.

Just as self-awareness for a person or company leads to consciousness, the acknowledgment of moral obligation leads to conscience. The concepts of morality and corporate conscience contribute to wisdom — and, indeed, enhance performance and effectiveness in our competitive environment.

The Pillars of Wisdom

Knowledge and experience are vitally important to our human development — they are the pillars of wisdom. However, being smart or learned or being observant or exposed to a variety of situations is clearly not the same as being wise. What we accumulate in our heads and hold in our emotional memory banks are really only raw materials. Once processed through our beliefs, once fired in Sirach's furnace of moral conviction, what we know and experience become transformed into insight, understanding, and perspective.

PILLARS OF WISDOM

Although depicted as distinct elements, what we know, experience, and believe clearly overlap. For example, what we know is given meaning by what we believe. What we experience may confirm or conflict with what we know. What we believe is stretched, challenged, or given currency by what we learn and do. Morality is the standard. It is what Marx calls the "superstructure" by which the intellectual and experiential aspects of life are given spirit and substance. This then is how we grow wise. While clear in theory, does the central pillar really matter? Is morality really a precondition for wisdom? And should morality even be an issue in business?

Before answering, consider these messy examples from the real, ruthless world of business:

• Intel, one of the most highly regarded and well-managed companies in North America, finds out that its premier microchip is flawed. It not only holds this information back, but it also resists offering a replacement until customer complaints grow so loud that it surrenders under pressure. Was this a bad business decision, a poorly developed sense of public relations, or a lapse in moral judgment?

• General Motors, suffering through yet another restructuring, has been sued by over five hundred pick-up truck owners because gas tanks positioned side-saddle under the vehicle sometimes rupture in accidents. Despite evidence of the danger, and despite having a new design for its new trucks, GM resists pressure for a full recall. Is this more corporate arrogance, another Ralph Nader episode of missing the public's expectation for safety, or a lapse in moral judgment?

• General Electric is one of the premier corporations in the world. Despite an enviable business record, GE has been embarrassed by a persistent string of scandals. It was fined for paying illegal bribes to procure contracts for jet engines. Most recently, its Kidder Peabody unit was embroiled in illegal securities accounting. With each wave of deviations from corporate policy, the CEO has issued a new generation of more explicit, more stringent guidelines. But is this predilection for bending the rules and breaking the law indicative of poor training, poor communication, or a lapse in moral judgment?

These are obviously serious companies, with firm commitment to established ethical standards. I cannot assume to know the circumstances in which these mistakes were made, nor to understand the intent of the people involved. The point is that strategies, crisis management scenarios, customer research, and employee training are not enough to protect the interests of a company (let alone those of other constituents) in the ambiguous and pressured world of global business.

Morality in Business

Moral obligation is usually seen as a type of air brake on business potential, mostly because people do not understand it. Morality in no way precludes the possibility for profit. It is actually a code for reciprocity. In *The History of God*, religious historian Karen Armstrong points out that the three major monotheistic religions of Judaism, Christianity, and Islam grew out of mercantile cultures. These were societies defined by trade, with all the same pressures, abuses, and greed that our modern securities exchange commissions are still trying to regulate. Out of this ferment of commercial interaction emerged a sense of morality. While the principles of morality also took on spiritual dimensions, they gained currency precisely because they facilitated an expanded, more complex system of trade and commerce. Morality gave legitimacy to business centuries before balance sheets and accounting practices.

Management today is done by sound bite. Competitiveness is the new doctrine. Productivity is the mantra. "Let the markets decide" is the justification. If a more thorough explanation is needed, then quote Adam Smith. Once again, modern business people are prone to teaching what they do not know. Smith was, in fact, a moral philosopher. His often quoted *Wealth of Nations* was only one of a series of works that tried to establish a moral framework for the interpersonal, political, artistic, and commercial interactions of a society being transformed by the industrial revolution.

Smith's "invisible hand" assumed that the dynamics of a free market were indeed best suited to determining economic progress and viability of products, companies, and economies. However, because of his training and beliefs, he was also convinced that a common moral obligation was the prerequisite platform upon which those market dynamics would be played out. Smith recognized that economic benefit from unfettered self-interest would be hopelessly lopsided. Without moral intervention, free markets would implode because of their own unfairness. (Smith's reservations seem justified when we look at those countries, such as China, Brazil, Russia, and India, in which a largely amoral market is allowing only a sliver of the population to extract the vast majority of the wealth from the economy.)

Whether morality has a role in the economy is a debate that continuously surges and recedes. In the early 1970s, economist Milton Friedman published an article that has become the rallying cry for those opposed to any intervention. Friedman argued that a business's responsibility is singularly to its shareholders. Everything else is irrelevant.

Protecting the sanctity of shareholders' interests serves a variety of agendas. For some, this means that the bottom line is the only line. For other companies, this is the reason for restructuring for efficiency. And for companies like asbestos manufacturer Johns-Manville, and silicone breast implant maker Dow Corning, this is the reason to seek bankruptcy protection from diseased, dying, or deceased consumers.

Friedman's position needs to be rethought for a couple of reasons. First, history shows that the market, as Adam Smith suspected, is almost always too adolescent in its behavior to balance the responsible with the profitable. Car companies, now preaching safety, forcefully resisted the introduction of seat belts and other life-saving improvements. Industry, now merchandising its enlightened environmental practices, only conformed to this obligation once forced to do so by law and the demands of customers. There were happy exceptions to this, but the point is that the market and its participants are not always mature enough to know what is their own best interest, let alone those of customers, the industry, society, and the environment.

A second reason for reevaluating Friedman's narrow definition of business obligation is that the very reality of doing business has been irrevocably transformed. In many ways, shareholders' interests are now actually advanced by strong moral principles. Companies used to transact business in a sequence: buying materials; creating products to which they added discrete value; selling those products to distributors or retailers; and then marketing them to the consumers who used them.

Mechanical and methodical, this system created a cycle of fairly predictable exchange. Each step in this process stood apart with its own driving considerations. Raw materials were commodities. Suppliers either procured these or added some basic function. The selling company would then engineer a higher value benefit. Once passed through the distribution channel, this value would be exchanged with a customer. Once the transaction was complete, the process of interaction would end.

CONVENTIONAL VALUE CREATION

Raw Materials	Suppliers	Design Make & Market	Distribution	Customer
☐	☐	☐	☐	☐

———————————————————————————▶

In the new model, one that Friedman would have had difficulty imagining, value is increasingly co-created by all the parties involved. The exchange of information and expertise creates much of the value of modern products and services. This exchange happens sporadically and spontaneously, in a random sequence or even simultaneously.

Think about Microsoft. An internal team of product developers work out the specs for a new product. Customers and hardware manufacturers are then invited into the development process to keep the product fresh and focused on the needs and capabilities of the market. Before a new program is released, thousands of prototype copies are sent out to customers and software writers. With the input from this extended circle, features are polished and problems debugged. Finally the product is shipped to customers. Almost immediately feedback from users begins to pour in through Microsoft's customer service center. This leads to intense problem-solving, as well as a run of new ideas. Upgrades follow. The cycle continues.

When knowledge comes into the value equation, the interaction among company, supplier, and customer is collaborative and irregular. The value that is created is produced jointly. And, because new knowledge creates new value, it is in none of the parties' interests to see the transaction come to an end. Shareholders' interests can no longer be definitively segregated from a company's other obligations. It is also the reason why companies are increasingly adopting the view, first articulated by Harvard marketing professor Theodore Levitt, that a company's only real assets are the relationships it has with its customers.

Since relationships increasingly determine a company's equity, the moral commitment of the company is a direct means for protecting and building shareholder value. Merck is one of the companies studied by James Collins and Jerry Porras. The pharmaceutical giant, consistently one of the most profitable, well-managed, and most admired corporations, long ago encoded as its primary responsibility a commitment to the health of individuals and the service of physicians. This obligation has often led Merck to make decisions that defy common business practice.

For example, after the Second World War, Merck gave away for free a proprietary drug to help large sectors of the Japanese population who suffered from a sickness caused by intestinal worms. This was not a tough decision; management understood that the larger purpose of the company was to use its expertise to give relief to suffering people. Merck could not have known and was not motivated by the fact that Japan would rebound, that it would realize an "economic miracle." Yet the generosity of the company has earned for Merck a unique and profitable place within the now robust Japanese market.

Fulfilling moral commitment is not always so noble, and its advantage may not always be so clear-cut. However, all companies are now in the business of relationship management, and the obligation and forcefulness brought to those relations determine viability and competitiveness. Those that ignore or take liberty with obligation are doing more than endangering reputation. They are also putting equity at risk because the very value of a company hinges on its ability to collaborate with and serve others.

COLLABORATION CLUSTER

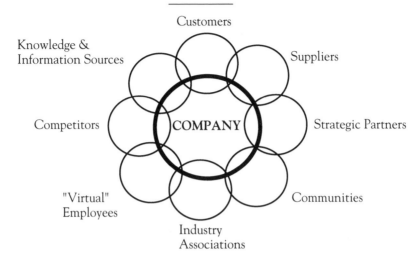

Any network is only as strong as the trust among its components. Trust is often regarded as sacred. It grows from a commitment of unquestioning obligation that comes from moral values. A highly developed moral sense is a prerequisite for wisdom since wisdom can only be expressed in regard for others. For example, Sony, while suffering some dislocation in Hollywood, remains one of the most highly respected high-technology companies in the world. Since its founding, Sony has defined its obligations in a simple but far-reaching statement called the "Pioneer Spirit." This statement calls on Sony to "serve the whole world" as a "seeker of the unknown." And to achieve this remarkable quest, "Sony has a principle of respecting and encouraging one's ability, always trying to bring out the best in a person. This is the vital force of Sony."

A commitment not to service, but to serve. A commitment not to sell, but to seek. A commitment not to productivity, but to respect and to bring out the best in its people. With its statement of "spirit," and with clarity for its obligations, Sony is ready for the chaotic unpredictability of its technological marketplace. Although the company does not know which of its products will succeed and which of its markets will take off, the company has the security and conviction of knowing what makes it Sony. Everything else is execution.

Obviously, for Sony, as for every other company, there are many risks, threats, and setbacks to be overcome. The global economy is neither friendly nor fair. However, the best way for successfully overcoming these perils is not to plan for every eventuality, nor to bury principle in the graveyard of expediency, but to define and anchor the obligations that will give a company "its vital force."

An Unpolitical Correction

Paradoxically, in an era of traumatizing change, the most effective management approach is based on unchanging obligations. A company's knowledge will grow old, and its expertise will become obsolete, but its moral principles endure, providing fuel for regeneration and relevance. The more perplexing the ambiguity, the more important it is to have the clarity, governance, and guidance provided by moral certitude.

The business potential of morality shouldn't be surprising. Interconnection and interdependence are inescapable, and these carry with them the logic of reciprocity, duty, and fair interchange. However, so strong is the resistance of some companies and individuals to this notion of moral responsibility that, while acknowledging the reality of mutuality, they settle instead for what we now call "political correctness."

Political correctness says all the right things, but has come to mean nothing. Unlike Sony's moral principles, political correctness does little to distinguish or drive an organization. In the absence of moral belief, the motivation is to produce the least offence — hardly a quality that creates dynamic and responsive business cultures. The politically correct tend to believe what the market research tells them.

How else can one explain a recent Cadillac advertisement, featuring one of the biggest car models on the road and claiming for itself environmentally friendly credentials? The details in the copy explain that Cadillac recycles parts and has made a contribution to an environmental organization. These are laudable initiatives, but is such a statement fundamentally right? With political correctness, positioning seems to be more important than truth, and deception is acceptable so long as it is only by implication.

When historians look back on the information revolution, they may well identify political correctness as the first electronically transmitted social disease. Information is so pervasive that perception has become the reality advertising people have always claimed it to be. Public awareness, now instantaneous, is the ultimate approbation. With political correctness, there is no penance for wrongdoing, no regret, only public relations. This is what happens when a whole culture has been spin-doctored.

Political correctness needs to be challenged because it provides people and institutions with a false sense of well-being. When individuals stop making rude comments because it is no longer acceptable to do so, they have only changed their behavior, not changed their beliefs and motivations. In psychological terms such repression is never constructive. Anger or prejudice or sexism that is subverted often turns up later in a more virulent form. Political correctness in business lets us feel like we are making progress in respecting obligations, when in reality we are only heightening tension. And when it springs back this tension will result in a more disruptive backlash.

In companies, political correctness undermines genuine renewal. If boundaries come down without an overriding moral context, then political correctness becomes the behavior code that fills the vacuum. If genuine principles are missing, then people settle for "niceness." If vision is empty of obligation, then the smartest strategy really is to be inoffensive. Such politicization is costly because it ends up draining the very passion and personal commitment vital for healthy change, for innovative competitiveness, and for genuine public service.

Correctness may be appropriate, but it is never inspiring.

The Obligations of Interdependence

The growing recognition of the value of interaction has been growing in recent years. In Peter Senge's work on learning, Michael Spendolini's exploration of benchmarking, and Stephen Covey's teaching of leadership, ethics, and moral principle are identified as critical to sustaining and enhancing the performance and renewal of companies, as well as individuals. The stipulation of morality from so many different sources recognizes that the modern economy, to a far greater degree than ever before, functions on an inescapable interdependence. No company is an island — in fact, increasingly enterprises are bound by complex networks of partnership, mutuality, and allegiance. In circumstances of such heightened interconnection, obligation becomes a strategic necessity as well as a moral responsibility.

Interdependence is forcing a dramatic redefinition of what it means to be competitive in virtually every product and service category. Visa and Mastercard are two very aggressive, usually hostile competitors. Each fights ruthlessly for consumer market share, for penetration of merchant acceptance, and for affiliation with sponsoring banks and affinity organizations. While the adversarial fight is intact, new technology is revolutionizing the whole business of financial transactions. In Europe, where debit and electronic cash tests are further advanced, these two competitors have had to collaborate — with each other and with smaller card issuers — to set the technical standards and to facilitate acceptance of the next generation of payment products.

Such collaboration is a financial and strategic necessity, but it also creates a host of obligations. The unified action of such industry heavyweights requires that the interests of consumers and retail merchants be respected, and neither compromised nor exploited. There is the legal obligation to avoid any antitrust or monopoly behavior. There is also the obligation within the partnership to share appropriate information and resources, and to negotiate equitable resolutions to the myriad of implementation problems. And while the companies have a mutual need and opportunity, such collaborations only work when there is also a deeply held and respectfully extended mutual obligation.

Obligation, a prerequisite for wisdom, has often been anathema to business people. In fact, the tension between obligation and business practice is a persistent and evolving one. The benefits of collaboration are, in a sense, being imposed because few companies have the wherewithal to really "go it alone." Investments in new technology and risks against new markets are often too burdensome for any one enterprise to face autonomously. But while the reality of interdependence is apparent, the appreciation and recognition of obligation is still very tentative. For many executives and for many companies, the ethic of independence is too established and honored to be rechanneled.

It would be wrong to assume that the only reason for respecting obligation is the defensive one of not making destructive mistakes. In some of the most successful and advanced companies, obligation is not a burden but a performance-booster. According to Collins and Porras, companies that operate with a heightened and more expansive appreciation for their obligations do not wallow in compromise, but tend to be more enduring and more profitable than those driven only by the bottom line. Hewlett-Packard, Merck, Rubbermaid, General Electric, and Disney are organizations that set standards within their industry for service, innovation, management, and financial performance. While these companies occasionally mess up, Collins and Porras determined that these results are achieved so consistently because of the pronounced sense of obligation within these companies.

A Competitive Conscience

One of the reasons so many organizations are unsettled is that restructuring has wiped away a set of long-standing obligations without creating new ones that will support and sustain them into the future. For instance, job security was an obligation won over generations of union and management negotiation. While the new economy may make such security insupportable, the elimination of this obligation has proceeded without much thought of what reciprocity will replace it. Consequently, companies are leaner without being unified, and more productive without being more competitive.

Even the most progressive of companies are struggling with the dichotomy between power and obligation. General Electric has for several years brought its most senior managers together for business review and strategy sessions. In addition to clarifying issues and goals, these sessions were also devised to create a commitment to cooperation. Even though managers were assessed and rewarded on measures of cross-divisional interaction and contribution, they resisted this ultimate test of cooperation — what CEO Jack Welch calls "boundarylessness." The culture is so steeped in competitiveness and control that even the dictate to cooperate has been hard to achieve.

This is very important for the many companies that are belatedly trying to impose higher standards of customer service in their organizations. Service resulting from imposed criteria will always be stilted and superficial in comparison to that flowing from the commitment dictated by conscience. While we have all heard a lot about corporate culture, there has not yet been very much discussion about that ethic of responsibility that makes a culture hungry to serve. Conscience is that reflex of personal responsibility connecting belief to behavior.

As the inner voice of obligation, conscience provides the guidance to do "what is right" from the perspective of the overall strategy and greater good. With employees wired amongst themselves and interactive with customers, managers can neither exercise control over every encounter nor issue policies to regulate every eventuality (nor should they want to). Unleashing employees to serve customers with individualized attention and commitment is a requirement of competitiveness. However, adherence to the code and behaviors that define one company from the next is still necessary.

Functioning like a corporate gyroscope, conscience maintains the constancy of workers and the equilibrium of the company even as the enterprise adjusts to the volatility of the current market by making itself up as it goes along. Conscience guides internal interactions between employees toward the corporate good, even when the strategic plan is cloudy and undergoing a rewrite. Conscience infuses craftsmanship with value. It creates respect in relationships.

One of the most successful appliances of the last decade is Matsushita's electronic bread maker. A technological marvel, the secret of the machine's engineering was achieved outside of the company's prodigious talent base. One of its engineers, befuddled by the technological complications of consistent kneading and baking, took it upon himself to go study bread making at the Tokyo hotel most famous for its baked goods. Studying the traditional craft opened the engineer to new possibilities for the machine. The humility to reach out for new learning and the sense of obligation that guided the engineer to do so were instrumental in creating a product that surpassed the needs and expectations of customers. This is an example of how total quality and full customer satisfaction depend on that personal accountability which comes from belief, and on that personal commitment which comes from conscience.

Of course, companies have a choice. They can demand these values from employees or they can engender them. Just as there are various grades of quality, there are various grades of obligation. The engendered obligation, because it is reciprocal and spontaneous, will provide the greater competitive leverage.

OBLIGATION FROM POWER	OBLIGATION FROM CONSCIENCE
Driven from top-down.	Grown from within.
Regimented by dictate.	Spontaneous by circumstance.
Motivated by fear of failure.	Motivated by gratification of result.
Leverage from superiors.	Leverage from peers, suppliers, and customers.
Reflexive response to measures.	Intuitive response to what is right.
Based on command.	Based on trust.
Limited by dependence.	Liberated by interdependence.

Conscience sounds like another impediment of responsibility, a millstone dragging down entrepreneurial risk-taking and innovation. Actually, it is a source of great confidence, a platform from which risk-taking is both more responsible and less isolating. In empowered environments, individuals are required to assume more responsibility and initiative. When the reciprocal obligations of conscience are clear and fair to everyone, workers can exercise their accountabilities with more individuality and creativity. The trust in the system of supportive mutuality encourages the trial and error without which real advance and innovation is impossible.

Business is obviously very difficult and testy. Even the most successful companies face agonizing decisions. Even the most balanced and responsible employees are put in situations of stress and paradox. Pressure will likely only grow. Tension and discomfort will only increase. This external reality of business will not change — so our inner confidence and fortitude become even more important. Conscience provides an assurance about what is right when all the options we face are muddy, mixed-up, and compromising.

In the collaborative work style now being adopted throughout the economy, the likelihood of conflict has grown exponentially. The more people to interconnect, the more reasons to disagree. However, conflict can be an important source of new ideas, and tension can be a catalyst for creativity. There are many approaches to managing conflict — everything from "getting to yes" to securing a "win-win." Conscience provides an underlying unity, the balance of obligation, that keeps conflict at its creative level, and keeps it from degenerating into destructive divisiveness. When there are no departments to retreat to, when there are no boundaries to hide behind, conscience provides safety and integrity.

Organizations often mistake policy for conscience. One bank circulates a code of ethics document to its traders once a year and asks them to read and sign it. After fulfilling its policy objectives to make all employees aware of its ethical standards, management turns up the heat to keep volume of trades growing. Brokers are primarily driven by the pressure to "do the deal," since that is how the group's profitability and the individual's compensation are structured. As financial instruments have become more complex, such a cursory genuflection to policy has been totally inadequate in meeting the information needs and ethical obligations to customers. While conscience can give expression to policies, policy cannot mandate a conscience.

Professor Robert Solomon of the University of Texas philosophy department explains that business ethics must "move from having rights oneself to recognizing the rights of others." Conscience is the inner conviction that recognizes those rights. While not undermining self-interest, this sense of responsibility to our larger social interactions ensures that self-interest does not undermine others.

In the following graph, I have depicted conscience as the critical guide for relationship interactions. Conscience flows from the beliefs and convictions held by both the individual and the company. Values, so important in the discussion of modern corporate culture, are also factors in conscientious behavior.

A CONSCIENCE MODEL

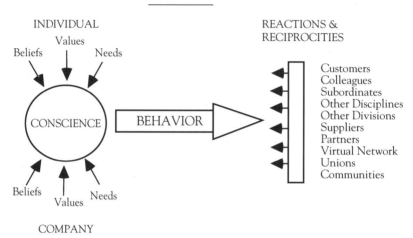

As the figure above shows, conscience is that personal judgment which makes us responsible in our behavior to others. In a perfect world, conscience would cost little because people would get proportionately what they give. However, in our imbalanced world, and in our messy business climate, conscience carries the price of conviction. Aristotle called this virtue the persistence to "do what is right and honorable" even when conditions make it painful to do so.

A more developed conscience would likely have prevented North American manufacturers from growing lax about issues of quality and service. With a heightened sense of obligation to customers, companies would have seen the ongoing cost of investing in quality as an intrinsic element of delivering value within the relationship. There is a certain sacrifice involved in doing the "right and honorable thing," but, as is usually the case, following the guidance of conscience is also the most efficient and effective course of action. Having scrambled throughout the 1980s and early 1990s to catch up on quality, many North American companies are still paying the significant price of having to make technology, process, and training improvements. The more expensive and perhaps irrecoverable loss is the human one — the trust and respect of customers who have taken their business elsewhere.

Creating the Value of Values

Given the growing strategic importance of moral clarity, how can an organization or an individual begin to bring the fuzzy elements of values into focus? How can the philosophy come into effective practice?

As with wisdom, each company will need to work through its own system. However, there are some lessons to be learned by looking at those organizations that have excelled as a result of their beliefs. One such company that has been repeatedly studied and written about is health-care giant Johnson & Johnson. Based on a review of the company, here are some of the building blocks for realizing the value of values.

1. *Values take time to build because they gain their substance from the countless interactions and communications that occur everyday.* J&J operates in one of the most dynamic, highly regulated, competitive, and knowledge-intensive industries in the world. Although atypical and sometimes baffling to outsiders, the company's structure and approach work exactly because they have been developed from within. Often compared to a centipede (not the most flattering of management models), J&J comprises 168 operating companies, clustered in thirty-three business lines, serving customers in fifty-three countries.

The company is highly decentralized. Management groups for each division and unit are free to pursue their own strategies and R&D. Even when J&J acquires another company, it usually leaves the existing management in place and tells them to call head office only if they need help. Seemingly random, totally flexible, and uncoordinated in its operations, J&J is actually held together and motivated by a rigid and permeating belief system. Senior management and employees do not pretend to have all the answers to the unpredictable issues confronting them. Instead, they have a clearly understood, tried, and tested moral framework for guiding them through the unpredictability, setbacks, and ambiguities of doing business. J&J faces the same chaos that perplexes all business people; however, as a growing and learning entity, it is sustained by the obligations and commitments it has absorbed at the cellular level.

Since there is no pretending to have the ultimate answers, people within J&J are not only free but also encouraged to experiment and test the unconventional. Failure is tolerated within the company as part of the price for creating new opportunities and for adapting to shifting pressures. This supplies the broad emotional support for innovation and risk-taking that psychologists identify as an essential condition for successfully managing short- and long-term change. Again, this represents a reversal of management orthodoxy. It turns out that a persevering culture (i.e., the centipede) provides much more fertile conditions for risk-taking than organizations prone to making fast, sweeping changes to culture.

2. *A moral context needs to be precisely articulated and managed in detail in order to provide effective guidance.* While J&J encourages autonomy, there is little flexibility when it comes to conformance to moral principles. These standards were defined by management in a formal and now famous "Credo." Written in 1935, in response to the devastation wrought by the Depression, J&J's Credo expressed the firm's beliefs and priorities. Central to these were its obligations to health-care providers, its employees, and communities.

J&J's Credo preceded the trend to mission statements by almost fifty years. This reflects a certain prescience, but also provides an important analog. Missions have become so common that they are almost generic. The problem with these statements may be that we jumped to mission without first defining their deeper principles. A credo says "I believe" while a mission says "I will do." The creed therefore provides the mission with its context and conviction.

A creed, even more than mission, implies deeper faith. Operating within this sphere of moral purpose is not simply ennobling but smart. J&J CEO Ralph Larsen explains: "If we can manage a high level of complexity coupled with a tolerance of ambiguity, that would be an important competitive advantage." The Credo provides the inner clarity that makes ambiguity tolerable and manageable. Even in the most uncertain of circumstances, the company's progress, defined by its higher purpose, continues. With a moral basis for the trust among the company and its divisions, employees, and operating units, J&J has been able to realize the full advantages of both empowerment and synergy — those much coveted accountabilities that have frustrated so many other companies.

3. *Credibility is a condition for effectiveness, so it is critically important to "practice what you preach."* Many companies have taken the half step of acknowledging the need for shared values. Without the full force of moral conviction, these values are often fairly safe and innocuous. As a result, employees in many newly "value-driven" companies have only become more cynical, while suppliers, customers, and other constituents remain

generally unconvinced. The problem is perhaps more complicated than not just living up to the language and promises of values. It may be that as business moves into the realm of obligation and relationship, the stakes are much higher than in transaction selling. By employing concepts of the spirit without the substance of belief, companies are suffering the backlash of having betrayed a sacred trust.

In *Reinventing the Future*, authors and business teachers Gary Hamel and C. K. Prahalad note the incongruity of endless companies spouting noble statements about commitment to employees one quarter, and then announcing cutbacks, firings, and plant closings the next. Such reversals indicate poor planning on the level of business, but represent a deeper hypocrisy on the level of relationship. While difficult action is sometimes required, companies must recognize that faith is fragile, that trust takes a long time to build and only a short time to lose, and that without faith and trust, values are just politically correct pabulum.

4. *It takes a tough company to stand by its convictions.* Morals are often referred to as "soft" business issues. Nothing could be further from the truth. Think of the swift and unequivocal action J&J took when its Tylenol brand was tampered with. The unfathomable implications of a totally unexpected and deadly contamination would have frozen even the most astute strategists. J&J acted without pause or hesitation to recall its entire inventory, not because the company had a preset series of answers, nor because marketing mavens had predetermined the PR implications, but because the Credo told them what was right. In the most tragic and un-predictable of circumstances, the moral framework provided an imperative for action.

Contrast this reflex of principle with Perrier's bungled denials and apologies after the benzene contamination of its mineral water. Or Intel's after the press picked up that its Pentium processor was (slightly) flawed. Andy Grove, Intel's CEO, is a remarkable and visionary leader. In times of difficulty, he has shown great compassion and commitment to his workers. But the company's hesitant and awkward response to Pentium's problem shows how tricky and difficult the obligations of relationship can be.

For several months after it uncovered the flaw, Intel kept silent. Only once the glitch was publicized on the Internet did the company come forward and recognize it. Even though customers complained, Intel re-sisted making any restitution, citing the statistical fact that the flaw would manifest itself to the average user only once every 27,000 years. While statistics have absolute value in engineering, they actually have little to do with the flow of trust in human relationships. The average customer did not like being averaged. For Intel, the problem was defined in the product terms of performance and reliability. For customers, the problem was defined in the human terms of promises, pacts, and betrayal. Only after IBM released its own assessment of the chip and applied the public pressure of no longer accepting shipments of Pentium did Intel capitulate and offer a replacement for any customer requesting one.

Intel is a smart company. It has learned its lesson, at least the marketing one that engineering realities do not necessarily reflect customer priorities. Only time will tell whether this situation has helped imbed the deeper obligations that inextricably accompany relationships.

5. *A moral code within a company must be followed by everyone, but not everyone can follow a moral code.* Paradoxically, credos inspire flexibility through rigidity. The more precise and fixed the beliefs, the greater latitude, adaptability, and creativity afforded to adherents. Larsen believes that "the quickest way to destroy morale is to issue edicts from New Brunswick [head office]. We do best when we take the time to describe the problem and let them [managers and employees] come up with a solution." Since the company has consistently lived up to its Credo, the people within the company are clear about what is expected of them, and have the confidence to persist even when the way is not clear.

J&J's Credo is not designed for mindless accommodation. In fact, because it imposes a set of moral obligations on its managers and employees, the code serves to filter out the people for whom those values are inappropriate or dissonant. Like the wisdom it embodies, the Credo is not there to avoid tough choices, but to provide the internal guidance for making them. That it operates on the level of belief also inspires the passion companies need to serve customers with innovation and enthusiasm. This, too, is a consequence of obligation, because, as theologian Matthew Fox reminds us, "there can be no passion without compassion."

The Bottom Line

Johnson & Johnson shows that values are inextricable from results. The company's performance has been as stellar as it has been steady. J&J has more than doubled investors' value between 1989 and 1994 — a period that included a nasty global recession, as well as considerable regulatory ferment and competitive price pressure. Innovation in the pharmaceutical industry is especially important for future revenue flow. J&J has recently introduced a variety of successful new products, including a revolutionary drug for the treatment of schizophrenia, which realized over $100 million in U.S. sales in only its first year. As a testament to the mercantile instincts that function in harmony with its moral code, J&J was named by persnickety Wal-Mart as its supplier of the year.

The Credo works for J&J because it comes out of the company's history and traditions. And it keeps working because the company tests, challenges, and affirms the creed in everyday operations and behavior. Morality is not an add-on, but an integral aspect of operations. It is not a burden or constraint, but a context for dealing with unpredictability and chaos. It is not a characteristic of culture but an expression of strategy. Morality provides the sense of obligation that produces quality. It informs interactions between managers and employees. It creates the expectations and standards for providing service and value to customers. What was once regarded as discretionary to business is now, in fact, essential to it.

A MORAL AUDIT

HISTORY	BELIEFS	OBJECTIVES	OBLIGATIONS
• What are the two or three defining influences that shaped the company and its business?	• List the beliefs that flow from these influences that explicitly or implicitly guide the company's operations.	• What are the immediate and far-reaching goals of the company? • How is success defined and measured?	• What are the values and obligations inside and outside the company that flow from these goals and are consequent to the success?
• How has the action of the company reflected the values it expouses?	• How are the beliefs communicated? • How clear are they? • What behaviors do they encourage, reinforce, and disabuse?	• How is adherence to values measured and rewarded? • How is accountability to obligation supported?	• What are the interdependancies and reciprocities governing corporate action? • How is obligation for these expressed?
• What is the biggest mistake or shortcoming that needs to be acknowledged in relation to the moral fiber of the company?	• Which beliefs must be: - Reversed? - Renewed? - Challenged? - Reemphasized?	• How can the company's objectives be restated to reflect the emerging or established moral construct?	• What are the priorities in time of conflict or uncertainty? • Which obligations are unassailable?
• Which unique or particular forum, format, experience, or insight that has shaped the company can be reactivated to create the "pillar" for supporting moral values and principles?	• What are the steps for introducing this pillar and making it an integral part of the company's daily interactions?	• How are the long-term goals and objectives served by this pillar? • How do they express it and give it immediacy?	• How does the pillar serve its obligations? • What are its enduring and sustaining qualities?

A MORAL FRAMEWORK

Professor Solomon posits that there are six "virtue ethics" that can be seen as the ingredients for a moral code. These are identified below, with questions I have developed to help give dimension to each.

<u>INGREDIENT</u>

<u>QUESTIONS</u>

1. COMMUNITY

- As social beings, individuals derive "identity and meaning" from the "communities" they work within.

- How are mutual interest and cooperation encouraged and encoded?
- What are the goals that provide broader meaning and purpose to the "community"?
- What are the underlying values of that "community"?
- How are those essential values reinforced?
- How are contrary values repelled?

2. EXCELLENCE

- Obligation not only prevents doing what is wrong, but also supports excelling in what is right.

- What are the goals, rewards, and reinforcements encouraging achievement beyond the job or project description?
- How has excellence been positioned and managed within the imperatives of productivity?
- When is pride nourished?
- Do policies simply restrict and limit — or do they also inspire and cajole?

3. ROLE IDENTITY

- Responsibilities and ethics are a function not only of an individual's values, but also of their role and accountabilities within their company.

- Are obligations defined as clearly as roles, processes, and responsibilities?
- How do obligations show up on the organizational chart?
- How are these measured and rewarded within the company?

4. HOLISM

• The virtues of life are not separate from those in business. It is time to halt that harmful schizophrenia.

• How are values defined and given priority?
• How are these aligned?
• How are they manifest in the internal and external behavior of the company?
• Are the values audited?

5. INTEGRITY

• Wholeness and honesty are criteria that apply to the individual as well as "community."

• Do internal practices align with external expectations for quality, value, and honesty?
• What are the integrators and unifiers?
• How are these activated during restructuring?

6. JUDGMENT

• Principles provide guidance, but in the gray reality of business, the right thing is often only discernible by judgment.

• How are judgment skills nourished and rewarded?
• What are the policies for going beyond policy?
• Is wisdom acknowledged?
• How is it addressed, measured, encouraged?

FOUR

BREADTH FROM WITHIN

Just as they have done with other management theories, many companies may immediately seek a model of strong moral purpose to imitate or implement. This is foolhardy. Each organization, like each individual, must take care to develop a personal set of convictions and principles. Those held by Johnson & Johnson, Hewlett-Packard, Matsushita, and Sony work because they reflect beliefs and behaviors unique to each company. To *borrow* a model for moral action is to admit the lack of the inner sensibility, obligation, and compassion for developing one. Indeed, many companies remove themselves from the actual content and experience that create perspective and wisdom by going outside for help. Morality, like wisdom, is not a concept to transplant, but one to nurture from within.

Implementing Wisdom

Businesses today face a number of perplexing dichotomies: short term versus long term; innovation versus economy; cost versus quality; learning versus doing; efficiency versus creativity; control versus consensus; competition versus cooperation. Dealing with these pressures is much harder than simply creating strategy or defining new revenue opportunities. Many companies hunger for new insight and new approaches. And they look for answers outside, turning to consultants who seem to have the right framework or model.

Outside answers have provided some meaningful information. But too often the research, training, and seminars have provided only a temporary spark from only a tangential insight. What more business people are finally realizing is that insights into business and enhancements to processes are most effective when they go through the difficult but creative exercise of developing them on their own.

As a consultant I am often regarded as the outside solution to an internal problem. In my previous role as a CEO, I, too, brought in outside specialists to provide perspective, expertise, or more credibility for an initiative I had already begun. I have realized that this cycle of looking anywhere but within for the solution is what is defeating so many organizations. Even though they subscribe to the importance of learning, many managers settle for a type of virtual knowledge, taking in the experience of others, and applying it against the problems they have been unable to express or define. This borrowing can never be as effective as that learning we create for ourselves. It can never have the full salience and relevance that we achieve when we construct a solution from within our own capability. While outside stimulation is always important, the greater value is the one from within.

How do we gain practice with this internal capability? What can companies do immediately to activate the inner resources of knowledge and experience? Where lies this inner wisdom? I have three recommendations:

1. Terminate all consultants immediately and impose a company-wide consulting moratorium for one year. Take the dollars saved and put half to profit. Use the other half to provide the time and support resources for an internal, interdisciplinary team to do the tasks originally assigned to outside consultants.

2. Suspend all market research for one year. Take the dollars saved and put half to the bottom line. Use the other half to free up everyone from the CEO to the receptionist to visit and engage customers on a one-to-one basis.

3. Initiate immediately an exploratory to create an opportunity for extravagant generosity to your company's customers. Think big and be ready to use the savings from the first two recommendations to make it work beyond expectation.

The premise of these recommendations is that knowledge and experience, as the dynamic ingredients of wisdom, are too important to be delegated to outside resources. Although they seem overly dramatic, each recommendation serves to jump-start the wisdom cycle of learning and doing.

The pressures confronting companies are generally presumed to be competitive, but more often than not, the trouble, splits, and confusion are internal. In Vespers prayers said by the Catholic clergy during Advent, wisdom is referred to as the light "strongly, sweetly ordering everything." These recommendations are "strong and sweet" practices to help companies and individuals achieve the needed "ordering" from within.

Beyond Borrowed Learning

The director of Total Quality Management at a multinational pharmaceutical company likens the use of consultants to a heart transplant that replaces a fundamentally healthy heart. Too often companies have this needless surgery, and then suffer the paroxysm of trying to have the corporate organism accept the grafted tissue. My own experience, as a provider and consumer of outside counsel, is that such external exercises only nominally engage the potential and imagination latent in the organization.

One client, facing difficult competitive and regulatory issues, hired one of the major international consulting firms to do a multimillion-dollar strategic review. After over six months of work, the plans and options were presented. I was invited, as were several other outside specialists, to provide a third-party perspective to this second-party's analysis of the first party's dilemma. The content of the recommendation was well researched and reflected the reality of my client. The format, however, was generic — the usual models and matrices used to deconstruct a centralized company into more autonomous business units. The strategic recommendations made sense and were adopted.

The recommendations were implemented, and the ideas pivotal to the restructuring began to cascade through the organization. Many of the managers who were now responsible for getting it done found the concepts simplistic and, in some cases, unworkable. They had been through the training and understood the mandate. But, as always happens with execution, some of the square pegs just would not fit in the round holes. Complaints mounted. Resistance grew. That the consultant's structure was so predictable had many people wondering why their own ideas for a similar reorganization had been ignored. Others felt that more would have been accomplished had they had the access to the CEO and board that had been extended to outsiders. Some felt that, in light of the cutbacks that went with the restructuring, the money for consultation should have gone to preserving jobs and retraining.

Some of this mumbling reflected the usual fear and bitterness of an organization struggling to renew itself. But it also contained a nugget of truth. Logic from outside, however compelling, is ineffectual without passion from the inside. This is not just a matter of getting "buy-in." This involves inclusion at that deeper level of mutuality, respect, and obligation.

There are times when outside counsel is indeed necessary, but it is important for the executives to realize that they are almost always paying a far steeper price than shows up in consulting fees. No matter how well intentioned, the process of consultation tends to drain the confidence of the company's internal resources. That a solution has to be constructed from the outside suggests that the potential ones from the inside are somehow lacking, somehow less effective, somehow less credible. Since consultants are often entrusted with the major issues of corporate strategy and customer learning, internal development of this knowledge is stunted. Even when we use others' questions, it prevents us from gaining the discipline and experience in formulating our own. As others have already observed, the investment in understanding made with consultants ultimately walks away.

Every level of a company is diminished by deference to an authority other than that inside the organization. At the most senior levels, the counsel of an outsider represents either an efficiency — get expertise not readily available inside — or another form of risk reduction. In both scenarios, the company loses. It is denied the opportunity to develop the expertise firsthand. And, while risk may have been reduced, an opportunity for originality, for testing judgment, has been foiled.

Another damaging aspect to idea borrowing is that accountability can often be avoided. When consultants have made their call, with all the credibility of their experience and expertise, then it is fairly easy for executive management and employees to disengage themselves from direct responsibility. I have seen this in organizations that have been through several generations of restructuring. Consultants are like a "no-fault" insurance policy. Whether this is conscious or not, the message deduced by staff (who are always watching such things very closely) is that the most senior people within an enterprise lack the wherewithal or courage to generate their own solutions. Such inference is hardly confidence-inspiring or commitment-inducing.

The borrowing of knowledge is something we have always done in business, but we have never done it in an information age, when knowledge itself is the product. Finding a shortcut to knowledge at any level eventually undermines an organization's ability to adapt.

Solveig Wikström and Richard Normann, business professors and co-authors of *Knowledge and Value*, say that knowledge is not a static unit achieved through learning or training. They explain that in the research literature from both business and the social sciences, knowledge is generally described as a sequential process:

- *generative* knowledge represents the new ideas and discoveries that come from direct problem-solving;
- this knowledge is then used in *productive* ways to make the products and services a company offers its customers come to life;
- and then this knowledge is manifest in the final product to the customer as *representative* of the company's expertise and ultimate value.

Logical and linear, this is a flawed model. In their analysis of how companies are struggling to adapt to the impositions of the information economy, Wikström and Normann offer a more dynamic view. These three processes, which represent how knowledge is transformed into value, are unstructured and rarely sequential. "Rather, in modern companies, the three processes merge with one another, and they are often simultaneous and integrated; they occur *reciprocally* and *synchronously*."

When knowledge is accessed from a source other than from within, it denies the organization the opportunity for the interactions in which value is made. We not only lose the chance to create, we miss the experience of interplaying with knowledge, of stretching its insight, and of exercising our curiosity. This dynamic involvement is the difference between what we learn and what we know.

This sounds abstract, but its implications are all too real. Teaching Total Quality Management, learning the new process skills of reengineering, and taking seminars on customer service represent knowledge in its old construct as a sequential commodity.

"Learn this new idea."

"Do it."

"And get better as you get more familiar with that new knowledge."

Many externally conceived initiatives at renewal have failed, or have not lived up to their promise, and the inference has been that the learning organization has been somehow deficient. Wikström and Normann suggest that knowledge is organic. It flows in many directions — chaotically and simultaneously. Companies miss this serendipity and expansion by experience when they implement ideas or solutions conceived elsewhere. Even a customized solution, when created by a consultant, does not have the cogency, immediacy, and applicability of knowledge created by those who will live with it and apply it.

As we have seen, the transformation of knowledge as a source of value creation involves customers, as well as peers. If we remove ourselves from the spontaneous development of our own knowledge, we risk not having the experience or the edge in co-creating this value with our customers. In other words, the issues we tend to delegate to experts and consultants are the ones that are essential for developing smarter, more complex relationships. The internal confidence and competence in originating and transferring knowledge is therefore not only an organizational enhancement, but also a competitive necessity.

Organizations cannot be self-contained knowledge factories. By curtailing the role of consultants, I am not suggesting that all outside stimulus be blocked (or even that consultants be banned forever). Expertise, new constructs, and fresh perspective are important sources of renewal. However, the value of learning depends on our capacity for dealing with it, on the confidence and wisdom we use to determine its relevance. When companies come to their own new concepts and ideas, they find ways of integrating and compounding that knowledge in surprising, value-expanding ways. They also derive far more satisfaction from this type of knowledge expansion, leading to higher levels of both commitment and accountability. Jim Burke, CEO of Johnson & Johnson, states: "Managers come up with better solutions and set tougher standards for themselves than I would have imposed."

The way to derive maximum benefit from knowledge is not to buy it off-the-rack, but to participate in the intimate exchange of its discovery. There are two important elements to this: intimacy and discovery. Our full human consciousness must be engaged. And the engagement must include the awe and joy of an expansive, challenging adventure. This is what Csikszentmihalyi calls "flow" — an immersion of self into the learning, doing, creating. Wikström and Normann found that companies expanded and used their knowledge most effectively when they put themselves into a type of flow, investing in learning partnerships with industry bodies, universities, and specialized institutes. Horizons get stretched through involvement rather than input. New ideas are interconnected and introduced, as well as new networks for processing and enhancing them. Since these outside investigations are based on mutuality, the (not-invented-here) blocks to absorbing the new ideas come down, at the same time that the motivation for integrating them goes up.

Knowledge is actually becoming a commodity. Expertise and specialization is readily available from a variety of sources. Consultants will need to establish their value not simply through the expertise they bring to a situation, but through the skills of integration and enhancement in the teaching, coaching, and implementation. Just as companies are increasingly co-producing value with customers, so consultants must co-produce solutions. Co-creation disrupts the relation between expert and trainee. It requires a heightened mutuality. Once the teachers have the humility to acknowledge also being students, the value they bring will again be worth paying for. Just as for the rest of us, their worth will be determined by their wisdom.

The Search Within Research

For many companies that I have worked with, market research is an ingrained and essential part of the decision process. With the help of ever more responsive computer and communications technology, these companies have far more information about their users than ever before. Despite this plethora of data, most remain distant from their customers and consumers, and many have suffered, not a closing, but a widening of the gap.

At its most destructive, this overuse of research represents an abdication of judgment. Using research to decide destroys confidence in the same way that importing a solution from a consultant does. Such research also condemns an organization to be an endless follower because, while research can paint a crudely impressionistic picture of what the current issues are, it cannot predict what will be nor, more importantly for business builders, what *can* be.

In the late 1980s I met Masao Morita of Sony when I was a partner and president of the advertising agency that had won the Sony assignment for Canada. Masao was in Canada on a two-year assignment to provide strategic guidance to the local Sony company, as well as to gain North American operating experience. Masao is the son of Akio Morita, the co-founder and recently retired chairman of Sony. In keeping with Japanese tradition, Masao's older brother had been given the managerial reins of the original family business — a centuries-old and highly regarded regional sake producer. As the younger son, Masao had to settle for going into the second family business.

Sony is one of those prestigious advertising clients who allow an agency to showcase their strategic expertise and creativity. As the CEO, I had several meetings with Masao early in our companies' relationship to define expectations and map out process. Like all North American marketing companies, our agency put great stock in formulating strategy. An important dynamic in that process at our agency involved developing a statement of "Brand Character." This personification of the brand was usually culled from quantitative market research, or perhaps from focus groups. In expressing and forming a character for a brand, we believed that it would be both easier and more meaningful for the customer to relate to the advertising proposition.

Landor & Associates, a U.S.-based research company that measures brand awareness and values around the world, had recently announced that Sony had surpassed Mercedes-Benz in worldwide recognition, and was now firmly entrenched in the brand pantheon that included Coke, Marlboro, McDonald's, and Disney. Knowing how other marketers measured and tested their brand properties, I assumed that Sony, too, would have rich supplies of market research to draw from. A brand of such great equity could only have been built with great deliberation, volumes of data and input, and a clear, perceptive strategy.

I asked Masao about the strategic documentation that went into the management of the brand's reputation. He was puzzled. "Sony is Sony," Masao said. "The strategy is always Sony."

I appreciated the Zen of that statement, but as a marketer and responsible advertising practitioner, I persisted after a strategy. If we did not have such information, then we would get the facts to construct a positioning for Sony through a formal national study, or through some qualitative sessions with small groups of customers. After all, we wanted our advertising to build on the brand equity already established. Without a strategy we would risk not contributing to, or even depleting, that precious equity. Masao finally retrieved from his files some press articles. "Read about Sony. Get to know Sony." And that concluded the strategic planning session for that day.

Among the articles was an interview with Masao's father, Akio. He had been asked by a reporter what made Sony so successful. The founder's answer surprised me. He said that it was his desire for the Sony name to conjure up the excitement, the tingling in the tips of the fingers, that people feel when they are opening the box and peeling away the packaging from a new Sony Walkman, or Sony Diskman, or Sony Trinitron. What I came to realize as I "got to know Sony" was that the strategy was implicit: it was based on sensation instead of facts. While I had wanted information to answer questions, Sony operated on a deeper experiential level. This insight provided our basic strategic guidance, and "the tingling in the fingertips" became the measure of whether or not we were delivering ideas that enhanced Sony's equity.

North American companies are, by contrast, addicted to market research. Others have already noted the North American propensity to "analyze" versus the Asian propensity to "do." The argument for using research more judiciously has usually been made in the context of breaking "analysis paralysis."

My reason for suspending research is different. Just as a company risks artificial knowledge with consultants, it risks synthetic experience with market research. Studying customer trends on a printout, or observing their reactions and discussion from behind the one-way mirror of a focus group facility, provides the kind of empty strategic answers that Sony, for its thirty-five year history before meeting me, had avoided.

Coca Cola's disastrous introduction of New Coke represented the ultimate exercise in quantification in the history of market research. The company performed over 500,000 taste tests to confirm its business strategy, and to support its marketing claims that New Coke tasted better. The numbers were irrefutable. New Coke was preferred. But all that research was, in fact, worthless. All that money wasted. All that time lost. The data, with all its bits and bytes and cross-tabs, failed to capture the essence of Coke, which is an experience. Ian Mirlin, the president of the Harrod and Mirlin advertising agency, wrote in an article at the time of the Coke crisis that while the marketing people had been busy measuring "share of mind," they had missed the fundamental reality that Coke was a "share of heart" brand.

Coke behaved as if they owned the brand and could make whatever adjustments to it they wanted. This mega-marketer did not understand that its brand was a property in which its consumers had co-invested, and which they, in essence, co-created. Consumers were not just "buyers" anymore because they had developed such a strong personal and emotional stake in it. Such consumer commitment is the dream and ambition of any marketer, but this more advanced relationship, this more intimate involvement, also carries with it far more responsibility. When ownership is shared, more consultation is required. And when ownership is experiential, more respect is demanded. Coke, with all its data, missed this essential mutuality.

Research is really a convenience for marketers and business people, and the more they indulge in this convenience, the lazier they seem to get. It is not that people are not working hard to ensure the integrity of the data. And it is not that they are not investing long hours in analysis and synthesis. The laziness is in accepting a surrogate experience rather than facing the trials, exposure, and risks of personal and direct contact with the consumers. The very assets marketers and their companies are dedicated to serving are often only known statistically.

The other great failure of research is that it tries to cloak in objectivity what is always and essentially subjective. The more complex the marketplace becomes, the more intimate the interaction with customers, the more ambiguity enters into the equation. The farther business moves from standardization, the less valid are the generalizations and yardstick measures derived from conventional research. That the investment in market research is inexorably growing represents the futile attempt to resolve ambiguity with numbers. Breaking the cycle of "spending more to get less" requires fostering a general appreciation for what I later call "substantial subjectivity."

This notion will be initially disconcerting for business people steeped in the doctrine of data. Yet, if we admit that the nature of value is being fundamentally changed by knowledge, then we must accept that how we collect and use the information forming the building blocks for that knowledge must change as well. Value-creation, once a function of manufacturing or transaction, now is generated by the free-flow of knowledge between people inside the company, as well as with outside suppliers and customers. It is impossible to dissect, measure, monitor, report, study, synthesize, and act upon each of these sometimes structured, but often random, spontaneous, and cumulative interactions. Not only would the data be expensive to capture and overwhelming to manage, but it would also largely be worthless because the random cannot be controlled, the spontaneous cannot be predicted, and the cumulative cannot be unbundled.

People will argue that to respond to customers more accurately and to serve their needs more passionately, companies must be constantly learning more about them. I agree, but conventional, rational learning in these unconventional, intuitive times is less relevant, less effective, and too wasteful. What we need is learning that is interactive and intimate. We need learning that puts even the most senior managers in personal, direct contact with customers — one-on-one.

Harley-Davidson, whose motorcycles are an icon for the independence of the American spirit, has recently also become a symbol of U.S. business resiliency. Like many organizations and individuals, Harley came by its now appreciated business wisdom through crisis. It was on the losing end of the quality and volume war with the Japanese motorcycle companies: Honda, Yamaha, Suzuki, and Kawasaki. Harley faltered, and looked like yet another in a list of global casualties to the relentless innovation, low price, and model proliferation strategies of these organized and deep-pocketed competitors. It was on the brink of extinction several times. Finally, with incredible effort throughout its operations and culture, Harley effected a turnaround that has now gone on for over seven years.

Many people already know the Harley-Davidson story, or will at least recognize the script. With their backs to the wall, everything had to change, and it did. Management stopped bickering with employees. The company stopped dickering with suppliers. Through disciplined systems innovation, continuous learning, Just-In-Time distribution and delivery systems, and a renewed commitment to its customers, Harley did the unthinkable and not only survived, but won leadership for its segment back from the Japanese.

Such case-study simplifications, however, can never capture the conflicts, the survival anxiety, the difficulties of change, nor the deep-seated doubts the company and its employees confronted and overcame. Richard Teerlink, Harley's CEO, puts it in perspective by explaining that human skills made the system work: "Top management must realize that it has the responsibility and obligation to provide an environment in which an employee feels free to challenge the system to achieve success. Once the employee is committed, the techniques become easy."

Any person to "feel free to challenge the system" must obviously have the confidence of his or her own convictions. Yet this freedom also carries with it the responsibility to ensure that subjective concerns of each individual have the weight of substantiality. And substantive thinking in any organization comes from the anchoring of an idea in a deep and expanding understanding of the customer. It is important that this understanding of the customer permeate an organization with the same intensity as the now nearly universal concern for quality. It is not enough to provide summaries of research learning to people. Beyond this factual understanding, all employees — including those in factories, on shipping docks, and in the executive suite — must have the opportunity to experience the needs of the customer in a way that encodes understanding at an intuitive level.

Buy Extravagant Generosity

Peter Reid, who has chronicled the comeback of American companies in his book, *Well Made in America*, talks of the need to "create occasions and opportunities for customers to tell you what they think, and then *listen* to the customers carefully. And 'close to the customer' should be a way of life for top management and all employees, not just the marketing department."

My recommendation to invest in an extravagant event in celebration of customers goes further. Many business people and workers now talk about the primacy of the customer, but the human behind the buyer or consumer remains a client code, a share point, or a percentage in some demographic data. To get to the intuition that is human we must get to know the human. Creating an event for intimate contact with customers is a way of accelerating the conversion of all the individuals within an organization into full-time, interactive market researchers.

The experience of the customer can never be fully anticipated in any research questionnaire. Nike's head office is designed as a huge, high-tech workout facility. Employees jog on tracks or toss basketballs in the gym. The company also brings athletes from virtually every sport and every competitive level to its "campus." These "guests" use the exercise facilities, interacting one-on-one with the designers, engineers, and marketers who create Nike products. Sweating with customers on a run, or tossing a pass to one in a game, tends to give a different insight to employees about who they are attempting to reach and serve. The language of business does not need to be translated into that of the street. Information flows in games, in challenges, in competition.

Guests are made to feel as much as possible as members of the "Nike family." They tour design facilities and product development labs. They get excited about Nike. And Nike's employees learn to see them as people. Nike is not perfect, but it has mastered a form of learning-event that is interactive and personal. While others try to understand what "co-creating value with customers" means, Nike is doing it.

Harley's CEO goes on long bike rides with customers. Scandinavian Air System's senior executives take turns at airport check-in counters. Wal-Mart managers spend time each month greeting customers at the door and helping them carry purchases out to their cars. Different companies. Different approaches to a more immediate, more personal interchange.

The key is to take the risk and expose ourselves directly as individuals to the individuals we are trying to serve and sell to. Many organizations have invested in customer service technology like 1-800 numbers. While this represents an important advance, much of the experience of the customer is still mitigated through a medium and delegated to a specific department. The contact may be personal (after navigating the appropriate touch-tone road map), but it is also disembodied. The experience of companies with customers is indeed more frequent and valid, but still remains once-removed from their humanity. Accessibility is not the same thing as interaction.

In only a few years Saturn has earned a strong reputation for respectful commitment toward customers. In 1994, the GM division took this dedication to a new level. In an original initiative, the company invited all its customers to come to its manufacturing plant in Tennessee for a weekend reunion party. Just inviting everyone was an opportunity for contact out of the ordinary. Three mailings were sent to each customer, informing them of the details, providing options for accommodation, and explaining some of the features of the event. Once a customer accepted the invitation, Saturn took care of everything. Hotels were booked and confirmed. Reservations for various events were made. Arrangements for customers with special needs were queried and attended to. All of this was handled over the phone with a casual, comfortable Southern graciousness.

Several weeks before the homecoming, customers received a box by courier. In their parcel were hats, pins, and other Saturn paraphernalia for all the family members making the trek. (One Saturn owner I know

added another person to the caravan after confirming the original details, and several days later received another box with more hats.) Each
homecoming participant also received customized maps showing the
specific route from their home to the Saturn plant. The map ingeniously
included the locations of Saturn dealers along the way. Customers were
invited to drop in for free hot dogs and car washes. Local communities
and chambers of commerce, alerted to the potential tourism boomlet,
included coupons, discounts, and attractions literature so travelers to the
reunion stopping at a particular dealer would also be encouraged to visit
and shop there.

With all the family members wearing Saturn stuff, it also made sense
to give some homecoming identity to the car. Each parcel included a
colorful foam ball for owners to put on their car radio aerial.

A student in one of my classes in Toronto received the mailings. Primarily for the opportunity to attend a Judds concert that Saturn organized
as part of the event, she decided to use her vacation time to make the trip.
She was overwhelmed. Saturn seemed to "have thought of everything.
And even special requests were immediately taken care of. Nothing was a
problem."

Once underway, the journey itself became a party on wheels. Saturn
drivers on highways and driving through small towns would congregate
at truck stops and doughnut stores where they saw clusters of aerial balls.
Visits to dealers in previously unheard of cities made the customers feel
very special and cared for. All these exchanges on the way to Tennessee
built anticipation for the event to come, while also making strangers feel
comfortable, cared for, and somehow surrounded by friends.

Once at their destination, Saturn customers were welcomed by the
employees of the company. In addition to the entertainment, customers
were invited to tour the factory. They met the people who had designed,
engineered, and manufactured their cars. Tents had been set up for food,
for an interactive display of new Saturn products, and for face-to-face
market research between employees and customers. As it had for
Woodstock, it rained during the Saturn reunion. And as with Woodstock,
inclement weather only increased the camaraderie of the 200,000 people
who had made the trip.

Customer satisfaction scores for Saturn were already strong, and the
homecoming raised that precious goodwill to an even higher level. The
attention to detail, which we know is so important in product quality,

was applied with similar dedication to the interactions between people. As worthwhile as it was to give something back to the customer, Saturn's event also enriched employees.

First came the opportunity to meet and engage these customers one-on-one. The needs and biases of car drivers are now present with each employee, not with the superficial understanding provided by a numerical research report, but with the fullness of experience that comes from a chat between friends. Second, the employees now know that they can build more than cars. The teamwork of their particular brand of manufacturing is transferable, helping pull off an incredibly successful event (despite rain, mud, and mass attendance). This confidence in their style and skills is important in helping Saturn workers adapt to the unpredictability of the market. Third, the pride of doing something that others appreciate turns a job into a commitment.

Personal exposure actually helps individuals adjust the "mental maps" that are so important to healthy change. Robin Skynner, a doctor and author who counsels on healthy growth and development, writes that experience is "the most direct connection we have with reality, so we can be more sure of it than anything we've been told. It can also have the strongest influence because it's always tinged with more feeling. We haven't just understood something with our head, we've understood it with all of ourselves, so it carries a special conviction."

The psychic rewards for Saturn employees probably match those of customers. My student still spoke with amazement about the experience six months after returning home. A vacation given over to a commercial relationship had rewarded her in ways she had not expected. She reported to the class: "I left with an annoying little squeak in my car. And now I don't even hear it anymore."

Saturn's event worked for Saturn, just like Nike's athletes' clinics work for Nike. A homecoming may be too quaint for other companies. It may be too expensive. The point is that each business relationship affords an opportunity for exchange, not only of value, but also of information, experience, and insight. To achieve the intimate understanding of what customers need, feel, believe, and care about, companies must get better at creating unique opportunities for this more human exchange. The generosity is not an expense, but an investment in reciprocity, in the mutual learning and experience that forges genuine empathy, conviction, and trust.

Integration Before Interaction

Face-to-face experience with the customer is important in management theory because of the common-sense insights it sparks and because of the symbolism of accessibility and personal responsibility it conjures up. In this age of renewed customer emphasis, such focus and direct contact is in vogue. Still, my experience is that companies will be as successful with fostering more intimate relationships with customers as they have been in unleashing empowerment with employees. The change is more fundamental than process renewal.

McGill University business professors Frances Westley and Henry Mintzberg explain that "visionary leadership is a dynamic, interactive phenomenon, as opposed to a unidirectional process." Interactivity is one of the great promises of the new computer–communications technology, but our understanding of it is still primitive. The word suggests give and take, but it is much more than the opportunity for a ping-pong exchange. It is not simply that business can achieve a faster result from its stimulus, but that the stimulus itself is dramatically changed by the interaction with the response.

Westley and Mintzberg use the analogy of the theatre. A play comes to life not only by the script prepared by the writer, nor by the rehearsal and staging of the artists. The experience of the theatre is complete only once the actors engage the audience and the two-way flow of attention, credibility, and emotion mingles.

A company's strategy, no matter how competitive or astute, comes to life only in how it is experienced by the customer. Westley and Mintzberg add: "Like a performance, a strategy is made into vision by a two-way current. It cannot happen alone, it needs assistance." This again is how co-creation of value is achieved.

CEOs and planners have long believed that the formulation of strategy represents their greatest responsibility. Their ability to synthesize market intelligence and create direction out of the competitive chaos is a big part of how they justify their keep. Strategy, as a type of corporate alchemy, could only be practiced by the initiated. Now, with the realization that the customer is not simply a "target" for a "sale," but an integral co-creator of the business relationship, the managerial exclusivity toward strategy development is waning. The responsibility of even the most senior executives is no longer passive — analyzing and studying — but rather dynamic — engaging and experiencing the customer on their terms.

This immediacy of experience has the same value at the operational level as it does at the strategic. The sequential process of customer survey to analysis, analysis to strategy, strategy to tactics, tactics to action, action to learning is clearly too cumbersome and time consuming. Organizations now require a simultaneous interchange of information and understanding.

If every employee in a company must sincerely focus on the customer, then each must have a deeper intellectual and intuitive understanding of that customer. In other words, the competitive reality of most businesses is demanding that every worker become a strategist, a service provider, a problem solver, and a market researcher. The wisdom for doing this can only come from within.

This may seem like a recipe for anarchy, but in an economy in which value is created by knowledge, understanding can no longer be sequestered in the executive office. It must flow horizontally as well as vertically within the organization, and ultimately externally to the customer.

Peter Drucker, in "The Discipline of Innovation," notes: "It may seem paradoxical, but knowledge-based innovation is more market dependent than any other kind of innovation." The market dictates which knowledge works, which is of value, and which satisfies their needs. As customers get smarter in co-creating and selecting the knowledge that is of value to them, companies have to get better in creating genuine inducements for that partnership.

The highly flexible, competitively adaptive organization takes continuous learning to the next level of continuous experience. Business organizations that have absorbed the principles and suggestions of learning advocates like MIT's Peter Senge have developed the skills for restructuring their "mental models." They have achieved a personal mastery of knowledge and have collaborated to make the learning integral to the functioning of the whole team. These learning systems, while essential, create value only in how the customer experiences them. So the benefits of learning, like those of strategy, are only maximized in their application and practice.

Through action, the learning is tested, validated, and augmented. The feedback from experience continues the learning, at both a rational and subconscious level. Senge writes: "The subconscious is not limited by the number of feedback processes it can consider. Just as it deals with far more details than our conscious mind, it can also deal with far more intricate dynamic complexity. Significantly, as it assimilates hundreds of feedback relationships simultaneously, it integrates detail and dynamic complexity together."

It is hard to imagine a flexible organization that operates on its own intuitive mix of ever-compounding knowledge and experience. While technology is creating the opportunity for radically new organizational approaches, companies have largely yet to develop the human capacities, confidence, and generosity to create such structures. Kevin Kelley reports on a group experiment at a high-tech trade show in 1991, which shows vividly how a group, freed from conventional hierarchies and learning processes, and using the instantaneous feedback afforded by the new technology, can quickly adapt and create its own higher wisdom to guide itself.

Just under 5,000 techies in the audience were given a placard. One side was red. One side was green. The group held up the placard on one side while a computer scanned the audience and, through some proprietary and exotic software, assigned a pixel to each card. There were large video screens on the stage showing the audience-placards as scanned by the video-computer. As the audience waved the placards, the display screen recorded and showed in real time the changing mass of color. The people in the audience saw themselves in an organic way: if they flipped from one side of the placard to the other, the color of their pixel on the huge video map switched instantaneously.

Loren Carpenter, the presenter and software wizard, started the demonstration by projecting Pong, the original video game, onto the screen. A white dot bounced within a square. Kelley explains: "Without a moment's hesitation, 5,000 people are playing a reasonably good game of Pong. Each move of the paddle is the average of several thousand players' intentions. The sensation is unnerving. The paddle usually does what you intend, but not always. One is definitely aware of another intelligence on-line: it's this hollering mob."

As confidence increased, Carpenter, without warning, accelerated the movement of the ball. "In a second or two, the mob has adjusted to the quicker pace and is playing better than before. Carpenter speeds up the game further; the mob learns instantly."

After taking the audience through a series of exercises requiring ever more precise dexterity from this unled, highly desegregated audience, Carpenter booted-up an airplane flight simulator game on the screen. People on the left were assigned control for roll; people on the right for pitch. With silent intensity the 5,000 individuals concentrated on landing the plane. Decisions here did not work with the precision of Pong. Different sides of the room shouted to each other as the plane they controlled on the screen lurched and wobbled almost out of control. Obviously about to crash, the mob aborted the landing, pulled the plane up, and turned it around.

This was an amazing feat of interactivity, but, as Kelley notes, it raises a key question: "How did they turn around? Nobody decided whether to turn left or right, or even to turn at all. Nobody was in charge. But as if with one mind, the plane banks and turns wide."

Transformed by the power of instantaneous information, each member of the group acted both independently and in unity. Whatever decisions were needed were made not at a rational level but an experiential one: doing; adjusting; taking responsibility; learning continuously; interconnecting observations into corrective and correct action. The information and action flowed in a continuous loop. There was no time for reflection and analysis, for leadership, or for even the most accelerated of conventional decision-making.

This is the paradigm we in business are inexorably moving toward. Information, competition, ideas, and talent will be moving too quickly to plan and control. Individuals within a company will use their knowledge to make autonomous but harmonized judgments. They will learn directly from their experience what works — in fact, they won't have the time to wait for instruction, strategy, or clarifying market data.

Flow will determine success: flow among workers, suppliers, and customers; between response and strategy; between intuition and intellect; and between mistakes and accomplishment. This is why work by necessity will involve individuals at a deeper, fuller level of their human capacities.

While the demands of this high-ambiguity business environment are already apparent, most of the managerial initiatives of the last five years have been in retreat, cutting costs and boosting efficiency. It seems few organizations have internalized Shoshana Zuboff's insight that "the behaviors that define learning and the behaviors that define being productive are one and the same."

In *In the Age of the Smart Machine*, Zuboff provides important lessons about how work is being transformed by technology. On this point, she adds: "Learning is not something that requires time out from being engaged in productive activity; learning is productive activity. To put it simply, learning is the new form of labor."

Restructuring and reengineering may provide a more efficient movement of products and information. But the infrastructure of human flow involves wisdom. The trust for simultaneity, the obligations for unity, and the extended commitment to customers are generated from within. Knowledge must be anchored in understanding. Experience must be embraced with confidence. The integration of the individual must precede the interactivity of business.

SUGGESTIONS & QUESTIONS

1. Whether you are a CEO, a manager within a division or department, or a part-time "networker" operating from a SOHO (small office, home office), the need for a more dynamic experience with your particular customer is invaluable. You may already be measuring key variables of customer satisfaction. But for the purposes of this exercise, imagine a reverse interaction. Imagine what you would do to demonstrate your commitment and loyalty to that customer.

- What gesture would you make beyond the basic business transaction to show your gratitude to customers?
- How would you engage them to get at the needs and issues beyond their purchase or usage?
- What would you most like your customer to know about you as an individual?
- How would you express your creativity, interests, and passions to your customers?

2. Imagine creating a forum for a more expansive exchange of attitudes and interests between you (your company) and your customer.

- What shape could this forum take that would be unique to your business, or unique to the type of knowledge-value exchange your business represents?
- How would you involve other workers, suppliers, and associates in creating and implementing this forum?
- If you achieved a profit windfall, how would you invest some of that to create your own expression of "extravagant generosity" toward customers, suppliers, and employees?
- What expression of care has made you feel particularly valued as a customer? How could you translate your experience into an enhanced expression of care for your customers?

3. Reflect for a moment on the degree to which you or your organization rely on the "borrowed learning" of consultants or the "synthetic experience" of research.

- What are the inner deficiencies for which these outside resources are compensating?
- Which of these attributes are indispensable? How can they be developed and nurtured as proprietary skills and resources?
- What cultural, process, and skill changes are needed to activate this essential learning internally?
- What are the risks of deactivating consultants and research for a period of time? How can internal capabilities be leveraged to minimize those risks?
- Which exercises within your company stretch and strengthen judgment?

FIVE

WISDOM AND WHERE THE BUCK STOPS

Growing wise involves taking responsibility for what we learn, do, and experience, and for fulfilling the requirements of our moral principles. Such responsibility changes the conventional view of leadership. On the one hand, it means that each worker in his or her own role must take on some leadership accountability. This is the personal initiative to work within a team, to contribute constructively to solutions, or to extend ideas and service to enhance the relationship between company and customer. On the other hand, it means that the leader of the organization must embody those aspects of wisdom that the enterprise is seeking to nurture and leverage. By expanding to include others, such leadership *extends* rather than *imposes* its influence, creating the power of momentum, commitment, and collaboration.

The development of wisdom as outlined in the previous chapters activates and gives substance to our capacity to lead, whether as a worker or as a CEO. Leadership then is a type of acid test for wisdom, an opportunity to gauge its practicality and measure its tangible impact. The acumen that makes us wise relates to the skills that help us lead.

A Leadership for All

As we saw in "Rock Two" of Chapter One, a feature of life and work in a time of sweeping economic transition is that many of the accepted roles, definitions, and distinctions in business have been rendered either obsolete or ineffectual. Jack Welch, the transforming CEO of General Electric, has termed this characteristic "boundarylessness." In theory, the greater efficiency is realized when different people and disciplines work in full collaboration, without the protocols and systems of territoriality.

Since Welch and his people coined this concept in the late 1980s, we have seen the emergence of the virtual corporation, which again involved an elimination of boundaries. Now projects are attacked by cross-functional teams, not only from within the sponsoring company, but also outside — with employees and freelancers working synchronistically across time zones and hierarchical levels. In both of these devolutions of structure, the work alone dictates the organization, pace, and roles to be assumed. People collaborate and do what needs to be done without regard for the imperatives of traditional territoriality.

The logic of this approach is obvious. In a telling reversal of management ideology, Toyota exported from North America the concept of boundarylessness to create a cross-functional manufacturing approach that is now the benchmark for its future organizational system. Shedding the inefficiency of compartmentalization makes sense; however, taking down boundaries has consequences that managers eager for improvement often fail to heed. Attitudes are complex. Traditions are entrenched. And the process of change as often as not proceeds in irregular and messy fits and starts.

Marty Myers, the chairman and creative director of the BAM advertising agency, explains that "the paradigm shift has just hit the fan." As the edges and margins that defined specific roles have been breached, workers have often reacted defensively. The elimination of established delineations has caused many people to suffer a loss of identity or a crisis of purpose. This may seem extreme, but we forget that territory is how people for centuries have defined their place and often even their worth. The dislocation of such important touchstones can therefore spark an emotional, irrational counter-reaction. In an article about transformation in *Fortune* magazine, Thomas Stewart writes: "The risk of failure is great. Snipers and cynics may be waiting anywhere — higher up in the company, among peers, among subordinates."

While the majority of workers may hold their fire and resist the urge to sabotage, they are still usually ill-equipped to handle the heightened responsibility and greater stress of working without boundaries. In addition to the competence of their discipline, individual workers must also have the competence of collaboration. Here is that issue of teamwork again, yet with a twist. Not only must people learn to cooperate, share, and communicate, but they must also take responsibility for many of the principles and activities that traditionally have been ascribed to the leader.

In a boundaryless world, individuals must create their own purpose, set their own mission, pursue their own goals, and live and breathe their own strategy. They must inspire confidence in others, work to the collective good, and manage the planning and skill enhancement for their own careers. Even when working within a larger company, employees are now as often as not essentially self-employed, needing to contribute and re-earn for themselves a place and a role in current and future projects. Whether autonomous or not, we are all essentially the CEOs of our personal corporation, and we create value by selling our individual skills, intelligence, and insights.

While eminently sensible, such universal leadership is again more complex and taxing than it seems. One of the reasons why empowerment has generally failed is that this issue of leadership was not clearly resolved. In many cases senior managers were reluctant to surrender the imperatives of leadership. In many others, employees were reluctant to assume its burdens. Responsibility was assigned, but accountability became fuzzy. And when everyone did try to take the lead, organizations found themselves so without confines that the result was a paralyzing anarchy. People have begun to give up on empowerment because the demands for leadership have become just too trying.

Here then is the paradox and the test. In the fragmented and fast-paced reality of business, companies need strong leaders at the top who are willing to lead without the power and authority of their position. As well, they need a workforce that accepts the mandate of personal leadership without the ego squabbles and sniping that have characterized the behavior of princes. Can this be achieved? What skills and sensibilities need to be activated for something as abstract as leadership to become a common element of everyone's job description?

The fundamental criterion for an organization without boundaries, and for a fully empowered workforce, is morality: the only way to function constructively without the rules and procedures of set boundaries is with belief in a common purpose, and commitment to a mutual obligation.

James MacGregor Burns, an historian and Pulitzer Prize winner who has studied leadership, observes that a strong moral premise is essential to advancing any transformation. He writes that such a leader "looks for potential motives in followers, seeks to satisfy higher needs, and engages the full person of the follower." The critical leadership for renewal is one that is essentially wise.

To advance this argument, I have taken the specific dimensions of wisdom outlined in Chapter One, and have defined the application and implications for both organizational and personal leadership.

WORKING WISDOM	*ORGANIZATIONAL LEADERSHIP*	*PERSONAL LEADERSHIP*
PERSPECTIVE		
Timelessness	• A context within a broad continuity and mission.	• A place within that context.
Clarity and Focus	• Clear, accessible, and motivating vision.	• Intuitive understanding of strategy.
Compassionate Detachment	• Empathy for human needs. • Courage for necessary sacrifice.	• Willingness to share information. • Surrender territoriality.
VALUES		
Truth and Honesty	• Earn the right to lead with integrity and openness.	• Earn reputation for honest input and commitment.
Justice	• Unimpeachable fairness in action to express moral code. • Create a culture that supports equity in all aspects of behavior.	• Reciprocity in all relationships to express the moral principles of the company in the everyday.
ACTION		
Unity and Integration	• Strategic and organizational sense for the whole to create a belonging.	• Collaboration and cross-functional cooperation.
Intellectual and Emotional Harmony	• Encoded and tangible respect for the emotional and intellectual needs of people.	• Participation at the full level of knowledge and experience.
Equanimity	• The ballast provided by self-knowledge. • The patience for innovation and risk-taking.	• Extend the balance to relationships within the company and with external stakeholders.
SUPPORT		
Substantial Subjectivity	• Use judgment to anticipate the needs of the enterprise.	• Use judgment to anticipate the needs of customers.
Mentorship	• Create an ethos that nurtures wisdom. • Choose successor, in part on his/her capacity to mentor wisdom.	• Take responsibility for identifying, nurturing, and passing on group wisdom.

There is a symmetry and cohesion to this chart. But what does it prove? Is it meant to lay out the ideal? No. Not everyone can be wise to the same degree. And not every wise person can be sagacious on every dimension at all times. The purpose for this chart is to show that whether we are a CEO or a line worker, our open-ended job description of today inevitably involves assuming some of the responsibility and perspective of leadership. This requires a consciousness and an integration that are of a different order of magnitude than we have usually been trained for. And this big-picture perspective flows from that remarkable human capability that I call wisdom.

Out of the Ashes of Folly

Like never before, the CEO has become as vulnerable to restructuring as any line worker on the factory floor. In only the last few years, IBM, GM, Westinghouse, Northern Telecom, American Express, Saatchi & Saatchi, Philip Morris, W. R. Grace, among others, have undergone high-profile dismissals of their most senior executives. Each of these circumstances was unique, but they collectively point to a widespread desperation to bring a redefined leadership to bear on an ill-defined business climate. John Kotter, author of *The Leadership Factor*, observed that North American companies "suffer from being over-managed and under-led." In other words, many people still assume that leadership is only an advanced form of management.

It is one of those ironies of human nature that leaders are often the last to understand the need for change. In *March of Folly*, historian Barbara Tuchman has given several graphic examples of leaders and institutions who stubbornly persisted in mistaken strategic behavior, even when it was obvious that this action would finally undermine the whole organization. When the Trojans accepted a gift horse from their Greek enemies, they were subverting the caution of their own experience and reaching out for a reward they thought they deserved. When the Renaissance popes sold indulgences to raise money for their own profligacy, they were selling passes to heaven while discounting their own authority. When the United States persisted in fighting Vietnam even after the resolve of the enemy was clearly understood, ideology became the victim of practicality. In Tuchman's analysis, these are examples of folly, of "policy pursued contrary to ultimate self-interest."

Folly, as the opposite of wisdom, represents the denial of new connections and interdependencies, rather than their synthesis and interpretation.

The growing gap between the compensation for employees and CEOs is one expression of leadership folly. Although a few executives have earned the respect of their employees — like Hollis Harris of Air Canada who voluntarily took a pay cut during his company's restructuring — most CEOs and senior executives have granted themselves increases in compensation, regardless of performance. This general trend has exacerbated the alienation of many employees who survived the trauma of downsizing. Increasingly, it also raises the ire of shareholders and board members. Such misjudgment at the top proves that although the language of business is now of collaboration, the behavior too often remains elitist and authoritative.

These fixed attitudes about authority and power are slowly changing. For a conference inquiring into "Tomorrow's Company," Sir Anthony Cleaver, chairman of IBM U.K., wrote: "The more single-minded business becomes in recognizing that there is no protection against the accelerating pace of global competition, the more it has to understand that all its stakeholders need each other. Few businesses can flower in an educational desert; few markets will grow in communities where the social fabric is cracking, and all business prospects are undermined if some companies destroy customer confidence by irresponsible behaviour." Companies in conditions of such interdependence need a leadership that builds bridges, creates commonalties, and achieves a balanced sense of proportion in everything from executive salaries to new product risk-taking.

A Model for Wise Leadership

To show how the leadership of interdependence works, I have drawn descriptions of the changing function of the CEO from business literature. The first column summarizes the accepted principles of leadership; the second includes the latest interpretation of the leadership art; the third represents my view of where organizational leadership is going.

TRADITIONAL	NEEDED & ACKNOWLEDGED	NEEDED NEXT
• Competitive Drive	• Cooperation & Collaboration	• Seductiveness
• Strategic Goal-Setting	• Nonfactual Imagination	• Fast Learning
• Self-Sufficiency	• Interdependence	• Reliance
• Provide Approval	• Provide Context	• Provide Morality
• Rational Analysis	• Intuition	• Integration
• Plan	• Coach	• Recruit
• Self-Interest	• Mutuality	• Empathy

Seductiveness

The very nature of doing business is changing. Where once the game simply involved beating the competition, today success requires interactions with other companies, suppliers, and sometimes even competitors. This is already obvious. In the future, companies will compete for fewer resources — be it natural, human, technological, or capital. In this world of growing scarcity, the leader will succeed not by driving organizations, but by "seducing" the talent and resources it needs for that company.

The heated competition to earn a place of partnership or investment in Dreamworks SKG is an example of this "seductiveness." Any company can buy a satellite. However, there is only one Steven Spielberg. It admittedly takes a lot of money to create an information infrastructure, but, more importantly, it takes a lot of talent to fill it. While not every software writer or knowledge worker is a Spielberg, the definition of value is changing as hardware becomes generic, and software increasingly provides the real competitive advantage and product differentiation.

We are right to worry about the "de-jobbing" of the economy, but the mobility of the "knowledge worker" described by Peter Drucker will continue to shift the power in business from those who have the money and jobs to those who have the ideas, knowledge, and creativity. This reversal requires leadership that, instead of granting the privilege of employment, will seek the privilege of engaging the best employees.

Fast Learning

CEOs have usually ascended to their position by accumulating important knowledge and experience, and by demonstrating the ability to motivate other people to follow their ideas and directions. In the knowledge economy, it is increasingly impractical and undesirable for the leader to be the grand and ultimate repository of information. Nor, with the complexity in the marketplace, is it feasible for the leader alone to be the source of the "big idea."

The notion of leadership as a "library" will give way to the concept of leadership as "laboratory." This will be scary for many. For the past decade, leaders have been talking in visionary terms, but for the most part behaving introspectively. Results have been achieved through consolidation and cost-cutting, sharpening only the reductive skills of productivity enhancement.

When creating value through knowledge, the expertise of efficiency is less important than that of catalyst. Fast change, quick innovation, and constant experimentation will be imperative because, just as the medium is the message, the company is now the product. This means that CEOs will need to be as good at learning as they are at judging, as willing to experiment with structure and strategy as they are at launching new products.

Reliance

The mythology of leadership includes the caution about it "being lonely at the top." It is getting lonelier, but not for the reason historically implied by this aphorism. The isolation of leaders, once a function of their rank or power, is now the result of greater and more limiting dependence. Instead of exercising power, more and more CEOs are finding themselves having to lead by soliciting and succumbing to the power of others. Think of Winston Churchill. The quality of his leadership was much more complicated than that of Franklin Roosevelt because he not only had to marshal, convince, cajole, and inspire his own nation, but also to beg, borrow, and plead with the Americans for their support. His leadership at home, no matter how brilliant and articulate, would not have won the war. Churchill is a paragon of leadership not so much because of how he used his power but because of how he used his dependency.

While most CEOs perceive themselves to have the power of FDR, the complexity and competitiveness of the modern economy has reduced them to the status of Churchill. The danger is especially great because they do not yet know it. Apple thought that leadership meant beating IBM when, in fact, leadership would have been to surrender its architecture to the clone-makers and software writers who have done the most to connect with and serve customers.

Even strong companies cannot exercise leadership purely from the traditional platform of power. With stock options, Microsoft has over 10,000 employees who may be multi-millionaires. Mike Maples, one of several people who make up Microsoft's office of the president, calls these employees his "volunteers." Obviously, typical corporate power structures are rendered ineffectual when the dependence of employee to company is reversed. Maples states: "We're able to keep them because their jobs are meaningful, not because they need the money. That really makes us think about how we manage here."

Not every company has the problem of millionaire employees, but every company I have studied relies more and more on the capabilities of its most talented, most capable employees. As competitiveness for customers becomes competitiveness for the most gifted employees, companies will find that this informally acknowledged reliance will become a burning dependency.

Provide Morality

There is wide acknowledgment that "top-down" decision-making is too time consuming and onerous in today's fast-moving economy. As befits the mold created by business heroes like Lee Iacocca, leaders must "set the standards," inspire "the troops," and then "get out of the way." While the demands of customization require ever-deeper, more genuine delegation, the one aspect of management that may remain in the realm of dictate is setting moral principles. As I have argued earlier, moral clarity is the generative energy needed for real vision. It is the essence of what the leader provides.

One of the lessons for GE from the treasury bond scandal at Kidder Peabody is that the autonomy of empowerment must be moderated by a heightened sense of morality. The greater the autonomy for the individual manager, the more explicit and demanding must be the moral direction imposed by the leader. It may seem contradictory to argue that CEOs should tighten their grip on the moral structure of the company at the same time that they are loosening the reigns of traditional power. However, while a CEO cannot anticipate and guide every business decision made by subordinates, the clarity of moral expectation ensures that the spirit of the vision set by the leader is upheld in every eventuality.

To earn the right to set such standards, leaders must also set the example. They must live, as well as define, the vision. Robert J. House, a professor at the Wharton School of Management who has studied business and political leadership, believes that the most effective people in spearheading change are those "driven by the satisfaction of building the organization, seeing people develop, and accomplishing things through others." The traditional motivations of money and position are secondary. Although the sense of practicing what is preached is obvious, the wisdom to do so remains rare. That may be because values have been embraced for their optics rather than from deeply held personal conviction.

Integration

Why do so many companies stumble? Why are the majority mired in mediocrity? Many argue that although most of the repairs have been done to the body of companies, the problem has really been in the head. Structures and systems need reworking, but the real crisis for many organizations is the failure of leadership. Despite the spate of books and seminars on the issue, the continuing dearth of leadership suggests that this may indeed be a quality that is "born not bred." However, the real culprits in this disappointment may be expectations that are too high, and systemic pressures that foster the wrong skills.

Throughout history, in every aspect of human affairs, leadership has been a scarce commodity. The needed intersection of intelligence, experience, intuition, and moral clarity happens infrequently. That is why we prize it so much.

Already a rare quality in individuals, leadership is further imperiled by the approaches many companies take to identify and develop it. Since vision cannot be quantified, companies use measurable criteria to define what leadership is, and who the candidates are for assuming it. The essentially competitive nature of this process ends up rewarding the almost adolescent characteristics of "who stands out," and "who has the drive and grit to make it to the top." While self-preservation is an important aspect of wisdom, self-promotion is not. Often, the individuals who have the necessary wisdom to lead have neither the ambition to fight to the top, nor the skills and personality that companies even value.

Patricia Pitcher, a professor of leadership at École des Hautes Études Commerciales in Montreal, has documented the deconstruction, specialization, and secularization of leadership in *Artists, Craftsmen and Technocrats: The Dreams, Realities and Illusions of Leadership*. In her research, Pitcher found that an adjective often used to define the business leaders she studied is "brilliant." As she dissected this quality, Pitcher found that it actually identifies a highly defined analytic ability. She explains: "If you conduct an analysis of something, it means you look at its parts and their interrelationship; you break down, somewhat artificially, some phenomenon into its constituent parts . . . But some things do not benefit from being broken down into parts; they lose their essence this way — an idea, a sunset, a poem."

For the most part, business people believe analysis to be the fundamental rigor of effective decision-making, so companies reward the most analytical, the most "brilliant," with ever greater responsibility. By prizing the skills of such rational "dis-integration," companies inevitably affirm those leadership principles geared to units and performance instead of those conducive to totality and vision. Pitcher calls this "the triumph of technocratic illusions."

The schism between leadership that comes from *rational competitiveness* and that which flows from *wise integration* is an ancient one. Buddha remarked to his followers that the "ferocity" required for leadership made it difficult to attain enlightenment. Competing obviously focuses energy outward and against others, while wisdom takes place on the inside and is embracive. Different cultures have sought to accommodate this dichotomy in various ways. The tribal groups of Native Americans recognized the importance of both roles, assigning the "chief" sovereignty over secular issues and the "shaman" leadership over the spiritual. There was no hierarchy in this split because the spiritual realm for the people of the First Nations is as rich and important as the empirical world.

In the West, the Catholic Church created the College of Cardinals to provide a reflective council to the Pope. Although the papacy has often behaved imperially, the structure was originally designed to protect and reflect the deeper needs of the collective organization. Here, too, the emphasis was on unity and equality. It was only in the mid-nineteenth century, as the Church's culture adopted the rationality of the industrializing world, that the papacy assumed the supreme decision-making authority of speaking "ex cathedra" — speaking from the chair of God.

Modern corporations have largely borrowed their institutional model from the Church (which several millennia ago borrowed it from the Roman empire). A board of directors, like the College of Cardinals, is entrusted to provide a wider perspective to senior management. Like the Church, companies have been through a migration of power in which professional managers have assumed more and more of the decision-making authority. While they may not claim to be speaking from the chair of God, many CEOs behave as if they are. And, until very recently, most boards served perfunctory roles. They were only really visible when they went through their own ritual of burning straw to send up the white smoke indicating the selection of a new CEO.

In the last few years boards have become both more liable and more activist. This development is usually seen as an issue of rebalancing power. At a deeper level, the invisibility and impotence of many boards — and now their new assertiveness — actually speaks more to an undervaluing and misplacement of wisdom. The voice of balance has been overwhelmed by the persuasive, if flawed, logic of the technocrat. GM's board gave Roger Smith and his successor repeated chances to implement their plans, acquiescing for a decade to the logic of analysis before succumbing to the messy reality of disgruntled customers and lost market share. Similarly, the board of construction giant Morrison Knudson allowed itself to be swayed by the logic of William Agee's turnaround plans, even though business, profits, and acquisitions were repeatedly ending up in a loss-making muddle.

The boards of the many companies that are suddenly forcing themselves to be more active are not showing themselves to be wise by intervening in crisis. If anything, such reactions are signs that these groups have themselves been seduced by folly. Making changes in management, while important, remains only a tactical solution. The real problem can only be addressed by exercising power with obligation, by acknowledging and rewarding sagacity, and by creating structures that embody the whole scope of human need and potential.

Buddha taught that "one's awakening awakens others." Wise companies flow from wise leaders. Therefore, the real issue in corporate governance has less to do with the split of responsibility between boards and executives, than with the integration of morals, knowledge, experience, and judgment into decision-making.

Recruit

Although overused, sports metaphors continue to be illustrative for business. Already, management has been compared to "coaching," spawning books of practical advice from Pat Riley while with the New York Knicks and Don Schula of the Miami Dolphins. (Certainly these are better than sequels from Attila the Hun.) Coaching is the position of highest accountability — hence the frequent firings and replacements each year.

The coaching metaphor is relevant for business because such leadership represents a control exercised indirectly. Only the athletes, using their prowess, reflexes, and commitment can actually play the game and win. The coach's strategy and will to win, no matter how astute, are dependent on the athletes for fulfillment.

There is yet another aspect of modern sports that may presage the future interaction between management and worker. Extending Drucker's view that the information economy will essentially belong to a group of highly mobile, highly flexible "knowledge workers," it may be useful to regard these as the next generation of "free agents." Highly skilled, wired, and imaginative, these workers will zigzag between projects, investing their sought-after skill and wisdom in those projects that provide the best package of fulfillment, reward, environment, and opportunity for continued growth. The CEO, who is used to having control over which employees to let go, will need to learn the more subtle skills of recruiting and retaining those essential employees without which "winning" is impossible. This is another example of the shift from "power over" to "power dependent."

Some of the more progressive companies have delayered by allowing employees options for early retirement or voluntary severance. In many companies, the workers who chose to stay often express the view that they lost some of the best people to such open-ended rationalization. Among the departures were exactly the self-starters and the entrepreneurial risk-takers whom the renewed organization desperately needs to remake itself successfully. Some of this may be recrimination, a response to the understandable sense of loss by survivors. Nevertheless, it points to the need for CEOs to also recruit the commitment of their most talented employees. While change may have to be imposed by necessity, the role of the leader is to secure the buy-in of those who must make the new organization work.

Frankly, most CEOs are struggling to either appreciate or realize this balance. When he was the CEO at Apple, John Sculley estimated that over 40 percent of his employees would leave the company after completing a project. The individuals found the original vision for the project so compelling that they devoted incredible hours and sacrifices to make the dream a reality. The Macintosh was created this way — as a product to change human history as well as build Apple. Yet, after completing the project, employees were drained not only of energy, but also of purpose.

This trend is apparent at many of the hot information companies, including Microsoft. It reflects a management by enthusiasm, without the balancing maturity to prevent what high-tech author Frank Rose calls "crash and burn syndrome." While managers in the autocratic style of legendary coach Vince Lombardi could once demand such sacrifice, the new workforce, like the new athlete, requires much more dignity, respect, and inclusion.

Empathy

Like other aspects of business, leadership has been defined by its "hard" and "soft" aspects. On the hard side are such characteristics as "smart," "tough negotiator," "brilliant with numbers," and "asks the best questions." On the soft side are things like "gutsy" and "good with people." In the old and still dominant mode of leadership, the hard characteristics are seen as essential, while the soft are considered important but discretionary.

In today's upside-down business world, the soft skills are increasingly the most strategic, and therefore the most essential. In *The Expertise of the Change Agent*, David Buchanan and David Boddy report from various studies that many companies have fumbled their way into the productivity improvements promised by new technology. The authors cite a survey in which "46% of information technology projects were delivered late, and 48% over budget." They concluded that: "Human performance in an information technology is as much a social and organizational accomplishment as a technical one." That these data were not obvious to senior managers shows how much business has underappreciated the very hard cost of neglecting the "soft" aspects of human need and motivation.

Wisdom involves empathy. Rabbi Joseph Telushkin summarizes the Talmudic teachings about leadership: "In short, if you wish to transform and elevate people, sympathy and preaching are not enough, because both compel the listener to concede the falseness of how he (or she) has been living until now. The first requirement is empathy. Only when a person senses that you identify with his/her circumstances and understand his/her truth, will he or she be open to change."

Several important insights in this warrant amplification:

1. Effecting change is not enough. The best leaders "transform and elevate," altering not only the consciousness, but expanding the very potential of the people being led.
2. Information is not enough. People not only need to hear the reasons for corporate change, but they must also sense that their reasons for fearing change are understood, appreciated, and taken into account by management.
3. Strategy is not enough. Employees need to hear "truth" reflecting both the goals of the organization and the reality of employees. Too often CEOs assume that the problems during change come from a lack of information and context. Since the real issue is truth, the real problem for CEOs is credibility.
4. Empowerment is not enough. Before asking employees to "stand in the shoes" of customers, leaders must themselves "stand in the shoes" of their employees.

Integrity at the Top

Some will argue that the capabilities of competitiveness, with its drive and focus, are essentially incompatible with those of a wider, more embracive intelligence. Many believe that only by exception will one person be able to achieve the position of command simultaneously with the lucidity for compassion. This may be one of those self-fulfilling limitations.

Companies are struggling to provide ever greater customization and quality to customers, while aggressively increasing efficiency. While companies have quickly adopted the efficiency of flatter, more horizontal organizations, they have been less effective in surrendering the vertical power flow. But by necessity, that is changing. Serge Huot, vice-president of Global Sourcing at GE Medical Systems, explains: "In a big organization each layer slows down the process. By delayering you are giving people the power to change."

In other words, the demands of the market are themselves forcing a leadership that is both fixed in its vision and flexible in its execution, determined in its strategy and accommodating by letting employees come up with solutions. The split between leadership and wisdom may never have been necessary — it is certainly no longer competitively tenable. That is one of the reasons why the precocious (although still sometimes immature) Microsoft has adopted a multi-member office of the president; it is one of the reasons why Sony and Nissan have both established positions for a "corporate philosopher"; it is the reason that Xerox created an office of quality that reports directly to the CEO. A balanced organization is impossible without a balanced leadership.

Ford is attempting to overcome generations of conventional management theory and establish its own working balance by creating "the kind of company the customer would design." However, despite advancing the principles of teamwork, Ford's processes have remained stubbornly vertical, with decisions, manufacturing, assembly, and marketing following in a progressive sequence. In customer service and satisfaction, Ford trails not only the Japanese, but also General Motors. This is a serious setback for a company that for more than a decade has invested hundreds of millions of dollars promoting its promise that "Quality is Job One." Humbled, the goal now is "organizing around four key processes that create customer satisfaction on the service side of the business: Fixing it right the first time, supporting dealers and handling customers, engineering cars with ease of service in mind, and developing service fixes faster."

Such horizontal makeovers are common. The trick in making them work is to encourage (to have the courage for) leadership qualities that are:

1. pervasive — operating throughout the organization, at every level, within every relationship and
2. embracive — wise enough to engender and support the necessary interactions and cooperation that go with such shared obligations.

Despite the flippancy with which corporate culture is often discussed, changing it remains among the most difficult of leadership's challenges. Think of how hard it is to change personality or to modify eating or drinking behavior that we already know is bad for us. Modifying culture fights the same slippery aspects of human personality, habit, and attitude. Yet culture must be addressed.

Alex Trotman, Ford's CEO, is attempting what some analysts call the "largest merger in history." He is combining the very separate, culturally distinct European and North American operations. It is the ultimate test of synergy, requiring the ultimate balance of forward strategy and cultural glue. The new collaboration must be established, and then reinforced in countless ways. *BusinessWeek* reported how "at ritualized meetings, managers pored over three-ring binders full of data. Trotman has banned the binders and instituted 'no-fault' meetings where managers can fess up to problems knowing that the problem, not the message bearer, will be attacked."

Culture, like wisdom, is created over time. The failure of so many restructuring schemes is due not to the validity of the implementation plan, but to the casual attitude toward generating a corresponding and supportive change within culture. As Trotman knows, each behavior, meeting, and action is an opportunity to change that culture or to be undermined by it. But this is not just a matter of conditioning. It again requires the full conviction of belief. The harmonizing of competitiveness with compassion within leadership is therefore not a consequence but a condition for healing the split between plan and culture, between performance and obligation.

During the major league baseball strike of 1994, it is highly symbolic that the last team to lay off staff was the team that had most recently been first, winning back-to-back World Series championships. Paul Beeston, CEO of the Toronto Blue Jays, comments on how the logic for winning and for the enlightened management of people are one and the same. "We don't have any mission statement. We don't have any written policies. We have an organization chart that I don't think anyone's ever looked at. We have a policy manual, but we don't pay attention to it. The fact of the matter is, you have got to treat every person in the organization as if they are the most important."

King Solomon, who before Churchill was the archetype of the enlightened leader, described wisdom as a flow that "moves more easily than motion itself, pervading and permeating all things." The boundaryless spontaneity demanded by the new structures at companies like GE and Ford will need exactly such a leadership — a seamless leadership that is itself "pervading and permeating."

Those organizations that have earned high marks for innovation and customer responsiveness have in a sense already mastered Solomon's wise leadership. Take 3M as an example. Consistently regarded as one of the best managed of North American companies, 3M generated almost $1 billion of its $15 billion in revenue from products launched within 1994. With a long history of innovation, 3M also registered 543 patents, an increase of 40 percent from 1991. And the company delivered profits of almost 20 percent. In an interview in *The Economist*, CEO Livio DeSimone attributed these impressive results to "appreciating the curiosity of your people." This seems like understatement, except that the culture at 3M, fashioned seventy years ago by William McKnight, has consistently respected the input and discretion of workers. Leadership at 3M flows not only from the top, but also from the sides, from below, and, most importantly, from within each individual.

In a time when virtually all companies are seeking leadership at all levels to accelerate product development, improve service, and advance productivity, the lesson from 3M is that the quality of execution hinges on integrity at the top. If the CEO does not practice and teach the moral as well as strategic values that guide the operation, then it will be impossible to achieve the initiative and accountability on the level of the individual employee who is finally responsible for the quality of the product, the intelligence of the decision, and the courtesy of the service extended to customers.

Integrity is often confused with honesty. Frankness, openness, and truthfulness are certainly dimensions of integrity, but these are its expressions rather than its definition. Integrity is to operate from the whole, to reflect the complete or the totality. This means incorporating the full range of human skill — listening, thinking, reflecting, learning, questioning, intuiting. However, the totality is not just the inner one of an individual's potential, but also includes connection with those outer forces and factors with which every human being interacts. Integrity is essentially a type of unity — a blending of inner capabilities with external influences. An executive shows integrity when the full range of that individual's character is dynamically involved with the issues and pressures of the external world.

A Model Manipulation

Integrity and moral conviction are so important because all organizational leadership, indeed all management, basically involves manipulation. Although it is rarely acknowledged as such, the shifting, cajoling, inspiring, and threatening that influence others to take a direction they otherwise might not is manipulative. Becoming a leader, or exercising leadership, inevitably requires using such devices of motivation, so each essentially involves a basic level of even gentle coercion.

Manipulation is not bad in and of itself. Arguably, it is an essential and intrinsic part of the pact between company and worker. Although it seems antithetical to the very precepts of enlightened management, there are times when manipulation is obviously needed. Consensus is not necessarily capable of all the judgments, timeliness, and perspective that the modern enterprise needs. There are times when the beneficial sense of inclusion and the ethics of participation must be overridden by the wider, less clear, collective good that only the leader can see and commit to.

As power within organizations continues to fragment, and as the self-interest of the organization is increasingly served by being more embracive toward workers, the skill of manipulation is open for abuse. That is, engaging employees, suppliers, and customers on the fullest terms of their human need and potential only as a device, not as a conviction, only as a strategy, and not as a moral belief. At this level manipulation becomes reprehensible, and the damage it does, particularly to the trust between parties, is irreparable.

Leadership without integrity encourages the most divisive type of politics and sycophancy. It will allow the destructive manipulation that is without conscience and personally aggrandizing. Some will agree that immorality is unacceptable, but that amorality is probably the best that can be hoped for when the market is dictating the priorities. Such logic is basically premised on a semantic game. In the interactions between people, there either is or is not a moral basis for trust.

Leadership that is whole, that is striving for integrity, will create organizations that are proper and practical, as well as companies in which there is constructive tension between committed "persuaders." Lest this sounds like negative idealism, it is helpful to recognize that companies successful in empowerment have done a better job than most in creating the manipulations and integrity to replace the command–control imperatives of old leadership. In these organizations, the commitment to ideals of service and behavior (integrity) are clearly articulated. The rewards and reinforcements (manipulations) for inducing the behavior geared to the goals are also clear and compelling. Peer pressure and peer recognition (more manipulations) are among the motivators for conforming to the goal.

Whether by conscious decision or by customer demand, virtually every company has delayered decision-making. Leadership, which used to operate by direct extension from the CEO, now tends to weave its way indirectly throughout a company. At 3M and Hewlett-Packard, engineers themselves determine where to invest a portion of their most precious research time. At Nordstrom, employees are encouraged to take whatever personal action necessary to solve a customer problem, complaint, or request. Having successfully devolved power, these companies have replaced the oppressive control of hierarchy with the pervasive control of shared values. Such empowerment may be seen as the ultimate manipulation, and it would rightly be regarded as intrusive and diminishing were not the strains of integrity so strongly developed and present within these organizations. Morality is therefore what gives manipulation its legitimacy.

Wisdom (or its opposite) is expressed in the interaction between the manipulation an executive must use to fuse organizational action and the integrity with which it is done. Chester I. Barnard, in his landmark book, *The Functions of the Executive*, explored this issue in 1938 while teaching at Harvard. Barnard wrote with great insight, but also from personal experience, having served as president of the New Jersey Bell Telephone Company, and before that, of the Rockefeller Foundation. Of all the functional responsibilities of the CEO, Barnard argued that "the distinguishing mark of the executive responsibility is that it requires not merely conformance to a complex code of morals, but also the creation of moral code for others." This encoding of specific moral principles within a company, and the nurturing of its obligations among employees, is not so much a spiritual intrusion as the necessity for creating genuine and cohesive values.

Personal integrity, while essential as a foundation, is not enough. To fulfill Barnard's responsibility for moral creativeness, a CEO must define, promote, and engender the highest integrity throughout the corporation. In the context of the 1930s, Barnard perceived "morality" as affecting not only the inner relationships of a company, but also the individual "crafts-manship" of employees. He understood that personal obligation was a precondition for quality, and that reciprocity between company and employee was a precondition for this heightened obligation. The cata-strophic decline of quality in North America through the 1960s and '70s reflects not only a managerial myopia, but an even more disturbing mana-gerial moral crisis. Fixing systems without infusing and encouraging the needed integrity has landed the majority of quality schemes on the or-ganizational scrap heap.

In a manufacturing economy, integrity reveals itself in the functional quality of the actual product. In an information economy, integrity is actually more important because value is created and transferred by a process of connections between people. Obviously, the quality and trust of each interaction depends on the depth of integrity at play. By promot-ing moral character, a CEO is not simply contributing to culture, but actually building the competitive momentum and differentiation to en-hance each vital connection. Henry Mintzberg writes: "It is this integrity — this sense of being truly genuine — which proves crucial to visionary leadership and makes it impossible to translate into a general formula."

History has already given us numerous examples of leaders who em-bodied and engendered integrity to build very successful enterprises: William Cooper Procter, grandson of the co-founder of Procter & Gam-ble, introduced enlightened profit sharing and employee ownership plans over one hundred years ago; Ray Kroch, McDonald's founder, reversed the conventions of franchising, serving and securing first the success of franchisees. While exceptional, these executives demonstrate that leader-ship wisdom can be synthesized in a single individual. The key variable is not so much talent as integrity.

Business culture assumes that leadership is a rare and very special qual-ity. This only reinforces its obsolete elitism. Wise people, while not abundant, are also not rare, but it takes a wise organization to recognize, nurture, and reward them. Mary Parker Follett explains: "Leader and fol-lowers are both following the invisible leader — the common purpose. The best executives put this common purpose clearly before their group. While leadership depends on depth of conviction and the power coming there from, there must also be the ability to share that conviction with others, the ability to make purpose articulate. And then that common purpose becomes the leader." Paul Beeston puts this in bottom-line terms when he says: "We win together. We lose together."

QUESTIONS OF LEADERSHIP

1. IN A WORLD WITHOUT BOUNDARIES

• Reflect for a moment about whether and how you have experienced the collapse of boundaries.

- What have been the implications for your work and for your job description?
- How have you accommodated this blurring of boundaries?
- What, if any, has been the source of your resistance?
- How has this ill-defined world stretched you?
- What have you or your organization done to re-create the sense of identity and purpose that the taking down of boundaries tends to compromise?
- What do you specifically need to function and thrive in this new environment?
- What does your work or company need?
- How have working relationships changed?
- How can these relationships be improved to reflect the reality of merged boundaries and cross-function teams?
- How are obligations expressed in the absence of hierarchy and job description?

• Imagine the future structure of your work, company, and interactions. Chances are that this will be still more fluid and less flexible.

- What are your anxieties and hopes going into that future?
- What would you like to accomplish? What would give most meaning to your work?
- How can you prepare for that realization?
- What are the specific skills you need to expand your flexibility?
- What is your plan for honing and nurturing those critical skills?

2. A LEADERSHIP FOR ALL

• The nature of work and the impermanence of jobs suggest that virtually every individual will need to function with far greater self-motivation and autonomy. Whether empowered or self-employed, each of us will increasingly be asked to contribute as leaders as well as specialists.

- How would you characterize your leadership style?
- What are the strengths? Gaps?
- Who do you most admire as a leader? Why?

• Take a few moments and complete for yourself the following leadership model:

WORKING WISDOM	LEADERSHIP IN ACTION
PERSPECTIVE	
Timelessness	• How do I reflect consciousness of the past and future for myself? My work? My company? My colleagues?
Clarity and Focus	• How clear is my personal strategy? • How conscious am I of that strategy in the tension of everyday decision-making?
Compassionate Detachment	• In what ways do I tangibly demonstrate empathy for peers, subordinates, suppliers, and organizational superiors? • How successful am I in keeping ego out of decisions and interactions?
VALUES	
Truth and Honesty	• Am I honest with myself about priorities, competencies, expectations, limitations, and needs? • How do I demonstrate my commitment to the truth?
Justice	• In what ways do I work to create and extend reciprocity and justice in this delayered, boundary-reduced work environment? • What is my accountability to myself? My company? My colleagues? My community?
ACTION	
Unity and Integration	• How do I work to eliminate separations and boundaries?
Intellectual/Emotional Harmony	• Am I respectful of the full spectrum of human need — for myself as well as for those I interact with?
Equanimity	• What do I do to work toward a genuine balance?
SUPPORT	
Substantial Subjectivity	• Do I trust my own judgment? • Do I exercise my own judgment sufficiently to earn that trust?
Mentorship	• Whom can I learn from? • Whom can I teach?

• As a more detailed project, research the leader you have identified as admiring most and go through the model from the perspective of what you have learned about or from that individual.

3. MANIPULATION

• In what circumstances or situations have you experienced manipulation?
  - How does that feel?
• When have you manipulated others?
• What are the issues or insights attending to that manipulation?
• Which values that you espouse and that you hold with others build trust?

II

Individual Quest, Collective Advantage

Six

An Opening to Wisdom

In seeking renewal, companies are open to possibilities that even a few years ago would have seemed remote. Encouraged by teachers like Charles Handy, Peter Drucker, Peter Senge, Matthew Fox, and Steven Covey, many business people have begun to understand that learning and leadership are as much a function of the spirit as the intellect. The frequent discussion of values is, in a sense, a code for this greater involvement of the human potential. It is widely understood that people who share purpose at a deeper level are far more likely to collaborate on the fiscal and performance objectives set by the enterprise.

Having looked at the need for wisdom in business, we now turn to how an individual person grows wise. Part II maps out this personal journey.

The "In and Out"

In 1992, while visiting Japan, I spent almost a full week at the twelfth-century Dogen monastery at Mount Eihei. With eleven other outsiders, I practiced meditation and participated in the monastic chores of cleaning floors, raking leaves in the garden, and preparing food. Each activity was taken on with a calm intensity, not as a diversion from the meditative practice, but as an extension to it. The doing was illumined by the sitting in meditation, and the sitting was made richer by the doing.

This was new to me. I had grown up in a Western tradition in which the immersion in the spiritual was done quite apart from the everyday. This split was not an act of hypocrisy, but a conviction that the sacred was special, and therefore apart from the ordinary. Instead, the sacred infuses the ordinary, and the ordinary defines the sacred. Both are made more relevant and more meaningful by the other.

My co-guests at Mount Eihei understood this. All were business people — men and women using their vacation time to reflect and reenergize. Those I spoke to were honest about how their coming to Eihei served as both a personal retreat as well as a mini-executive management program. In mastering more advanced meditation disciplines, these executives were seeking to manage stress better, to maintain better balance in ever more demanding business circumstances, and to see issues of personal and career development in a wider continuity. For them, the week was one long intake, the benefits of which they would apply throughout the coming year.

This seamlessness makes sense. We are spending more and more of our time in business, and it is involving more of our personal commitment and creativity. How we work and relax, learn and seek entertainment, are being integrated into a continuous mass. If we are now expected to work even harder and even longer, then the pressure for the career experience also to open the door for wisdom only increases.

In the literature of both Eastern and Western culture, wisdom involves a continuous, expanding process of ascent and descent. As an ideal and an action, wisdom serves as both a source for personal realization, and for pragmatic group problem-solving. This duality involves "ascending" to a new level of consciousness, and then "descending" to apply that consciousness in real life. New learning is then realized, which helps the "ascension" to yet a higher level. And so the cycle continues.

The "up and down" characterization of this movement is not a value judgment: each phase feeds and is indispensable to the other. This dynamic is what the medieval scholar and mystic Meister Eckhart called "outflow and flow-back." There is a filling and an emptying, a theorizing and a putting into practice, an exploration of the perfect and a testing of the pragmatic. The flow parallels that of breathing — in fact, this most essential and natural of human capacities is often used as focus for reflective meditation.

The practice of breathing as a spiritual discipline is very familiar to Oriental business people. And while North Americans have sought to implement quality programs in the straight line progression of a logical plan, the Japanese, Koreans, and Chinese see quality as a continuous process of going back and forth — from management to employees, from employees to management, from company to customers, from customers to company. Incremental advances are continuously achieved. And in a very short time these advances compound, and huge gains are made in both learning and quality.

Ascending and descending can only be done with consciousness, but that does not mean that it always requires great effort. Mindful practice brings familiarity, efficiency, and intuition into play. For those who seek it, the in-and-out progress toward wisdom eventually becomes as natural as breathing. For example, companies that have mastered the in and out of quality eventually see it as an intrinsic process. It may have taken effort to get quality consciousness started, but once entrenched, it flows with its own natural momentum. For these companies, quality is not an added value, but an essential value.

The Path to Wisdom

The dynamic movement of ascending and descending is common to all wisdom. Spiritual writings in both the East and West often compare the quest to climbing a mountain. Although there is a common destination, the route and pace each individual takes are unique. Cyprian Smith, a Benedictine monk and teacher, explains that there is an infinite variation of two basic approaches: "The first is a winding path, approaching the summit gradually, pausing at each stage. It is slow but thorough. The second assaults the summit directly, ascending the steep rockface without hesitation or delay."

Each individual has different strengths, characteristics, and biases and will ascend in different ways. The important thing is for the individual to be conscious of the ascent and to have sufficient self-knowledge for it to be meaningful and appropriate.

Again, the experience of North American companies with quality is very telling. While some have followed a deliberate winding but purposeful approach to managing quality, others have tried to zoom to the top. (Many have given up, not because quality became less important, but because their approach did not have the self-awareness to recognize the unique approach that would have worked for them.) Procter & Gamble and Toyota have been following the deliberate winding but purposeful route to quality for years. They set the pace based on their own (often prodigious) capacities.

Others, like Xerox and Ford, have come to realize the importance of quality when the competitive threat became so acute as to threaten their very survival. After these companies scrambled with great urgency to climb straight to the top of the quality mountain, they learned that the descent — the consistent day-to-day application — might, in Smith's terms, be "slow and gradual." They ultimately persisted, mastering skills appropriate for their particular culture and competitive circumstances. Those that have given up completely have lost not only the chance for consistent quality, but also the opportunity to learn about themselves. They have yet to realize that if wisdom is an asset, self-ignorance is a liability.

That each path is unique again confirms the folly of trying to borrow wisdom from consultants. Nothing permanent has been invested, so nothing permanent has been gained. This need for individuation — for styling a distinct and specifically relevant path — is one of the enriching opportunities for those people who have remained within corporate structures. This creation — this freedom to invent oneself — also motivates and sustains the self-employed. To compete in the marketplace of knowledge effectively, each company and individual will eventually need to create a system, path, and expression of wisdom that is matched to their unique nature. Wise employees will be valued for their ability to provide the constructive self-awareness that each entity needs to ascend the mountain.

To understand the progress toward wisdom, it is first necessary to explore the tentative steps, forceful strides, and imaginative leaps made by individuals in their own journey. This will feel uncomfortable for those whose management sights have been defined by the traditional dictums of "setting objectives," "planning strategy," "implementing with excellence," and "monitoring and measuring." However, the skills for bringing order to a group cannot be the same as those for liberating the full potential of an individual.

Many companies understand the need for greater customization, and acknowledge the role of fully engaged employees in delivering both innovation and service. But they want to implement these graduations to more individuality with the control, precision, and authority of the old managerial order. No wonder that empowerment was stillborn. When the paradigm shifts, we need a new language, and fundamentally new skills to cope.

As it was for me initially in Japan, many will find this is an awkward mingling of two distinct spheres of human endeavor. There are several reasons for persisting. Again, one of the features of this era of transition is that long-established boundaries and segmentation are losing their cogency. This merging together of what had previously been distinct and separate is affecting individuals as well as institutions. The same logic that reaches for the efficiency of cross-functional teams in business applies to the individual in their modern life. Specifically, how we work and relax, and learn and seek entertainment are integrating into a seamless (sometimes confusing) whole. We are spending more and more of our time in business, and it is involving ever more of our personal commitment and creativity. This makes work a logical activity from which to also derive reflective meaning.

The quest for wisdom has been a central preoccupation of human beings for as long as the species has had self-consciousness. (Homo sapiens means "man who knows, who discerns." "Sapiens" is actually the Latin word for understanding or wisdom.) The myths and ancient literature that have shaped the meaning and values of modern civilization are largely preoccupied with the challenges of attaining wisdom. These and the many mystical writings from both the East and West provide rich descriptions of the wisdom journey. While different cultures express this quest in different ways, they mostly share a basic structure:

1. Wisdom flows to those who desire it. If one does not seek, obviously one will not find. More importantly, if one does not seek, one usually pays the significant penalty of not being even aware.
2. Any sage perspective first requires self-knowledge. Although the catalyst for growth may come from an outside circumstance or crisis, the foundation for wisdom is clarity from within.
3. As one delves deeper into self-awareness there emerges a strong recognition of the wider unity (or interdependence) that humans all share. This "connectedness" is based on what the Talmud describes as the profound understanding between *cause* and *effect*. Connectedness flows through time, across generations, cultures, and individuals.

It all starts with the wanting. However, to go after wisdom simply because of its advantages and its potential as an asset is like setting a building's foundations on quicksand. The effort, no matter how valiant, cannot succeed because the base is too unstable to support the weight of the generated superstructure. The many imbalanced attempts to seek excellence, build learning organizations, or empower employees are ultimately abandoned because the supporting foundation is never properly set.

Desire for this type of personal growth comes about because of an inner longing. This longing may reflect an innate spiritual sensibility. Or it may have been caused by an external disruption or crisis. In either case, the ascent has a deeper personal value than whatever career benefits can be gained from the climb.

Setting out on this expedition is not the same as establishing a goal in business. The objective is not so much to be *attained* as to be *learned from*. Success is therefore in the progress, in the individual steps, and not just in the final conquering. Companies that have developed the maturity to innovate continuously know this. The failures, setbacks, and dead ends are as important as the win. In fact, no win would be possible without them. With such awareness of the process as well as the purpose, the judgment of failure becomes irrelevant because its value is at least as great as that of success.

Desire is not the same as drive. Business people already have an overcapacity of drive, but the self-motivation that propels it is not necessarily based on self-knowledge. Drive often masks an inner deficiency. It can serve as a compensation, seeking to create out of sheer willpower an external value that will make up for an internal flaw. Such drive seeks the goal with single-minded purpose. The objective is what matters because the objective holds all the value.

By contrast, the desire for self-knowledge and truth is more of an opening than a purpose. The value is on the inside, so the enrichment happens along the way as well as at the top. The reward is continuous and cumulative.

Companies have valued drive, but they have recently, and mostly inadvertently, also created desire. The flattening of organizations has left even the most career ambitious employee asking: "Is this all there is?" Workers who have been "rationalized" have had to face an even more wrenching reappraisal. Having devoted themselves to winning the perks and promotions of career, the endless reengineering has left many people drained not only of hope, but also of self-worth. Some who have slipped off or have found themselves stuck on the career ladder are now starting to climb the ladder of personal development. They are seeking a value that is not dependent on external accomplishments and acquisitions, but on internal consciousness.

Some companies are now deliberately nurturing this desire. For example, General Motors has added to its educational and training programs courses that respect the spiritual aspirations of its people. Issues of the soul are seen as part of the remaking of the company. Of course, there is a pragmatic as well as noble aspect to this. In a time of cutbacks and freezes, the traditional business inducements are no longer available. Giving attention to the more mystical meaning of life is therefore a way of making work more rewarding. In this continuity, the individual grows to the company's benefit and the company succeeds to the individual's benefit.

Although this may sound like extended selfishness, I believe that there is more at play. By allowing people to express their desire for inner growth, companies like GM are allowing individuals to ground themselves. This inner development helps them be more resilient to the upheavals that will likely continue. It gives people the sense of self-confidence to tackle the greater autonomy with which each employee will inevitably be entrusted. And it provides a personal capability that individuals can take and apply to whatever job, project, or association the future may hold for them. In a time of little job security, this is an investment in the security of self-potential.

Not everyone values self-consciousness, so not everyone will express the desire to seek a meaning beyond the functional, the rational, and the material. However, while this dimension of questing may be undernourished or neglected, it does exist as part of the basic makeup of human beings. Look at the need for balance. Even people who relish extremes in behavior and experience know that they are removed from balance. The way we move from grief to acceptance, for example, is an intuitive adjustment toward that equilibrium. The desire to know oneself is, in a sense, the desire for balance — having the inner constancy to withstand life's turbulence.

Immanuel Kant defined beauty as "purposiveness without purpose." Beauty has its own value, and does not need a function or achievement to realize it. Desire for wisdom operates in this same realm. Even if the desire for wisdom does not yield the expected result, the act of desiring opens a person to the rich possibilities of their individuality.

Self-Starting: A New Definition

Wisdom is sometimes mistaken to be altruism or selflessness. A wise act may be altruistic, involving self-sacrifice, but wisdom does not abnegate the self. In fact, as we have seen, all wisdom practices start with self-knowledge, including healthy doses of self-appreciation and self-respect. For all the education we receive, most of it is concerned with giving shape and form to the exterior world. Little academic energy is expended in our formative studies to try to explain the workings of the inner world. Self-awareness may be what distinguishes humans as a species, but, until the formalization of psychology (and, for many, even since then) this was not considered as important a field of study as mathematics, science, or art.

In this information age, individuals, companies, and communities struggle with the overload of newly generated information. The knowledge most appreciated is still that which is made up of facts. A "smart" person knows a lot of facts and can recall them from memory at the time when they are needed.

Facts dominate the knowledge landscape. The *New York Times* now publishes a synopsis of news for travelers that, with euphonistic appropriateness, it calls "Times FAX." *Harper's* magazine publishes an "Index" of juxtaposed and therefore revealing facts, while CNN's *Headline News* uses dead air time between commercials and programming to transmit its own arcane "Factoid." When business people engage in arguments about policy or decisions, it is considered essential to back up a position with facts. Likewise, politicians quote statistics from polls, which are their own supporting facts.

Despite this almost unnerving abundance of facts, business and society remain impoverished when it comes to *meaning*. Facts tend to be constructions of only one part of human nature: reason. Self-knowledge respects the value of facts, but does not assume that these are by any means the full measure of a human being. To know one's self requires what wisdom teachers have called a "new way of *knowing*." In addition to the knowledge provided by the senses, this "new way of knowing" includes the intuitive. Intuition is not activated by resorting to impulsive emotion or the stirrings of the gut — it requires contemplation, or reflection.

With reflection, connections that are not obvious on the surface become clear and compelling. For example, the Synectics Corporation pioneered a process for structured brainstorming that has received wide acceptance in business. In their process, the people entrusted with creating a solution are fed all the relevant facts. Once the information is clearly understood, the Synectics approach uses word and visual associations to move ideas laterally into new areas. An important aspect of Synectics is that critical judgment is suspended. To do this, the Synectics people encourage a playful forgetting of facts, which are too "heavy" and weigh down the creative process. Only when facts are subsumed can the interconnective energy of creativity take off. That we need to relearn how to create, that we must have a formal system for forgetting facts, shows how dominant and oppressive these bits and bytes of data have become.

Peter Senge advocates that organizations develop the skills and structure for continuous learning, and begins with a concept of personal mastery. In *The Fifth Discipline*, Senge argues that the spirit as well as the intellect must be involved in such deep-level learning. Learning has the most value when it fits into a wider construct of meaning. Whether in a corporate training program or in a classroom, the questioning an individual brings to new information is a way to fit that stimulus into the wider conception of self. The more the self is engaged, the more that self is understood, the more developed and valuable that knowledge becomes.

The issues of self-development are of much interest today. The expanding literature in psychology, the growing list of self-help books, and the renewed interest in spirituality point to a real need shared by people in every strata in our society. The head may be stuffed with information, but the heart and soul have been left terribly undernourished. The remedy is not to cram more data into the cranium, but to begin to explore the self with the tools and questions each of us already have.

Author and Tibetan monk Sogyal Rinpoche sees the process toward self-knowledge as one that is both simple and endless. We start by listening. We proceed by reflection. We then do by meditation.

Listening

Listening is like breathing. We do it "naturally" and we do it without thinking. Yet we may be doing it with such inefficiency that it actually impedes self-development.

Eight years ago I started jogging. After several years of casual running I began the more disciplined training to do a marathon. As I increased the running distance, I found myself frequently experiencing that painful runner's affliction known as "side-stitch." It turns out that my diaphragm was being strained because I was breathing in a shallow way, with breath being taken into the chest rather than into the belly. In my mid-thirties I finally learned to breathe in a way which best served my body.

The fact that we hear sounds does not mean we listen. Even in one-to-one conversations, our minds tend to be off on their own hyperactive wandering. We hear other people, we nod as we take in their concerns, but our minds are often busy in these interchanges, already formulating answers or readying the next question.

Technology has, in effect, given each of us much bigger ears. The telephone, television, fax, Internet, and e-mail serve as electronic filaments that capture widening waves of material for us to attend to. While we are more informed and up to date because of this technology, all this stimulation has only distracted us further from the essentially personal process of listening.

Companies have fallen into the same trap, equating the accessibility provided by new technology to the human art of listening. Intending to be more responsive to customers, large and small businesses have installed the already noted and pervasive 1-800 numbers. A growing number are now opening kiosks on the Internet. Despite these new access points, customer surveys show that a majority of people believe service has actually been declining. In the pursuit of cost-cutting, even the technology of service has been vested with expectations for productivity. Turnaround speed for customer service representatives is often a higher priority than comprehension. This is why, as market researcher Max Blackston puts it, most of us still feel "like a digit or customer code." We may be attended to, but most of us do not feel as if we are being heard.

Attentiveness requires making space for what is being heard. This is not just a matter of focus, but also of what spiritual masters call "emptying" — the respectful silencing of our inner voice and the releasing of distractions. This is not an arbitrary process. As in meditation, the point is not to deny distractions but to see them for what they are, to understand their source, and then to move gently back into focus. Recognizing what is intruding helps us understand what is keeping us from listening effectively.

Denial or suppression, as we know from psychology, is never constructive. What we do not pay attention to eventually emerges and undermines other activities, preoccupations, and relationships. Attending to others and undergoing "emptying" would seem to be forms of self-denial. Instead, the opposite is true. Listening and emptying requires being so fully attentive to oneself that all the personal distractions, pressures, and needs are recognized and given their due. Listening with such completion is respectful to the person being heard, as well as to the self.

This is the point often neglected in corporate training programs for improving communications. Attention to the outside stimulus does not determine the quality of listening; it depends on the awareness of self that we bring to those exchanges. Emptying actually involves complete mindfulness (another one of those fun contradictions in the realm of wisdom). By knowing who we are, we can hear another for who they are. By understanding our inner strengths, issues, and concerns, we can listen without imposing our own agenda. Such mindfulness frees the individual to listen without distortion, and to be affected by what is fully heard.

In the Quaker practice, such mindful attention to another human being, or another's circumstance, is called "witnessing." Quakers are known as pacifists who oppose all violence, but they are also activists who commit themselves personally to a wide variety of issues involving social justice. While fervent in their cause, Quakers do not judge their efforts successful based only on the outcome. The act of participating, the process of "witnessing," provides transformation and growth. The lesson: It is not the result (although that is important) but the doing that opens us to wisdom. For those of us who are goal-oriented, this is particularly difficult to accept.

Buddhist and Jewish wisdom teaches that each word and each action, no matter how small or casual, has consequences. "Witnessing" respects the formidable power of such words and actions. It involves the consciousness to participate fully in life — even in those situations that our involvement cannot change. Such consciousness opens us to comprehension, understanding, and the possibility for wisdom.

Many of us, however, feel that we simply don't have the time for such deliberate "emptying" and for such mindful "witnessing." Our minds are already in dialogue with what is being absorbed. You may be thinking: "OK, but how?" or "can't do it because," or "nice in theory but tough in practice." Attentive listening does not seek to stifle these considerations. It tries to legitimize them by going to their source. Why does this approach make sense? Why does it make us uncomfortable? Why do we resist, embrace, or deny it? As we see the answers to these questions, we get to know yet another aspect of ourselves. With this insight we can then relax the concern and focus again on the listening and learning.

Sounds again like a laborious, time-consuming interaction. And at first it does take time to give what distracts us its due. Like anything else, getting into the habit of attempting to know ourselves requires investment. However, as self-awareness grows, the skill for recognizing the tangents and peripheral preoccupations becomes reflexive. The mind is not sequential, and it is usually operating at undercapacity. With so many synapses firing simultaneously, it is possible to gently still the distraction and refocus attention within a single breath. (Here is that "in and out" again.)

While not promising perfection, practice at least brings facility. One of the lessons provided by both spiritual teachers and psychologists is that the issues of our inner voice may cover a wide spectrum of concerns, but they usually reflect a consistent and possibly singular need. (In my case, most roads lead to impatience.) By finally recognizing the cause behind the concern, an individual can practice the higher form of listening Rinpoche advocates — a listening that honors the value of the information being provided, while at the same time enriching the understanding of the listener.

Can this happen in the hallways and meeting rooms in which so much information is transacted? Is such mindfulness possible when handling a fax, reaching for a ringing phone, or downloading data on a PC? Most of us feel too harried for even that single deep breath. And that's exactly the point. The amount of information intruding into our lives will not decline. Unless we develop the self-awareness and listening skills to deal with the exponential growth of information, life will only get more harried, more out of control, more disquieting.

Reflection

Reflection demands the same reversal in thinking. Taking time to consider and to create context is almost impossible to imagine in the productivity-obsessed environment of business. Yet time, projects, and people feel squeezed because organizations are trying to correct past unreflective judgments. For example, productivity improvement is both so pressing and so painful today because many companies failed to envision, comprehend, and invest in the training and human resource development they now need to be competitive. Without the understanding that comes from reflection, companies have been left scrambling to catch up and scampering to survive. Without reflection, there can only be reaction.

Some again will argue that the remedy is as difficult as the disease. Indeed, reflection requires dedication and discipline, time, instruction, and adjustment — valuable commodities that are in short supply. We need to remember that the problems of work and career are themselves very complex. Although we might wish otherwise, the reality is that any solution must also be complex and demanding. Shortcuts based on quick fixes have contributed to the churning and demoralizing status of modern business. To try another magical remedy is to invite not only disappointment, but also cynicism. When it comes to reflection, we need to follow the advice of Buddhist masters and "make haste, slowly."

Reflection works. How do Japanese car makers justify investing ten times as much training time for employees as do their North American counterparts? Why do they continue to make such investments when the soaring value of the yen has put such incredible pressure on costs? Obviously, the leaders and managers of companies like Toyota are convinced that the time to learn at a deeper level — to reflect on new procedures and practices — will realize much greater efficiency in operations. Production details will be more thoroughly understood. Process and technology problems will get de-bugged earlier. Workers will know what is expected.

Toyota recently reconfigured one of its Japanese plants to serve as a prototype for its systems and processes for the future. Having already revolutionized manufacturing in the 1970s with innovations like "Just-In-Time," Toyota's initiative has received lots of attention. As reported in a recent issue of *The Economist*, the plant is the opposite of what most of us would imagine the factory of the future to be. Machines and robots are in the background. The work space — bright, airy, quiet, and free from clutter — is designed for the maximum comfort of workers. People move alongside the assembly on conveyor belts so that they do not have to move themselves while attending to their task. There is less crouching, less reaching, and less stretching. Some employees actually follow the assembly on mechanical swings.

In gearing for the productivity demands of the future, Toyota has chosen to invest in making the work easier for people. Machines, robots, and computers have their place — not as replacements for workers, but as tools. Individual judgment is the company's most precious asset. The further Toyota pushes out the envelope of quality, the more fervently and supportively it practices the human touch of craftsmanship.

Using an individual's faculty for discernment and reflection helps to develop a personal relation to what they may be learning and experiencing. This is why Robin Skynner argues that healthy change involves a time to adjust, to reconstruct one's "meaning map." In reflection, connections are made that are at first not obvious. This is where learning becomes fully assimilated and active. Evelyn Underhill, the first woman to lecture on theology at Oxford, compares this deeper integration to the root system of a tree. All of us recognize the size, spread, and grace of a great tree. This visible magnificence is, of course, matched by an invisible one, "the vast unseen system of roots, perhaps greater than the branches in strength and extent, with their tenacious attachments, their fan-like system of delicate filaments and their power of silently absorbing food. On that profound and secret life the whole growth and stability depend. It is rooted and grounded in a hidden world."

In reflection we ponder questions: "What does this mean?"; "How does this affect me?"; "What is really behind this?"; "What is the truth?"; and "When will I learn?" Formulating answers to these questions must involve more than inductive and deductive reasoning, or the answers would have already been apparent (like the branches of a tree). Instead, the answers connect or leap into focus with the same bisociative energy that Arthur Koestler defined as creativity. Thoughts, experiences, values, hunches, guesses, and intuition go through a still mysterious blending to emerge as understanding. This is not the superficial understanding tested by comprehension and memory, but the profound and internalized understanding that flows from being rooted.

In their response to containing costs, many companies are saying that career development is now the singular responsibility of the employee. Some will provide opportunities for improvement, but most are only committing to providing a project for a time. In such a job market, the onus is obviously on individuals to make meaning out of their particular circumstances, and to create a value from among their repertoire of skills, talents, and experiences.

Someone else is *not* going to fix whatever it is that is not working. The only respite from the stress and distress of a situation is created from one's own ingenuity and reflective faculty. The good news is that, in practicing reflection, individuals not only solve their problem, but also build an asset that goes with them in whatever work or situation they find themselves. While the chaos in the economy may force great change, such people are firmly grounded in their own great common sense.

Meditation

The third developmental practice releasing self-knowledge is *meditation*. I know from my first book, *Meditations on Business*, and from my own practice with it, how off-putting this concept may seem. Listening makes immediate practical sense. Reflection is at least widely acknowledged to make good sense. Meditation is something else. It conjures up religious imagery, with all its rules, spiritual subjectivity, and proselytizing. Having already been co-opted by the Beatles and most of California, meditation is widely known but also highly suspect. Even those with open minds tend to regard meditation as a fringe obsession.

Of the three inducements awakening self-knowledge, meditation takes the most time, is the least doable in an office environment, and requires the most faith that the outcome will be worth the practice. As you would expect from this profile, it is also the most important and rewarding.

You have probably already heard, and have likely remained unmoved by, the benefits of meditating: the calm; the refreshment; the stress release; the insights; and the perspective. If such personal advantages have not won you over, why should a business or career reason?

In the first place, these are incredibly unconventional times in business, calling for unconventional thinking and unconventional practices. Charles Handy has already called this "the age of unreason." The impotence of logic alone to sort out the issues confronting business people is a point I have stressed throughout the chapters of this book. If reason fails us, and it has, we have no choice but to seek to engage the other potentialities of our human nature. Meditation is the tool for unleashing such potential.

When we calm our minds and concentrate, the stillness is not for denying or forgetting the exigencies of real life. Meditation is to see these problems, preoccupations, and conundrums for what they really are, so that we can ultimately see beyond them. The Dalai Lama explains with forceful simplicity: "Our ordinary mental state is one of distraction. Our ordinary minds are too uncontrolled and weak to be able to understand the nature of reality . . . It is therefore necessary to develop the mind into a suitable tool for investigating reality, like a microscope."

In normal work mode, people struggle to manage consequences. Through the magnification provided by meditation, they can finally see the cause.

Meditation is an internal act, and one of great intimacy. The clarity achieved within the concentration depends on the clarity of self-knowledge. This is why meditation has also been used in psychotherapy, stress management, and crisis recovery: to open doors to the mind, psyche, and soul. In the progress to self-awareness, sincere and purposeful listening provides the input. Conscious and consistent reflection leads to connections. Focused and aware concentration leads to an awakening or enlightenment.

Every major spiritual tradition includes meditation in its practice. After years of searching, Buddha achieved enlightenment while sitting under a tree. Moses broke away from the wandering tribe of Israelites and retreated alone to Mount Sinai. Jesus Christ spent forty days in solitude in the desert before assuming his ministry and teaching.

As a result of their concentration, each of these remarkable individuals also returned from their awakening with a code. Through their meditation and self-realization, each had ascended to a new level of understanding (in Moses' case this was literal as well as figurative). With this awakening, each also descended to the "real" world, seeking to teach, alleviate the suffering of others, and make their idealized vision practicable. Buddha introduced the Four Noble Truths; Moses presented the Ten Commandments; Christ taught the Golden Rule.

Hans Kung, the noted and controversial Catholic theologian, has also written comparative studies of what he calls the "great world religious river systems." In each he discovered an integral practice of meditation. Confucian followers were exhorted to do "quiet sitting" to recapture the equilibrium lost to daily living. Jews and Christians have used scripture as their primary inspiration, following a "tradition of point-by-point reflection" on biblical passages. Buddhists have developed a variety of techniques for "stilling the mind." Some practice visualization of "the master" to focus concentration toward the truth. Zen has taught a more ascetic "emptying" to arrive at the "vacant place of truth."

There are two lessons from these masters and traditions. The first is that the awakening to wisdom without some practice of quiet concentration is very difficult, if not impossible. The second is that the style or form of this practice is highly variable, affording a variety of approaches and routes for individuals to pursue.

The End Result

It is amazing, given the diversity of human cultures and the dissimilarities of time frame, that wisdom is universally acknowledged and that its practice involves such congruity. Leave aside the religious dressing. What is clear is that human beings have imbedded within them a searching, which, when followed with purpose and discipline, yields a higher consciousness and a clearer understanding. Life, society, and business have irrational and destructive aspects to them, yet these are the reality. The breakthrough to wisdom does not reorder the chaos. Nor does it resolve the tension created by the contradictions and conflicts. Instead, wisdom provides a depth of perception so that the connection between cause and effect is clearer.

This may sound simple, but why do so few companies fulfill the goals outlined in their mission? Why are employees too busy working to do the right thing for the long term? Why are customers generally less loyal even as companies commit themselves to more passionate service?

As these quandaries suggest, there is a gap between plan and execution, between objective and strategy, between cause and effect. The Dalai Lama asserts: "Compared to other faculties, like faith, mindfulness, effort and so forth, wisdom is said to be more important because it is only through the force of wisdom, when complemented by other faculties, that one can actually combat the force of delusions."

The transformation of business to "value-through-information," even its reengineering and quality initiatives, are often defeated by such "delusions" as:

- Dependence is a sign of weakness.
- Cooperation is less effective than competition.
- Information must be hoarded like gold.
- Control must be centrally imposed.
- Management and labor have separate priorities.
- Profit has more priority than the customer.
- Work is meant to provide only a living, not an opportunity for greater meaning.
- Value for shareholders rests on efficiency and productivity, not on creativity and innovation.
- Managers learn from past mistakes.

Without self-awareness, the gaps between cause and effect remain a source of frustration and confusion. Only with inner clarity can the implications and opportunities within these gaps be understood and turned to advantage.

If the disconcerting news is that all wisdom flows from some type of meditative practice, then the encouraging news is that this path is highly flexible. In fact, each person must find his or her own balance and way, based on self-appreciation, needs, and approach to discipline. Rinpoche stipulates that the goal is not meditation for meditation's sake, but for "meditative doing." Wisdom is not something gained or achieved, it is something that is done and practiced. This is particularly important given the pressure and pace of our modern lifestyle.

There are numerous books, tapes, and seminars that will help one find an effective practice. Choosing the right approach is a matter for each individual to determine. However, whatever steps taken on this path should not be taken casually. Ours is a society obsessed with a contradictory expectation for both convenience and results. Diets promise quick weight loss with minimal denial. Exercise machines promise hard bodies in only minutes a day. Financial agents promise old age security with minimal investment. Meditation practice that comes from this psychology of instant fulfillment — however popular it may seem — is likely to be as effective and enduring as spray paint cover-ups for balding heads. The test for such practice is not self-help or self-improvement, but self-knowledge.

A program of serious reflection and contemplation is not at all meant to be a retreat from life. Christ and Buddha and Moses walked among their people, engaged in the tough issues of their society, and did the work of life day by day. The benefit of being rooted and centered is that the activities, confrontations, and challenges of each day are met with mindful recognition rather than distressed reaction.

Many of the business practices currently employed by companies are attempting to give structure to the reaction. Through benchmarking, companies try to measure, match, or surpass the standards and innovations of competitors. Through quality management, they try to reduce the errors and flaws that impede performance. These measures and systems, while very important, only bring companies up to the prevailing standard. To get ahead of the turbulence, companies must move beyond the formalization of reaction and become agents and catalysts for their own future. This can only be done with a clear, honest, and mature sense of self.

There is a huge power in self-knowledge, but there is an equally destructive power in ignorance. As mentioned earlier, psychologists know that the personality traits and needs an individual may suppress or ignore eventually "sabotage" them. This is recognized in words attributed to Christ in the Gnostic *Gospel According to Thomas*. Discovered by a peasant in Upper Egypt in 1945, these ancient manuscripts capture the writings and traditions of an early group of Christians. While their interpretation of Christ's mission was eventually subsumed by the orthodoxy of the Roman Church, the Gnostic writings provide yet another window into the realm of wisdom. In *Thomas*, Christ is quoted saying: "If you bring forth what is within you, what you bring forth will save you. If you do not bring forth what is within you, what you do not bring forth will destroy you."

United By Cause and Effect

Across all cultures, as individuals develop a deeper awareness of themselves, they also inevitably develop an appreciation for the essential unity between all things and all people. How can this be? Why would an act of individuation create a consciousness of boundarylessness?

The awakening experienced by Moses, Buddha, Confucius, and Christ included the central realization that what creates suffering for human beings is consciousness of "separation." By being apart, by behaving without regard to the whole, individuals inflict pain on others, and experience pain themselves. Hence the reason Moses delivered commandments, Buddha taught compassion, Confucius extolled virtue, and Christ preached charity and love. This is a simplification, but having "ascended" to an insight, each of these teachers felt such a unity with others that they "descended" to put the illumination they realized into helpful practice.

Beyond the great masters, we judge people wise when they see connections between issues and occurrences that are not clear nor obvious to the average person. They see a unity where most only see fragments. Wise people also seem willing to give of themselves, to sacrifice today for an improvement tomorrow. This again is a consciousness of unity. Wisdom is not masochistic: the sacrifice is calibrated against the broader need and the broader gain. The continuum between sacrifice and greater reward again reflects an appreciation of unity.

The awakening to unity operates on numerous levels. One level is internal — the integration of personality traits, skills, needs, desires, ambitions that we all have. In such integration, what we have initially regarded as strengths and weaknesses meld into one.

How often have we heard about people whose strength really turned out to be their weakness? Consider how IBM's seemingly unassailable strength in big computer systems created the very weakness that led to the ascendancy of Microsoft and Intel. What we typically regard as opposites are already one and the same. Individuals and companies fail to see the continuity and so experience dramatic and jarring swings from one extreme to the other.

Another level includes "others" — other people, other species, anything "other than me." Self-awareness is important, but we are completely and inextricably linked into a much greater unity. We depend on the sun and earth for plants and oxygen. We depend on other species for food and biospheric balance. We depend on other people for work, for wealth, for basic services, and for sustenance. No one could survive outside this unified web, although again, we do not automatically have the consciousness to realize this. Wise human beings see themselves as part of this complex whole, not because they are selfless and noble, but because they are pragmatic enough to be cognizant of a rather self-evident truth.

The response demanded at this level is not self-abnegation, but reciprocity. Christ was not just a teacher, but a healing teacher. In the culture of his time (not too different from ours), people who were sick, blind, or crippled were regarded as incomplete. The many acts of healing recorded in the Gospels were undertaken in part to reunite the ostracized and displaced with their community. This restoration of physical unity celebrated the individual. And with this personal integration came the responsibility toward the broader unity: "Do unto others as you would have them do unto you."

Yet another level can be called "nonjudgment." In the awareness of how all things interconnect and interact, an individual strives to stay above the emotion and subjectivity of judgment to better see the link between a cause and an effect. C. S. Lewis explained in one of his popular, war-time radio broadcasts that "pleasure, money, power, and safety are all, as far as they go, good things. The badness consists in pursuing them by the wrong method, or in the wrong way, or too much. I do not mean, of course, that the people who do this are not desperately wicked. I do mean that wickedness, when you examine it, turns out to be the pursuit of some good in the wrong way."

The recognition at this level is what activates a sense of morality within human beings. As with wisdom and its practice, the basic definition of what is "right and wrong" is surprisingly consistent across cultures and time. Actions that respect the unity (compassion, charity, virtue) are judged as moral. Those that deny or disrespect the unity (separation, selfishness, inhumanity) are immoral. In responding to those who do not recognize such a universal code, C. S. Lewis asked readers to imagine a culture "where people were admired for running away in battle, or where a man felt proud of double-crossing all the people that had been kindest to him."

No such human society exists. Indeed, as Lewis observed, people have "differed as regards what people you ought to be unselfish to — whether it was only your family, or your fellow countrymen, or everyone. But they have always agreed that you ought not to put yourself first. Selfishness has never been admired."

Moral obligation is basically how wisdom expresses itself. Here is how the experts have expressed it:

> **King Solomon:** "Wisdom will not enter a shifty soul, nor make her home in a body that is mortgaged to sin. This holy spirit of discipline will have nothing to do with falsehood; she cannot stay in the presence of unreason, and will throw up her case at the approach of injustice."

> **Confucius:** "You are humane if you can practice five things in the world: respectfulness, magnanimity, truthfulness, acuity and generosity. If you are respectful, you won't be despised. If you are magnanimous, you will win people. If you are truthful, you will be trusted. If you are acute, you will be successful. If you are generous, you will be able to employ people."

> **Buddha:** "There is this Noble Truth of the way leading to the cessation of suffering: It is this Noble Eightfold Path, that is to say: right view, right intention, right speech, right action, right livelihood, right effort, right mindfulness, and right concentration."

> **Jesus Christ:** "Do good to those that hate you, bless those who curse you, pray for those who abuse you."

Although expressed differently and with varying degrees of emphasis, the essential connection to others carries with it an intrinsic and inalienable obligation. As Hans Kung notes: "Being human without this dimension would be stunted."

Turning from the philosophers, we can see examples of the awareness of unity and the acknowledgment of the obligations that go with it in business. As discussed earlier, General Electric's aspiration to become a boundaryless organization requires a morally defined reciprocity among divisions, levels, and employees. In another example, the relationship between parts maker Magna International and Chrysler is so integrated, that the supplier often initiates R&D and delivers productivity-enhancing ideas unrequested by the buyer.

The testing of unity principles will also determine the viability of many other companies: Apple, as it manages the arrival of Mac clones; Boeing, as it distributes to outside partners the design and manufacturing responsibility for the next generation passenger plane; and virtually all of the players — the entertainment creators and the technologists and distributors — who must cooperate in the creation of a commercially viable information superhighway.

Detachment and Compassion

There is one final stage in this process. After coming to self-knowledge and after awakening to the intimate interconnection between "self" and "other," two fundamental responsibilities are activated: "detachment" and "compassion." As befits a wisdom quest, these are both complementary and tension-inducing. In psychological terms, detachment is achieved when the ego is conscious — when it is understood and under control. Sogyal Rinpoche sees the unconscious ego as the "absence of true knowledge."

When we detach from the clinging preoccupations of ego, we have the opportunity to see situations without the distortion of unconscious self-interest. We may still have a self-interest, but we are at least fully aware of its root and implications. Detachment affords the objectivity that is needed to deal with paradox, and to see beyond irreconcilables.

Compassion is how obligation to others is fulfilled. This stems from both an intellectual appreciation for human connectedness, as well as empathy from the heart. In compassion, the virtues defined by Confucius and the charity demanded by Christ are extended. This is what contemporary Chinese theologian Fu P'ei-jung calls "the unity between knowing and doing."

Detachment and compassion will also be explored later. They are important to this discussion because they are essential elements for creating, extending, and leveraging trust. They have very different expressions, but these essentially balance each other.

DETACHMENT	COMPASSION
• Release preoccupation with self	• Preoccupation connects with others
• Objective deliberation	• Personal and urgent involvement
• Distance for perspective	• Proximity for intimacy
• Risk assessment	• Reward motivation
• Clear awareness of cause	• Full recognition of implications
• Nonjudgmental	• Morally passionate
• Seek the truth	• Ensure justice
• Perceive the continuity	• Appreciate the consequences

All this seems like a lot to expect of people, particularly when business is already so tough. But we must ask ourselves: what are the alternatives? Society, the economy, companies, and individuals are struggling to come to terms with a major realignment. Is mindlessness an option? Should people continue to pretend that the old economic paradigm is still valid, and that job creation is just around the next quarter? Is it realistic to expect that the management model for manufacturing things will have any relevance to a knowledge worker? Can the strategy and control structure inspire continuous innovation? Can it facilitate temporary networks to bloom? Can the logic that calibrates machines hope to stimulate, inspire, and reward the imagination of human beings?

Shoshana Zuboff challenged business people to address the managerial and skill implications of computerization. The regimens perfected for machinery were proven in her research to be totally inadequate for the changes in business produced by electronics and microchips. She suggested that companies not only *automate*, but also *informate* — provide people with the learning, knowledge, and access to help realize the full benefits of high technology. On Zuboff's continuum I would now add *integrate* — consciously moving management and employees to that higher knowledge that gains insight for the individual and new value for the corporation.

PLOTTING A NEW TRAJECTORY

1. Life offers a fullness that in our modern cleverness we find ways to avoid. Is there anything that you regard as essential for a full life currently missing in yours? In your work? Is there anything that you would regret not having done?

2. We listen with our heads as well as our hearts. In a difficult meeting, take stock of what you feel. Ask yourself: Why do I feel this way? What is behind the feeling? Follow the trail to the source. What does the source of the feeling tell you about what you need?

3. In most exchanges during the business day we have the overt agenda relating to the project or the problem. Then there is the covert agenda — what we or the others in the interaction really need. During another heated meeting or one-on-one session, check your feelings. What is your interior agenda? Also try to discern the covert agenda for your meeting partner(s). What have you learned about yourself? About your associates? How do the interior agendas align? Conflict?

4. The modern business day has become a morass of conflicting pressures. "Fire-fighting" is often full time, and then there is the regular, turbo-charged-through-rationalization job to do as well. "There is no time to think" is the mantra at most companies. How can you find ten minutes to simply reflect? What can you do or put off to allow you this time to see beyond the horizon of the day? The point is not to plan, just think, ponder, collect impressions, connect ideas. If you cannot find the time, what can you do to break this unending cycle before it breaks you?

5. Take a deep breath. Take several. Evelyn Underhill noted that people cannot provide perspective or wisdom if they do not have it themselves. She wrote: "But that means giving time, patience, effort to such a discipline and cultivation of your attention as artists must give, if they are to enter into the reality and joy of natural loveliness and impart it in their work." What are you creating that is giving scope and purpose to your life? Your work? How are you advancing the craft required for that creative task?

6. One of the reasons (or excuses) given by people whose work pace is frenetic and reactionary is that the situation is out of their control. They are not the boss, nor are they the customer, nor did they set such an unrealistic time frame. The next time you find yourself in a situation that is out of your control, experience it as a "witness." What do you observe? What do you observe about yourself? How are you influenced or changed by what you experience?

7. Most of us are painfully aware that work now operates with many complex interdependencies. For one day, draw a map of the necessary linkages between you and others. Which of these interconnections also involve reciprocity? Are there any that would be improved by your initiating a more reciprocal exchange?

8. Choose a trying relationship or problem. Imagine removing yourself from it. To the best of your ability, release any emotional stake. How has your perspective changed? If you had no involvement, how would the solution look? Why does your being involved complicate the situation?

9. Choose another trying relationship or problem. Imagine the solution that would solve the need or issue for the other party — completely from their perspective. What would you have to give to remedy the situation? What sacrifice does that entail for you? What human need is being served for your colleague? How would you feel if you gave what they needed?

10. What does "integrate" mean to you? What would it mean in the circumstances of your job? What does it mean in the context of enhanced customer service, value, and interaction? What changes does this suggest?

SEVEN

THE EXTERNAL PRACTICE: ASCENDING

W isdom, like human learning, does not flow in a straight line. As we grow, we tend to skip and deviate, test and intuit our way through facts and experience until we create a personal life view. Nevertheless, we need some mileposts to guide our advance. These mileposts are the ten separate dimensions of wisdom, clustered into four distinct categories, that were introduced in Chapter One. For the purposes of this analysis, and to suggest the continuous movement of ascent and descent, I have expressed this topology as a series of steps.

Although the structure implies that some steps are going up and others coming down, each attribute actually involves both ascending and descending. For example, there may be a stretching to gain a new perspective, then there is a functional and practical implementation of that perspective in daily life. For each dimension there is an ideal and a practice, an up and a down that recur again and again.

I have chosen to define the first two clusters, perspective and values, as generally ascending, and the last two clusters, action and support, as descending. Again, both sets involve up-and-down dynamics. My reason for this split is that perspective and values tend to drive us toward seeking wisdom, while action and support generally tend to be how we apply it.

Specifically:
- • Perspective: The context and sense of self to see beyond what is apparent to make judicious decisions.
- • Values: The girders and frame for building wisdom. These are the precepts that fuel the conviction of the wise.
- • Action: The day-to-day action and interaction that bring wisdom into practice.
- • Support: The attributes that develop personal wisdom, as well as nurture its development in others.

These categories are dynamic, discrete but interconnected: perspective guides action; values feed perspective; action brings accumulation. In any configuration or order, these clusters build upon each other. The figure below simulates how wisdom is assembled, activated, and reinforced in the unpredictable circumstances of real life.

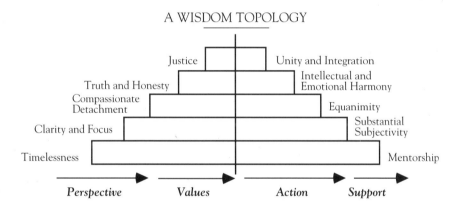

A WISDOM TOPOLOGY

Why even create such a structure for a commodity that is admittedly beyond any cookie-cutter definition? Simply, companies and the individuals in them tend to do what is measured: Xerox, Toyota, and Ford measure and reward quality; Microsoft measures and rewards progress on projects; Rubbermaid and 3M measure and reward new product innovation; Disney and Four Seasons measure and reward customer service.

To integrate the attributes of wisdom into the consciousness of business requires converting principles into actionable and measurable increments. The details for each dimension allow business people at least to start the process of creating the new tracking and appraisal tools. This provides input for training and cultural development, as well as for performance.

Perspective
Timelessness

For the most part, North American companies suffer the dual disadvantage of having amnesia and being myopic. The danger to organizations focused only on the latest quarter has already been well documented. Despite understanding the consequences, the exigencies of business are such that few organizations are even spending as much time on decision-making and analysis as before. The complaint I hear most often in my consulting is that people simply do not have the time to consider all the implications of their projects, programs, and assignments. It seems that the productivity and efficiency improvements of the last five years are exacting a substantial hidden cost — draining both the ability to understand fully the lessons of the past, as well as the confidence to imagine the future.

Thinking in continuity is a strategic necessity. The pace of change is confusing people into believing that they themselves must change to remain current. In fact, those companies and individuals that have successfully managed the most challenging transitions have done so by adapting new behaviors while maintaining essentially the same character. In other words, the ability to handle new, unpredictable circumstances most effectively comes not from prescience but from self-knowledge. The mastery of the future, no matter how ambiguous or complex it may be, depends less on what you do than who you are.

Cutbacks have often cut roots. As delayering has forced people out of companies, memory, tradition, and informal pockets of heritage have also been shed. So, too, has the time to place new events into a broader perspective. Middle managers have been seen as the enemy of productivity; they have been the most affected by restructuring.

Yet the consequences of erasing so much of the memory capacity within an organization have yet to be fully felt, or fully accounted for. In rushing to splice away the inefficiency of the past, many groups have also wiped away the elements of history and heritage that would have differentiated them in the future. They share the characteristics of productivity with other reengineered operations, but many now lack the substantial character to stand apart and influence customer choice and selection.

The past expresses itself not in quaint traditions but in belief, conviction, and confidence — there is a concrete and significant advantage in looking backward. Frederick Turner, a poet and professor, makes the point that tradition, usually assumed to be stifling and restrictive, is actually "the realm of true freedom." Turner supports his position with compelling historical examples. He writes: "Paradoxically, the civilizations that have set themselves to imitate the past always have been the most creative and truly innovative ones. The brilliance of Japanese culture follows from its devotion to classical Chinese culture to the extent that one of its three scripts (Kanji) and two of its three major religious traditions (Buddhism and Confucianism) were imported from China. The European Renaissance was fired by the ambition to recapture the art and thought of ancient Greece and Rome."

Respect for the past is respect for the self, which is why it is so important in the progression toward wisdom. In the rush to restructure, business people, in particular, have forgotten that tradition actually affords a great efficiency because it frees people to operate on a current or intuition or standard that they implicitly trust. The past therefore is not a museum but a furnace in which creative regeneration is fired.

Procter & Gamble is famous for re-making itself almost every decade. The goals, structure, processes, and operations of the company are recast to capitalize on the peculiarities of any given time frame. While dramatically changing what it does, P&G has yet to change what it is.

Edwin Artzt, recently retired as P&G's CEO, puts his legacy in this perspective: "What happens is that companies drift away from those fundamentals, and every once in a while you have to knock it back into place. What's critical is a company's ability to perform successfully across generations of management. That requires culture to be passed down from generation to generation. I've restored the culture rather than changed it."

Respect for employees, which was institutionalized in the 1880s, stands firm. Attention to quality, conceived even earlier in its history, is affirmed. And moral commitment to community, evident throughout its operations, only grows. Knowing itself so well allows P&G the advantage of adapting to the future with more flexibility. King Solomon wrote, "With difficulty we guess even at the things on earth, and laboriously find out what lies beneath our feet." If we strain to meet all the exigencies projected by futurists without protecting the values that define us, we do indeed risk missing what "lies beneath our feet."

Inventing the future requires diagnostic and scenario-building skills, but again, these are not so much new competencies as the continuous practice of self-awareness. The same reflective interconnection used in introspection is actually essential for imagining the future, along with its implications and its requirements. The more practice people have in seeing within themselves, the more practice they will have in looking into the unknown to come. And the more they recognize about themselves, the clearer their sense of the opportunities and vulnerabilities they face will be.

To achieve this presence of self, some individuals and companies intuitively recognize several things:

• Past, present, and future are only constructs of our scientific mind, but our whole mind zigzags continuously and simultaneously through each. To be mindful means to be conscious of the continuity of time, rather than its ever-shifting segments. The sixty- and one hundred–year plans of some Japanese and Korean companies provide less of a formal blueprint for strategy than a touchstone for such consciousness of continuity.

• History is important because it holds the knowledge of self that is necessary to be fully conscious of the present and fully engaged in embracing the future. Max De Pree, retired chairman of Herman Miller, says that company "storytellers" provided key lessons and behavioral clues for new employees in new circumstances. The stories do not prescribe a certain solution, but reveal the character of the company that is brought to problem-solving.

• Throughout history, the future has always required great leaps, big adjustments, and new skills of the people living through transition. They survived, just as we will survive the current dislocation. The issue is to maintain one's integrity. Integrity suggests totality or completion. People can only be whole if they are also carrying their past forward with them.

• Spirit endures. The executives, managers, and creative people at Leo Burnett, the largest ad agency in the United States, quote Leo in almost every meeting, even though he has been dead since the 1960s. Engineers at Hewlett-Packard use stories about David Packard and Bill Hewlett to inform their decisions, even though the founders are long since retired. For these and other companies, what the anecdotes reveal about the past are indispensable in helping them deal with the ambiguity of the present. The principles within the anecdotes enrich and give substance to the strategy.

• Even with the best diagnostic tools one cannot predict the future.

While futurists offer interesting and thought-provoking scenarios, the excitement or threat of their guesswork should not distract us from understanding deeply what is. Twenty years ago Alvin Toffler envisioned many of the disturbing adjustments we are now living through. Forearmed with knowledge, many still stumbled. It is the character within that determines outcome. And character is not predicated simply on what we may know.

Clarity and Focus

Perhaps the most consistent surprise in my consulting work is finding so many dedicated people within companies, including many senior managers and executives, confused about the real mission, objectives, and strategy of their organization. In part this shows how quickly we have exhausted the meaning of many of the words and concepts for renewal.

Not only is the language of company renewal muddled, but it is also increasingly heard through cynical ears. Jack Welch of General Electric has written that: "For a large corporation to be effective, it must be simple. For an organization to be simple, its people must have self-confidence and intellectual self-assurance. Insecure managers create complexity. Real leaders do not clutter."

Business is highly unpredictable — the economy, the industry, the competition and customer, and the ever-shifting organization itself — but *obscurity* is an internal condition. Confusion is not what reality does to us; it is what we bring to reality. Once again from Solomon: "Fear is nothing but the abandonment of aid that comes from reason; and hope, defeated by this inward weakness, capitulates before ignorance."

What we do not know about ourselves is what makes the unknown so fearful. I have worked with some very frustrated CEOs who have defined and communicated their company's mission very effectively, yet still find employees who don't understand or are confused. What we learned is that the confusion expressed about strategy is actually about that individual's relation to that strategy. The confusion is interpersonal, not intellectual.

There are numerous suggestions for how organizations will need to function to survive in the future. Some advocate the "post-entrepreneurial company" to produce innovation and small batches of value-added products systematically. Others see a business world comprising "dynamic networks" in which companies will couple and uncouple in irregular and customized combinations to bring exactly the experience, expertise, and resources needed for a project or product. Many have talked about the "virtual corporation," an amorphous organization in which expert freelancers and part-time employees work with a skeleton company staff to quickly serve and advance a requirement or need of a customer. In the view of Solveig Wikström and Richard Normann, the model will be a "value-creating partner system," which embraces not only a company's suppliers and strategic allies, but even the actual individual customer. As different as they are, these operational models have several important commonalties.

First, they are all viable, indeed tenable. Each is already emerging or already in place. In its evolutionary progress, business structure is likely to take a variety of forms similar to those the analysts and academics have so far defined.

Second, each of these organizational models depends to a significant degree on the quick, precise, and *creative* exchange of knowledge to work. The communications and specific meaning structure of an organization must be accessible, recognizable, and, most importantly, relevant to the many disconnected constituents that will be involved.

Third, efficiency and effectiveness within any enterprise of dynamic relationships hinges on mutual trust. Authority, which used to flow from power, must instead be created through cooperation. In such evolving organizations, communication, meaning, and trust are of therefore strategic, rather than cultural, importance.

Organizations devolving from a command–control structure to one based more on a network of interconnecting parts must deal with an identical transition in communication. Direction, once driven from the top, detail by detail, must now flow interactively and in fragments among all involved. Even people who are not part of such an organization — those who are simply "hired hands" — will need to be able to contribute not only to the project, but also to its direction. They, too, must therefore have a familiarity and facility with corporate semiotics. Communication at this level of complexity demands a clarity beyond what most companies have today — primarily the internal one of self-awareness.

Hewlett-Packard has a deeply developed sense of self. As mentioned, in meetings throughout the company, long-retired founders Bill Hewlett and David Packard are still quoted as if they are members of the smallest project team. Their precepts are captured in the formal code and informal practices people call the "H-P Way." Lewis Platt, the current CEO, offers his view of the strength of this clarity in corporate self-awareness:

"If employees understand that the core values of the company are the anchor they can hang on to, it gives you a fair amount of freedom to change."

Wise people are perceived as such for being able to reduce a complicated and unclear situation into something understandable by others. This reduction is not the result of superior analytical skill — although it may well involve analysis — but of more practice in seeking and uncovering truth. We can recognize wisdom in others because what they reveal resonates with an inner truth we know intuitively, but have not developed the facility for seeing ourselves.

- Clarity is a beacon that attracts people and gives them guidance. If a strategy or mission evokes only a passive acceptance, it likely lacks the insight or illumination to be compelling and competitive.
- Clarity works like an invitation. Those with clarity do not generally need to impose their direction because the insights they provide make such sense that others seek them out.
- Without honesty, there can be no clarity. Companies have become expert at using the skills of public relations and marketing to "position" information to employees in the best possible way. Spin-doctoring distorts the truth. This is why so many employees in so many companies have become so cynical.
- To "be able to comprehend what is the breadth and length and depth and height — a splendour of realization" is what Saint Bernard called "the business of all business." This is particularly important as knowledge becomes the new idiom of economic value.
- Learning more facts will not make a situation necessarily any clearer. Most business people will recognize the tendency to throw information at a problem. The goal is to see the knowledge beyond the facts — what Buddhists call "penetrating delusion."

Compassionate Detachment

While many business people I know are open to considering a more multidimensional time frame, and while many also readily accept the need for greater clarity, few would be caught dead with something called "compassionate detachment." These are not very strategic words. They do not add marketability to a resumé. As a concept, these words have not yet even made a dent in the more accommodating consciousness of corporate culture. However, this ungainly combination of empathy and distance represents a vital balance for dealing with interdependence.

When IBM began to lose market share, it was assumed that the reasons were technology and price. As mentioned earlier, the company had been pushing mainframes despite the proliferation of PCs because those products generated more revenue and profit. The company's cost structure, as a vertically integrated, full-service, and bureaucratic monolith, resulted in higher prices.

This diagnosis is accurate on one level; however, as always in these situations, much more was involved. During this period IBM was convinced that its solutions were the only way to go. In everything from dress code to software, IBM had the answer. This, in part, created the perception that the company, for all its success and resources, was arrogant.

As other businesses invaded IBM's turf, customers found themselves with new choices, new services, and substantially lower prices. While the industry redefined itself, IBM persisted on the course of action that was right for IBM. In the context of this wisdom dimension, IBM lacked the compassion to understand the needs and pressures of its own customers. And, in persisting in pushing mainframes, it lacked the detachment (lack of ego) to offer solutions beyond those that would serve itself.

It may seem strange to find fault with a company that only tried to sell its own products, but this is one of the ways in which interdependence is redefining the very terms of business. Self-interest works in a world in which market share is the only measure. But when success also hinges on relationship, the ability to see and respond to the interest of others is critical. This is the capacity synthesized in compassionate detachment.

Extending something as abstract as compassion or having the reflective ability to detach from self-interest requires an advanced sense of self. Is this even possible for an organization? In an article in the *Harvard Business Review*, Ikujiro Nonaka, a professor at the Institute for Business Research at Hitotsubashi University in Tokyo, explores the characteristics of a "knowledge-creating" company.

He writes: "A company is not a machine but a living organism. Much like an individual, it can have a collective sense of identity and fundamental purpose. This is the organizational equivalent of self-knowledge — a shared understanding of what the company stands for, where it is going, what kind of world it wants to live in, and, most important, how to make that world a reality. In this respect, the knowledge-creating company is as much about ideals as it is about ideas."

Self-awareness for an organization is the same as for an individual. Behaviors, biases, and prevailing emotions are all at work. They also all have a source. Chrysler's mini-vans have again been rated by consumer magazines as among the most defect-prone in this category of vehicles. The company has already recognized the need to improve quality. It will likely uncover the process or engineering issue behind the defects. But to solve quality for the long term, Chrysler must ask itself not what the solution is, but why the defect occurred in the first place. What is the behavioral, cultural, or historical reason for the continuous slip-up? I am not criticizing Chrysler, only asking whether their questions are going deep enough into the issue to yield more than a stopgap solution.

Companies comprise people. They have all the traits, strengths, and flaws that humans have — only magnified because they are bigger. Companies are also engaging in a new type of economic activity, not only making things, but also providing value-added to customers by packaging ever more knowledge and understanding into products and services. This involves a much more dynamic exchange than simply money for a product or service.

Wikström and Normann explain: "One consequence of this integrative process is thus that the borderlines between the producer-seller and the user break down. A marketing logic is replaced by a logic based on the establishment of long-term customer relations." While a seller of a thing can behave like a machine, in a relationship, elements of personality, trustworthiness, vision, clarity, empathy, and selflessness become integral to the transaction.

Companies and individuals operate unconsciously with attachment, so much so that it often can be seen as an addiction. The hard-nosed sales culture at Xerox so emphasized the closing of a deal that its gratification became a type of "hit." The pressure and impossible tasks of working on a big project became like a "high" for people working at Apple. In both of these cases, the lack of self-awareness prevented either compassion or detachment. Customers and employees became victims of abuse or burnout. And the attachment to what served the company — the expensive leases that generated revenue for Xerox, or the proprietary operating system that Apple refused for so long to license — became the companies' greatest liabilities.

Non-high-technology companies can also operate unconsciously with attachment. Banks have remained attached to old models of security, so they defy the logic of the new economy and lend almost exclusively to big corporations (or real-estate developers). Airlines are so addicted to seat-load measures that they underprice each other to the point of losing more money in the last eight years than the industry had achieved in the previous seventy years of its existence. Attachment defeats innovation and represents for many companies the major impediment to business and consciousness growth.

Buddhists believe that "ignorance, attachment, and anger are the causes of relentless suffering." Ignorance is the denial of truth. Anger is action without regard to cause or effect. Attachment is clinging to concepts or things that actually impede the path to self-awareness. These basically stand as the opposites of compassionate detachment.

Detachment may be a Buddhist term, but it is not an abstract issue for business. Roberto Goizueta, CEO of Coca Cola, said in an interview in *Fortune*: "If I could have a New Coke situation every decade, I would. Absolutely." As discussed earlier, this was one of the greatest, most public business mistakes. But New Coke forced the old Coke company into some deep introspection. The company finally released the marketing, research, and decision-making approaches to which it had become blindly attached.

Methodology, no matter how tried and tested, can eventually become just another attachment when it substitutes for concerted and detached mindfulness. Goizueta believes that another detachment — that toward failure — is also critically important: "We became uncompetitive by not being tolerant of mistakes. The moment you let failure become your motivator, you're down the path of inactivity."

At both ends of the spectrum, among entrepreneurial companies such as Nike, as well as such established monoliths as General Electric, the race to innovation and productivity involves breaking through departmental "silos" and attitudinal "boundaries." Territoriality is a direct function of attachment, and any company that wants to realize the efficiencies of cross-functional, inter-company boundarylessness will necessarily have to deal with it. It's no use telling people that they must give up the power and boundaries that used to define their role and importance without creating a new, expansive, and supportive consciousness.

Detachment is the peeling away of unconscious, addictive, and ultimately destructive behavior. This is what most agents of corporate renewal miss. They suggest models for change, which are valid in themselves, but fail to attend to the emptying that must happen first. New growth requires clearing away the old assumptions and beliefs. Such conscious detachment is rarely done, so even though people genuinely try to embrace the new, they are undermined by the unconscious attachments that were never aired, never acknowledged, never understood.

This is what IBM finally mastered. Through the fire of crisis, attachment to even the most sacred of operating modes was finally broken. To earn the respect of customers, IBM remade its vaunted sales force into a service consultancy. The new imperative was to find the solution, not the sale. As a result of this greater empathy and detachment, IBM now actually recommends and installs machines made by other vendors. In 1994, about one-third of IBM installations included computers from DEC and other competitors. And 1994 was the year in which IBM reversed its revenue slide.

One lesson is that our attachments run deep. Another is that the things we value are often the ones that damage us. And a third is that generosity may be counter-intuitive to our competitive thinking, but it is increasingly the defining term of competitiveness. Compassion earns trust from others. Detachment provides the inner and outer clarity to participate in constructive, mutually beneficial interaction. Activating this consciousness requires breaking through the web of self-interest and addictive behavior.

Compassion is the generous empathy that links a company with its employees, customers, suppliers, partners, and communities. And, along with detachment, it provides the wise balance that makes the manipulation inherent in management both effective and responsible. This is quite a conceptual mouthful, but is nevertheless important. Detachment provides the objectivity and determination necessary for difficult decisions, while compassion ensures that the effects, both positive and negative, are shared equally among all those involved.

Values
Truth and Honesty
One of the difficulties in writing this book (or any book) is discovering truth and faithfully communicating it. For example, the use of company examples presumes not only a familiarity with facts, but also an intimate understanding of motive, circumstance, and options. In previous sections I have used General Motors to illustrate behavior: in the case of its Saturn division, GM's behavior was wisely respectful of customers, but in the circumstances of the side-mounted gas tanks on pick-up trucks, it has been callously foolish. The facts are accurate, but what is the truth in either situation?

Truth has always been befuddling, but it assumes a different context, and perhaps even a higher scale of magnitude, in a society that is being radically reshaped by information. We may know more facts, but are they bringing us closer to the truth, or distancing us from it? With clutter and competing interest there is widespread misinformation, contributing to much misunderstanding. But there is also a genuine and growing demand for accountability and truth.

In its survey into the changing habits of Canadian consumers, MarketVision discovered that an astounding 25 percent of the buying population had boycotted a product in the previous year. This activism was usually unknown to the manufacturer. What most often compelled people to reject the offering of a particular provider was a misalignment of values. They felt that certain companies had distorted the truth.

This is an example of how important truth is within relationships. In business, a certain degree of truthfulness has been mandated by law. Gas pumps must be accurate. Advertising claims must be substantiated. Guarantees and warranties must be honored. However, the truthfulness implied in wisdom goes further. Truth is a value judgment, so an individual's ethical context must be fully engaged. Truthfulness requires honesty, the courage to see what really is, and the internal balance to deal with its full implications. The more truthful we are about ourselves, the easier it is to recognize and deal with truth in the circumstances around us. Truthfulness is hard to sustain, but harder to be without.

Truth does not belong to the realm of facts and knowledge, but to intent. This is why it is so tricky for companies adopting the new dynamics of relationship. In moving into this greater intimacy with customers, companies will be judged by their values as well as by their products, by their intentions as well as by their actions. Truthfulness in such interaction requires first an advanced honesty within. This again speaks to the need for self-awareness. It also requires that accountability to others called integrity.

Teamwork is an area of corporate performance that demonstrates this heightened need for truth. Overused as a concept, sometimes misused in application, a team involves an intimate interaction among specialists. Trust is understood to be essential for advancing the agenda of the team, for dividing responsibilities, sharing decisions, and resolving conflict. Fundamental to that trust is truthfulness. In *The Wisdom of Teams*, Katzenbach and Smith explain: "At its core, team accountability is about sincere promises we make to ourselves and others, promises that underpin two critical aspects of teams: commitment and trust. By promising to hold ourselves accountable to the team's goals, we each earn the right to extend our views."

Truth is the meeting point for reciprocity. By selling a DEC machine, IBM keeps its promise to do what is in the best interest of the customer. It earns the right of relationship.

It is commonly understood (at least by mothers) that truth usually wins out. Some companies are still learning the sagacity of this.

• Philip Morris spent $30 million to help finance Proposition 188, a referendum in California that sought to supplant "strict local smoking restrictions with a much looser state-wide law." The company kept its involvement well hidden, which worked against it when opposing forces finally revealed the source of the "pro–188" funding. Voters rejected the Proposition. And Philip Morris's reputation, already besmirched, became a little more encrusted with mud.

• Miller Brewing (a Philip Morris subsidiary) recently launched a new beer to compete within the popular micro-brewery segment. For marketing authenticity, Miller deleted any reference to its corporate brand on the label, instead designating the brewer as Plank River (a brand designation it owned). The new product gained an immediate following, particularly among younger beer drinkers. Proving again how "street-wise" consumers really are, people soon uncovered the truth about Plank River. In an example of electronic backlash, Miller's duplicity was posted on bulletin boards on the Internet. With the wired set, the "cool" became the "fool."

• Upset with leaks to the press, Procter & Gamble hired private investigators to track down the responsible employee(s). Even individual telephone records were scrutinized. When the truth of this hard-nosed approach became public, P&G received even more of the negative press attention that had originally raised its ire. The story eventually led to a book, which again hurt the reputation of the company, as well as the very precious morale of its people.

• For years, Bausch & Lomb sold the same contact lenses at two different prices to consumers. The identical "premium" lenses were priced up to sixteen times higher than the "economy" versions. B&L lost a multimillion-dollar class action suit in Georgia, and received many millions more in bad publicity. A product for clear vision was badly tarnished by a murky corporate pricing strategy.

Many people argue that business ethics are impossible because morality is a subjective value. In reality, morality is an ingrained notion — something fundamental to our humanity. Regardless of whether people espouse a specific religion, or align themselves with a set of beliefs, deception is judged to be wrong, and the deceiver is seen to be bad, while truthfulness is admired, expected, and respected.

• Ricardo Semler runs a very successful conglomerate in Brazil, and has earned an international reputation for innovative, sometimes maverick, management experiments. In a *Harvard Business Review* article, Semler defines his iconoclastic style. "I don't govern Semco — I own the capital, not the company. Semco could govern itself on the basis of three values: employee participation, profit sharing, and open information systems." Sounds like fairly conventional new age language. However, Semco's effectiveness has emerged from the truthfulness to which these values adhered.

When the economy turned sour and revenue dropped, employees all had the information to understand the implications. Semler met with groups of one hundred employees and asked for ideas. As a group they worked through each concept, actually implementing those with merit. These did not achieve the needed efficiency. After exhausting their collective ideas, a shop floor committee went to management and offered a 30 percent pay cut to prevent job losses. In that reciprocity of truthfulness, they also stipulated three conditions: that management take a 40 percent pay cut, that profit-sharing with employees be increased, and that union representatives co-sign every cheque written by the company. With these accommodations, Semco began to make itself over against "a radically new principle of organization."

• When American Express withdrew its revolving credit Optima Card in the early 1990s, it did so in part because a handful of executives were so intimidated about presenting "bad news" that they deliberately hid $24 million in losses. A winning culture had become so rigid that it left no room for failure. Since then, the company has introduced a progressive 360–degree review process, in which peers and subordinates, as well as bosses, evaluate a person's performance. This, and the opening of an internal ombudsman's office, has created an environment in which honesty and candor are invited and appreciated.

• For Richard Barton, president of U.S. customer operations at Xerox, reorienting the company to providing open information management counseling to customers includes honestly acknowledging past shortcomings. Barton states: "This is a time when companies will succeed or fail on the quality and integrity of their human capital. It is not about making sales, but about earning the trust of customers. We especially need to find genuine solutions, and not just opportunities to move more boxes."

• As it faced up to larger than expected customer losses in the expanding long-distance wars, Bell Canada chose to admit to its customers that it had screwed up. John McLennan, the CEO, appeared in television commercials in which he acknowledged the bureaucratic and monopolistic tendencies of the past. He also told customers that they would see a difference, that over time he and his employees would "re-earn" their trust and business. The frankness of this approach went a long way toward diffusing the cynicism of customers, and refocusing and inspiring employees.

These examples reinforce the adage that "honesty is the best policy." They also show that truthfulness is difficult, that it sometimes involves sacrifice and courage, and that it only flows from a heightened sense of self. If individuals and companies do not strive for truth, they forsake not only the opportunity to grow wiser, but also genuine, transforming learning. C. S. Lewis observed: "If you look for truth, you may find comfort in the end: if you look for comfort you will not get either comfort or truth — only soft soap and wishful thinking to begin with and, in the end, despair."

Justice

A wise act draws its moral authority from being just. All the empathy of compassion, the understanding of self, and the recognition of truth are, in a sense, only the preparation for practicing justice.

In our social and economic context, the responsibility for justice has been largely delegated to the legal system. Good corporate citizenship is defined within the parameters of conformance to federal and local law. Corporate officers (and their phalanx of internal and external lawyers) are therefore primarily concerned with the legality of performance and behavior. The question remains: is this really justice?

In wisdom, justice is more of a passion than a deliberation. Its intent is to extend fairness to others rather than defend what is due to the self.

Theodore Levitt, in *The Marketing Imagination*, provides the commercial context for this when he writes, "there is a system of reciprocal dependencies. It is up to the seller to develop the relationship beyond that supposed by the simple notion of keeping a customer merely for the contribution he (or she) makes to the seller's current revenues and profits. In a proper relationship both the buyer and seller should have a 'profit.'" This is the mercantile justice needed for exchange.

With information, justice evolves to another level. As people within companies put more of their creative ability into their work, the need for a fair and stable reciprocity is heightened. Wikström and Normann write: "An element of uncertainty will always accompany the generation and application of new knowledge. Anything untested can always give rise to anxiety, which in turn can discourage the generative process. But when the climate is one of psychological security, and allows an understanding of failure, then the conditions are good for risk taking and the generation of knowledge." This is the interpersonal justice needed for creativity.

As the economy continues its transition into knowledge, and as a much less segmented, defined, and bounded construct emerges for value-creation, justice again jumps to another plane. In many ways the very definitions of individual and company, person and product, are blurring. Who owns intellectual property when the collaborative team that created it comprises autonomous, self-employed specialists? In this case the extension of justice becomes more abstract, even as it becomes more essential. How are rewards divided? Who is invited back to the next project? How are decisions made and conflicts resolved?

Mary Parker Follett viewed the separation of self from the group as inherently flawed. She wrote in the 1930s: "Man advances towards completeness not by further aggregations to himself, but by further and further relating of self to other men. We are always reaching for more union; most, perhaps all, our desires have this motive. The spirit craves totality, this is the motor of social progress; the process of getting it is not by adding more to ourselves, but by offering more and more of ourselves." This is the synthesizing justice needed for wisdom.

Our capacity for justice is about to be even more seriously tested because computerization has really only begun to displace workers. Anderson Consulting, a subsidiary of the huge accounting firm, estimates that in the banking sector alone, "technological and management changes will eliminate 30 to 40 percent of the jobs in the next seven years."

Throughout North America, this translates into a staggering total of 800,000 jobs. In industry after industry, technology is making redundant not only the factory workers who have borne the brunt of past transitions, but also the more educated.

For the first time ever, even the professional disciplines are being affected. Already software programs that provide basic legal and accounting help are eroding the franchise of lawyers and CAs. A California firm is testing robotics that will be able to perform hip replacement surgery. Soundtracks for commercials and movies are now created almost exclusively with synthesizers. The argument that workers dislodged by technology can be retrained and redeployed is being rendered suspect since doctors and artists are being made superfluous. Advancing technology without advancing justice risks creating a society and economy in which people lose their livelihood, and companies lose their customers.

Again, it is not progress that is good or bad. Morality depends on the judiciousness of human beings. The lack of consciousness and respect for justice is unfortunately pervasive in companies. The fact that people are generally working harder, longer, under more pressure, and with fewer supports is essentially unjust. That many workers are becoming unemployed while others are so stretched is unjust. That fear of more job cuts is used to extract concessions and efficiencies from employees is unjust. That CEOs continue to earn salaries disproportionate to those of the company's other workers is unjust. That executive salaries continue to escalate even when their company's performance declines is unjust.

Some companies have started acknowledging the interconnection between business performance and wise justice. Both BMW and Hewlett-Packard moved several manufacturing plants in Europe to a four-day work week system. This decision reflected management's concern for the growing loss of jobs, with the rising number of permanently unemployed. Workers' wages were kept the same, because, although they now worked fewer hours, most also had to take turns working different shifts. Both Hewlett-Packard and BMW achieved major increases in productivity. Workers who would have lost their jobs maintained the dignity of working. And all employees gained more time for leisure, self-development, and family pursuits.

Motivation, quality, and productivity are essential for business success, and the justice of the solution worked out at these two companies helped realize all three. The majority of employees believe that the trade-off between more time off and shift work is more than worth it. As people use this time to bring better balance to their lives, they also seem to bring more constructive ideas and refreshment to their work.

These initiatives represent only a partial solution to a complex problem. A lot more courage and creativity will be necessary to deal with the displacement and deconstruction of the global economy. A profound sense of justice is increasingly valuable because it is the mechanism by which people as a group share the inevitable cycle of pains and gains that are part of business as well as life.

A Pause on the Ascent

Justice and truth do not simply reveal themselves in the imprecise world of day-to-day business. They must be sought, exposed, discovered, and championed. The sense of self, the beliefs that guide us, and the empathy we feel for others provide the constructive tension for undertaking the search. This is the interplay between perspective and values in which we personally grow wise.

It may seem daunting to ask so much of ourselves. Yet in many ways this represents a fulfillment, an opportunity to experience our humanity in its deepest and widest potential. When we slip into unconsciousness, when we withhold empathy or avoid truth, when we accept injustice, we inevitably are also accepting limitations not only in our growth as individuals, but also in our performance as companies. We may choose not to seek wisdom because it is so demanding, but there is no other way to face the challenges of the new economic order.

So, aware, obligated and committed, honest and fair (or at least trying), we are now ready to proceed toward the descent.

EIGHT

THE EXTERNAL PRACTICE: DESCENDING

We now move to the phase of growth and realization that involves the application and practice in real life of the perspective and values revealed from within. Aristotle called this "excellence in art," meaning wisdom is a constructive, creative, and tangible intelligence that changes our very interpretation of the physical world.

Remember, although I am presenting this as a descent, the sequence (the "in and out") is continuous. After his enlightenment, Buddha taught and meditated every day. Christ also retreated frequently to the desert. Action feeds our contemplation just as contemplation gives meaning to our action.

Action
Unity and Integration
Wisdom is essentially a perspective of integration: cause with effect; self with others; need with obligation; detachment with compassion; reason with emotion; spirit with body. Wise decisions have this integrity; seemingly divisive differences are simplified into something cogent and cohesive. Everyone wins a little bit, but everyone must share equally in the sacrifice to get there.

This integration operates on a variety of planes. There is first the internal unity achieved by an individual, arrived at through self-knowledge, in which goals and fears, strengths and weaknesses, and desires and repulsion are understood as *parts* of a totality. Mary Parker Follett reflected, "It is not my uniqueness which makes me of value to the whole, but my power of relating."

On another plane, there is the integration that the individual achieves within a larger group. Again through conscious introspection, differences within the social construct are acknowledged, understood, and respected. The diverse parts are amalgamated into a whole — not melted so that the boundaries of the individuals are lost, but united so that their identity is derived from the interaction within the group.

The planes of integration continue to graduate. Group with group, community with community, country with country. At the highest level, human consciousness also embraces other species, recognizing the fundamental interdependence of all living things on the planet that sustains us.

What does this have to do with business? Let us follow the graduation of integrity backward to see. At the macro level, there is finally widespread acknowledgment that the economy and ecology function as an integrated biosphere. This symbiosis is evident from Canada's depleted North Atlantic fishery to California's congested highways. Managing fish stocks and producing electric cars are essential for both jobs and a livable environment.

The global economy is creating another unity. Goods, services, capital, ideas, information, as well as many workers, now flow across borders with a fluidity unimaginable only a couple of decades ago. Cultures are resisting this melding, but more than ever there is a common interest as even the Communist regimes of China and Vietnam embrace aspects of market development. In this unity, distinctions vanish. The Third World used to be a separate place. Increasingly, there are Third World neighborhoods within First World communities, and First World pockets in Third World countries. Computers, modems, faxes, MTV, and the Internet have all added to that unity.

On a more micro level, companies have been forced out of the economies of scale and into the economies of customization. This has meant moving from the self-sufficiency of vertical integration into the collaborative matrix of horizontal integration. Boundaries among divisions, disciplines, suppliers, and customers are more porous. Ideas, service, and value are now combined rather than assembled.

Rubbermaid, one of the companies to achieve a high rate of continuous innovation, has also earned a reputation for outstanding management effectiveness. In 1995, the company was at the top in *Fortune's* "most admired" list for the second time. In an interview, CEO Wolfgang Schmitt offered a glimpse into a large established company that behaved so consistently as if it was just starting up. "Our business teams are as nimble as entrepreneurs. The teams can reach anywhere in the company for resources. We want an organization that gives us the best of both worlds."

Out of a sense of belonging, individuals take responsibility for personal as well as group needs. The more pronounced the unity, the smarter, more efficient the interaction. In relation to customers, unity represents the next level of connectivity and relevance beyond service. *Service* implies giving of yourself to another. *Unity* recognizes that giving to another is now the same as giving to yourself.

When the Pentium flaw became public, Intel's hesitation created a fissure between the company and its customers. Dell, which sold Pentium-based computers, responded in a radically different way. As described by Niklas Von Daehne in *Selling*, "within three days, the entire sales and service organization in Austin [Dell's home base] and the account executives in the field were briefed on the issue. Then the sales representatives started calling every single one of Dell's institutional customers to explain the extent of the Pentium problem."

The action resolved the anxiety of some clients. A few wanted immediate replacement chips. The key, though, is that because Dell did not see any distinction between its customers' anxieties and its commercial interests, it increased its usefulness, credibility, and importance to customers. Unity, then, is what propels growth in an economy without boundaries.

The logic of unity, like that of morality, makes great sense. But it is still practiced by exception rather than by rule. In each of the planes described above, self-interest defeats even the most obvious common good. Although the benefits of trade are obvious and irrefutable, countries still play costly games with quotas, subsidies, and tariffs. Companies still dump illegal chemicals into rivers and lakes, breaking the trust of their communities, as well as the law. Managers and employees embrace the language of teamwork while fighting a more lethal battle — not for more benefits but for work and dignity in the face of productivity and technology. Executives cut costs even when that means depleting morale and stifling innovation. Employees understand the need for commitment, but opt instead to oscillate between cynicism and entitlement.

To disregard unity is to disregard moral obligation. In "The Law of Human Nature," C. S. Lewis wrote: "These then are the two points I wanted to make. First, that human beings, all over the earth, have this curious idea that they ought to behave in a certain way, and they cannot really get rid of it. Secondly, that they do not behave in that way. They know the law of nature; they break it. These two facts are the foundation of all clear thinking about ourselves and the universe we live in."

We may not be able to stop ourselves from breaking the "natural law." Nor can we necessarily stop the craving for what is right. As Hans Kung reminds us: "The human being should not be inhuman, antihuman, but rather live an entirely humane life. Humanness must be realized in all its dimensions." A perspective of unity is an expression of that heightened sense of humanity.

How do we get to such a consciousness? What can be done within the "divide and conquer" practices of day-to-day business to foster unity?

Many companies already do an exercise called "gap analysis." This involves looking at an industry, customer need, or trend, and, through a range of analyses, pinpointing openings — unfulfilled expectations, new technologies, new insights — that may represent an opportunity for business growth. Gap analysis on a different scale has been used by wisdom teachers to create a more profound consciousness for unity. The purpose is to study the gap to see the whole.

All of us are victims or casualties of disunity. We are all struggling with gaps, such as those between:

- the time to act and the time to reflect;
- the pressures to react and the desire to proact;
- the efficiency needs of productivity and the needed deliberation for better service;
- the freedom of autonomy and the obligations of interdependence;
- the demanding requirements of career and the inner fulfillment of balance; and
- the collaboration for teamwork and the accountability to perform as an individual.

Since unity is by definition a collective, it makes sense that gaps exist on a broader scale than just for the individual. On this level, gaps exist between:

- economic activity and ecological preservation;
- technological advancement and human resource utilization;
- management business goals and employees' need for security;
- corporate vision and daily performance;
- meeting the bottom line and adding extra value;
- achieving greater efficiency and increasing innovation;
- setting the strategy and achieving the result; and
- stating values and the reality of behavior.

We may find ways to close the distance in some of these gaps, but disunity and strife persist. To be without boundaries does not alone bring unity. That can only come from consciousness and obligation. Meister Eckhart taught that enlightenment was "something that can be grasped only within the tension of opposites." To flip that around, what keeps us from seeing the unity is what keeps us from becoming wise.

Intellectual and Emotional Harmony

For several centuries, business has functioned by reducing a human being to the capability or skill that could most cost-effectively produce value. Manufacturing extracted labor; management segregated reason. The whole human being showed up for work, but only a small part was sought, engaged, and paid for. This, of course, has changed radically in the last few years, but the bias to break down tasks and to assign specific expertise still runs deep. The pace of competitive change and technological advancement is demanding a more integrated approach and is forcing even the most skeptical business people to see the benefits of a more "holistic" approach.

Struggling to give dimension and measurability to this totality, companies such as Xerox have called the fully developed, fully engaged resource "human capital." This is a major redefinition because it explicitly connects return, long associated with investment, to human potentiality. This connection was largely ignored in North America until companies there developed a new respect for the Japanese approach to management. Although capitalist, Japan's companies operate with a heightened sensitivity to their society, communities, and employees. Already emulated by Korea, Taiwan, and Malaysia, Japan's construct has been labeled "human capitalism."

Robert Ozaki, an economics professor at California State University and author of *Human Capitalism*, has defined three specific aspects in which "a company under human capitalism significantly differs from a traditional capitalistic firm. First, management and workers of the humanistic firm constitute an integrated group, assume primary sovereignty, and behave as if they jointly own the firm."

By now the stories of humble executives are legend: senior Japanese executives cleaning the toilets in newly opened auto factories; managers and workers eating as a single group in the company cafeteria; no reserved parking spot for the president. While dramatic, these actions do "speak louder than words," conveying a unity and sense of common purpose that invites a full and equal participation in the work to be done.

Second, according to Ozaki, a humanistic firm "both competes *and* cooperates with other firms in the context of an organized market." This requires an ethic combining calculated generosity with mutually beneficial competitiveness. For North Americans weaned on the principles of competition, this is also very difficult to practice. Old divisions, definitions, and rivalries are hard to break.

Third, "management and workers substantially share decision making." Many of the companies I have worked with do, in fact, encourage more participation, but this still tends to be in the execution of decisions or direction set by executives. Reengineering, for example, has usually been imposed by executive edict — the "substantial sharing" does not start until the difficult phases of redesign and implementation.

Since any business involving knowledge is essentially an exercise in human capitalism, the implications of Ozaki's observations apply to virtually all enterprises.

What do we draw from this? One implication is that any fragmentation in function or authority upsets the unity, and therefore intellectual and emotional harmony of the whole. There is inefficiency when employees feel separated in their interests from those of management. There is waste when market players focus exclusively on competition. There is apathy when workers are left out of the decision loop.

A second implication is on the human level. In not belonging, or feeling vulnerable or underappreciated, individuals tend to hold back their involvement. In that reservation they are also often withholding the precious creativity and spontaneity so vital for growth and innovation. The structures and behaviors that segment by expertise tend to also fragment, deconstruct, and isolate the contribution of the individual human being.

Since the explosion of scientific thought, "enlightenment" has come to mean primarily intellectual clarity and logically precise reason. It is ironic that "enlightened" has become a modifier of a mental process, not necessarily of wisdom. As a result, all the passion of emotion, the mystery of intuition, and the intangible energy of creativity have been devalued for not conforming to the expectations of reason. Companies have flourished in this logical disunity — until now.

To function in this new economy, there is a need and opportunity for companies to invite their human resources to perform at a higher level of abstraction and creativity. Note the word "invite." The key to transforming data into knowledge that customers will pay for is the interpretation, insight, and judgment of fully engaged and fully motivated individuals. The basis for engendering this type of work is genuine respect for the whole human being. *Invitation* reminds us that the role of management has irrevocably changed in that it must provide the support to elicit this enlightened performance. Without wisdom in the company, there can be no wisdom extended to customers.

Toyota's new manufacturing plant, mentioned earlier, is an example of moving technology to stand *behind* the worker, whose ingenuity is the real source of company value. Since converting to this new system, output per individual has increased by 20 percent, while defects — the principal measure of quality — have fallen to only 12 percent of the average of the old. Human involvement and human inspiration are proving to be the real and lasting determinants of competitiveness.

When people have the freedom to express the full range of their human talent, a job ceases to be just work. It is a place of growth, of belonging, of contribution, and of meaning. So begins the cycle of genuine productivity improvement. From a heightened intellectual and emotional harmony flows the commitment for more innovation. The greater the group's achievement, the more satisfied and fulfilled the individual. As Ozaki explains, employees "do not have to suffer the strain of unnaturally having to compartmentalize their lives and go through a daily metamorphosis as they report to work, because their firm is a mini-community, an extension of life itself."

The realization still emerging in business is that to create a boundaryless organization means not only dissolving the walls between people, but also the ones within them. Heart, mind, and soul have a place in business, because the products companies need to produce to be competitive are those that involve the practice of human understanding and creativity.

Such deepened involvement may strike some as just a higher form of exploitation. This is exactly why obligation is imperative. Without the other dimensions of wisdom — the clarity, compassion, respect for truth, and justice — this potential for higher value will only result in a reality of deeper cynicism. Wisdom is the ethos that earns for companies the right to enjoy this advanced contribution from their employees. And it is the ethos that allows individuals to retain personal balance and purpose in trying times.

Cyprian Smith writes that "the truest knowledge and deepest wisdom can never be something of the brain only, but must emanate from the core of the whole human being, flesh and blood, bone marrow and sinew." For both the individual and the enterprise, the scope of such growth at work represents a liberating potential and a strategic necessity.

Equanimity

Equanimity is how we often recognize wisdom in others. And imbalance is what often compels us to seek it for ourselves. Yet for something so obviously beneficial, balance remains elusive. Despite all the self-help and how-to books, the pressures of time, information, competitiveness, and personal activity seem to make balance an even harder virtue to realize.

Part of the problem is that we have accommodated imbalance for so long that we now accept it as normal. In the human body, the real risk of high blood pressure is that it wears down the electrical nodes regulating blood flow. When those circuits burn out, which happens when the organism is under continuous stress, the body is left without a system for managing its own blood. It cannot moderate the pressure changes needed to respond to either a serious threat or a relaxing nap. In accepting the abnormal as normal, the body's mechanism for maintaining its own fuel supply ultimately becomes stuck at a permanent and dangerous level.

In business, the imbalance as status quo is effecting a similar burnout of the circuitry for judgment. Workers in all departments, at all levels, accept as normal "not having time to think." Executives accept as normal the careening from one management orthodoxy to another. And society in general accepts as normal a situation in which many people are permanently unemployed while many others are chronically overworked. These and other such accepted "normalities" suggest an institutionalized imbalance.

Imbalance, with its conflicting pressures and permanent reactivity, occurs when organizations and individuals lose their sense of self. Good judgment, common sense, and even wisdom are lost or unattended as we try to live up to agendas other than our own. The off-center becomes the new center; cause and effect cease to have any connection; and change-fatigue becomes permanent.

A familiar sensation to many in business, this perpetually off-center position causes companies to adopt solutions without having the patience to fully master them. New skills are introduced into training without a clear understanding of how they will relate to a larger cause. Alliances are formulated overnight without the heightened mutuality to make them viable. It is no wonder that when imbalance becomes the average, we begin to accept the foolish as the reasonable.

Most of the problems confronting people in business would be much easier to solve if we allowed ourselves to experience our instinctive bias toward equanimity. Every tension we face can be seen as essentially a struggle for symmetry. Short-term profits versus long-term sustainability; cost-cutting versus investment in innovation; efficiency versus efficacy; margin growth versus customer-service enhancement; productivity versus jobs. Any issue (especially those filled with ambiguity and pressure) concerns balance.

When any problems are resolved with imbalance, then that solution will likely be both temporary and damaging. And as long as companies rationalize such incongruity as the price of competitiveness, they will pay the even more costly price of missing the opportunity for genuine renewal.

For example, RCA invented flat panel TV screens in the mid-1960s. Where are they now? Out of the business altogether. Who dominates and most benefits from this vital and exponentially growing market? Sharp Electronics. Does anyone care? IBM does. The computer company lost incalculable sales for its hot-selling Thinkpad laptop because it could not initially get enough of the high-quality, flat screen displays.

Beyond the issue of lost revenue, the jobs for designing and making these very complex screens — soon to be used in cars, home appliances, TVs, as well as computers — are exactly the high-value-added, knowledge-intensive jobs that the new economy most covets. Without such jobs, consumer confidence erodes, as does the tax base, and ultimately also the opportunity to invest in future social requirements like education. A balance issue for RCA — whether to make short-term profits or invest in new technology for the long term — has had real impact on the balance of trade between North America and Japan.

Balance affects interdependence. Imbalance may be painful to those who practice it (RCA lost first market share, and then the market), but it is not restricted to them. It ripples and creates tension through the whole interconnected web of society and commerce. Asymmetry does more than make stress for the individual or company involved. It also compounds into disunity, injustice, disregard for cause, and disrespect for effect. As society gets more wired and the economy more interconnected, the imbalance of one creates volatility for the whole.

Competitiveness is a threat. Globalization requires change. But if the lessons of the past three decades reveal anything, it is that business must be practiced with more deliberation, not less. Continuous expediency will not win out against competitors who practice continuous learning, continuous improvement, and continuous value-enhancement.

Robert Waterman, the consultant and author who helped start business on the search for excellence, states: "Corporate cultures that tend to put their constituencies — shareholders, customers and employees — on the same plane, as opposed to putting shareholders first, are perversely those that do best for shareholders." Obligation to others is a form of self-interest because by respecting our fundamental unity, it sustains balance.

If imbalance is the norm, how do we re-orient ourselves?

First, it is important to realize that poise under pressure may be a function of temperament and training, but in its wisest iteration, equanimity comes from the quiet confidence of deeply rooted self-knowledge. Inner certitude provides outer calm.

Second, a situation is stressful or painful because we attach such high stakes to it. Buddhist teaching suggests that *impermanence* is the cause of all suffering. Things inevitably change, so when we vest the familiar and comfortable with disproportionate importance, we suffer separation pain when these are taken away from us. Enlightenment in the Buddhist sense follows when humans release attachments to things that are transitory. (This is detachment again, now in the context of equanimity.)

To surrender an attachment is not to surrender what is important to the self. In balance, the continuity of need between an individual and the group, a company and its employees, and a company and its customers is unbroken. Detachment is what maintains balance. It allows an individual the equilibrium to determine what is just and to decipher what is true.

Why do we want judges in our judicial system to be both balanced and impartial? Legal disputes involve many facts, but reason alone is not enough to make judgments. Relations between people are inherently ambiguous, so detachment and a sense of balance are critical for determining what is right. As the commerce of things becomes supplanted by the commerce of relationships, the ambiguity in business will only grow deeper. At both levels of leadership and operations, companies need individuals who have the presence and impartiality to maintain balance.

Some companies have actually used equanimity as a competitive strategy. BMW has engineered its cars to achieve balance on a number of dimensions. On the functional level, its cars are designed with almost equal weight distribution between front and back. This improves road-handling and performance. As much as 90 percent of its newer models are recyclable, and are designed for relatively easy disassembly. This helps match the needs of the environment with those of production and customer satisfaction. The manufacturing process combines high technology with traditional human craftsmanship. This produces cars that are not the most luxurious, nor the least expensive. Peter Drucker uses BMW as an example of a company that is big enough to compete globally, yet small enough to be entrepreneurial.

The evidence that both productivity and people benefit from equanimity is growing. In a study tracking 115 Harvard Business School graduates since 1974, John Kotter determined that: "Success at work for most people means a job that is economically and psychologically satisfying, that makes a contribution to society, and supports a healthy personal or family life." Getting the job done is not secondary, but nor is it primary. Rather, it is simply a part of a continuum.

The issue of equilibrium is as old as society. History offers two examples that provide particularly useful models. In establishing the principles of democracy after the War of Independence, Americans wanted to avoid tyranny and anarchy. Based on the Enlightenment's view of the fully dimensionalized human being, the fathers of the country created a system of "checks and balances." There would be an Executive to lead, a Congress to represent, and a Court to adjudicate: three autonomous power sources that work to keep each other in balance (most of the time).

The French were solving a slightly different problem after their revolution: interdependence. Once again, to achieve balance between the individual and the community, the intelligence that framed French law created a troika of principles. "Liberté. Egalité. Fraternité."

Balance between two polarities seems to require the intervention of a third force. For the French, liberty depends on the legal and social acknowledgment of equality. But if everyone were free and equal, that would not necessarily assure the reciprocity needed to function in society. Hence the ethos of "brotherhood." Brotherhood ensures that one's liberties do not intrude on another's.

The imbalance in business may be that a third factor is continuously missing. Short term pushes at long term, efficiency pulls at efficacy, employment struggles with unemployment. Reconciling such diverse needs requires that the independence of each side be balanced with interdependence. And the factor for realizing this balance is again reciprocity.

Below is my construct for this triangulated model of balance. Part A is drawn from the historical lessons discussed above. Part B explores the implications for business.

A)

Personal Self-Interest	Other Self-Interest	Reciprocity
> Liberty	> Equality	> Fraternity/Sorority
> Representation	> Leadership	> Justice

B)

Corporate Self-Interest	Individual Self-Interest	Balancing Reciprocity
> Control	> Empowerment	> Redefined system of justice for shared results and accountability
> Job Flexibility	> Job Security	> Truthful development of mutual flexibility options
> Productivity	> Learning	> One-on-one knowledge and wisdom enhancement
> Competitiveness	> Balance	> Formal attention to developing head/heart/spirit
> Innovation	> Creativity	> Release from the fear of failure

Most organizations plan with an objective and a strategy. These may not be enough. An objective has cogency for business based on transaction, but those objectives based on relationship benefit from also defining the "reciprocity." This will provide a presence for the customer, worker, and supplier within the plan, and create terms for the strategy that appreciate the company's continuing need for symmetry.

Support
Substantial Subjectivity

When we go to the wise, we are seeking their subjectivity. Objective opinion or quantitative analysis would be apparent to anyone who can think logically. We respect the wise for their personal judgment — the benefit of their knowledge, experience, mastery of specific disciplines, breadth, intuition, and beliefs. When we discuss a problem with the wise, we generally want context or insight, not facts. If anything, we seek a synthesis, a revelatory understanding that will free us from the burden of too many irreconcilable facts.

Facts have been devalued for a couple of reasons. First, as we have seen, there are now too many of them. So much research and information are available that anyone can take a stand on any issue and find corroborating data. Facts, like dollars, suffer inflation when there are too many of them in circulation unsecured by knowledge and understanding. Second, the rate of change is such that facts now have a much shorter shelf life. They are constantly being displaced by new information. The instability of facts has allowed companies to delayer because it reduces the importance of mid-level "fact-managers" and of head-office "fact-police."

The dependence on facts and the reluctance to trust the subjective are holdovers from that mode of management that sought value-creation in segments. Value is now generated through synthesis — the merging of facts with the knowledge, experience, creativity, and interactions of the workers, suppliers, and customers who customize it. Facts are a raw material in that knowledge–innovation combination, but alone are weightless and impotent. Hence the need for the substance of experience and creative interpretation. Still, only an advanced judgment can solve the complex problems attending this new type of value creation; only personal insight can deal with situations of pressing ambiguity. Hence the need for substantial subjectivity.

Like compassion and detachment, the new economy requires that substance and subjectivity be linked. Substance is derived from the commitment to truth, justice, and fairness allowing personal judgment to come to fruition. And while value relies on the individual's interpretation, the insight is not self-serving. This is what gives enlightened subjectivity its authority. Wise people are motivated by the larger concerns and interconnections already discussed. Their commitment to truth and justice, their compassion for others, and their detachment from personal gain free their judgment from the personal bias and self-benefiting motivation that made the need for facts so logical and essential in the first place. As a creation of the human spirit, substantial subjectivity does not deny the importance of facts, but recognizes their limitations. Insight, created by reflection, intelligence, experience, and morals, reaches to a conclusion that facts alone do not lead to. This internal, personal substance is wisdom.

Think of all the situations in which work is becoming interpretive. Customer service representatives may have formal manuals to refer to, but real value for customers is created when solutions are improvised for personal needs. Improvisation within a strategic context is one such interpretive act.

As companies resort to more cross-functional teams to improve quality and accelerate project work, judgment, creativity, and conflict resolution require more than an ability to follow instruction. Such interactions are interpretive. The expertise of any single person, like an engineer, researcher, or MIS specialist, may involve lots of objective data, but their effectiveness within this interplay of team–project–customer hinges on skills of interpretation.

Jobs in traditional industry and manufacturing sectors have evolved to be much more knowledge based. Even on the factory floor, productivity is increasingly a function of interpretation. In her study of the organizational impacts of technology, Shoshana Zuboff noted that "most managers approached the technological conversion with the belief that the technology would eliminate, not exacerbate, the need for operator understanding."

Computerization provides greater standardization of outcome, but, ironically, it requires more mental dexterity and interpretation from the people interacting with the technology. The realm of subjectivity is like that of software: the more hardware coming on stream, the more developed and complex the interpretation and insight must be to instruct and operate it.

When Aristotle defined wisdom as "excellence in art," he was also implying the creative essence of judgment. Art springs from a highly personal interpretation of reality, yet it moves others because it resonates with some universal truth or emotion. The personal is art's subjectivity. Its universality is what makes art substantial. The opinion, passion, and experience of an individual is not a weakness, but instead represents the fundamental source of art. Subjectivity involves the same creativity. When wise teachers tell us to view our lives as a work of art, they are suggesting this creative potential of enlightened judgment.

Substantial subjectivity is a culmination — it is how an individual reflects growth. The perspective of continuity within time and community is part of that substance. Compassion, the dedication to justice, and the hunger for truth ensure that subjectivity is free from the distortions of unconnected self-interest.

This is sounding very ideal. The subjective part, because it is human, keeps this grounded in reality. Not every one has the desire or inclination to reflect and consciously develop these inner capacities. And not all who do seek such growth attain the same level of substance. The variability is as great as our humanity. For businesses, for workers in this new environment, and for entrepreneurs creating value on their own, the skills of substantial subjectivity must be addressed because these are the ones driving knowledge.

While not every one can be wise, virtually every individual in every job must have at least some of the skills, insights, and abilities of this substantial subjectivity. Whether thinking up strategies or operating new painting technology on the assembly line of a car plant, workers must learn to create their own view: their own understanding, interpretation, and expression.

Fostering within individuals the inner awareness and confidence to express their "artistry" is the major role of management. Training and procedural policies within companies have actually stunted the growth of such artistry. And in the recently flattened structures of business, linear problem-solving is no longer possible. Instead, management must encourage individuals to take more responsibility, extemporizing solutions with ever changing combinations of other colleagues, specialists, and resources.

This realization led the Canadian Imperial Bank of Commerce to take the unusual step of abolishing training programs. As detailed in a 1994 article in *Fortune*, CIBC was caught flat-footed by the last recession, and suffered particular exposure to overdeveloped real-estate properties. The accounting and lending methods of the old economy, based on hard assets and formal analysis, no longer generated wealth. To stop its conventional thinking and practices, CIBC stopped its conventional training.

Acknowledging that more abstract interpersonal skills were needed for dealing with the vagaries of the new knowledge wealth, CIBC now allows individual workers at all levels to design their own learning programs. The bank identifies the needed skills, provides tools for personal analysis, and resources for study and experience, and lets people explore the opportunities for their own growth. In conjunction with this individualized approach, CIBC is also testing a range of new indices to help determine progress and gaps in this effort to activate the full potential of its "intellectual capital."

With substantial subjectivity, the goal is not to unleash unbridled personal opinion, but to ground people with elements of thoughtful consciousness and to allow them to express their insight in constructive ways. Substantial subjectivity fosters a profound and primary respect for the truth, a compassionate commitment to justice, and a willingness to see self-interest served via mutuality.

If wise subjectivity is essential for lasting corporate renewal, it is also a critical competency for the self-employed. As more of the economy converts to the networking of independent workers, expertise or specialization will become more generic. Differentiation for an individual entrepreneur will therefore be a function of this subjective artistry. The substance of real knowledge is important, but the full value of the "networker" will be in *creating* solutions — and the enthusiastic acceptance of those solutions.

One of the benefits of unplugging from a conventional job structure and networking is that it affords the individual the flexibility to develop the interests and capabilities that are most fulfilling. In Aristotle's terms, the wise are "the most self-sufficient" because they can "practice the art of contemplation" by themselves. Not everyone operating from his or her own office relishes being isolated. Even those enthusiastic for this independence struggle with a different concept of security, more administration, and the need to invest in their own "brand equity." But in most cases, this form of work also affords more opportunity for reflection, self-analysis, and perspective. In relying on the self to make a living, people exercise their wits, as well as their brains — which is exactly the combination demanded by the unpredictability of the current economy.

Mentorship

In all traditions, the wise perform the essential role of teacher. Moses, Christ, Buddha, and Confucius all had followers and disciples whom they taught. Having ascended to the realm of understanding, each accepted as part of the responsibility of wisdom the obligation to descend and help others realize their own awakening. In a reversal of conventional thinking, they taught not because they could not *do*, but because they had already *done*.

Mentorship on the plane of wisdom involves both leading others to the potential they already possess within themselves and raising their consciousness of the interconnections and obligations we all share. The unity of inner depth with outer breadth is the essence of wisdom teaching. Modern business management has been likened to coaching a team or to leading an ensemble of musicians on a harmonious improvisation. These are valid metaphors. The focus of wisdom is to develop a fuller awareness of skill, talent, expertise, and confidence, releasing the artistry of the "athlete" or "musician." At the same time, it creates the generosity and cohesion to make the larger unit work as a totality.

Teaching wisdom requires a formal discipline or practice. Wisdom is rare because it is not accumulated casually. Its teaching therefore often seems rigid. In fact, a formal structure is indispensable. Within the discipline of an established framework of seminars and workshops, the individual is free to explore issues at depth, without repeating the usual mistakes, or exhausting the dead ends that make the path inward so tricky.

These formal approaches may vary widely in content and structure (although there are some inescapable similarities), but the point of the discipline is to focus on what is really important. Usually, this is within. Peter Senge speaks of this learning as a "personal mastery," which "goes beyond competence and skill, though it is grounded in competence and skills. It goes beyond spiritual unfolding, although it requires spiritual growth. It means approaching one's life as a creative work, living life from a creative as opposed to reactive viewpoint." The potentiality is again described as an artistry. And artistry is almost always achieved by a persistent and disciplined practice of craft.

In *Creating Minds*, psychologist and teacher Howard Gardiner explores the similarities among Freud, Einstein, Picasso, Stravinski, Gandhi, Martha Graham, and T. S. Eliot. His analysis contains important lessons for those seeking to develop their own artistry, not only as creative people, but also as wise ones. Gardiner shows that genius alone did not explain the breakthroughs achieved by these giants. Each worked very hard to master his or her basic craft, to grow proficient in his or her field. Once acknowledged as standouts, each only worked harder to raise the level of their art and personal artistry. (For example, Einstein's writings from later in life are valued more for their sagacity than for their physics.)

As we know from how the arts have been taught for centuries, mentors themselves must embody the skills they are passing on. The relationship is not one of control (even though there may again be considerable discipline), but one of shared passion, respect, and deep affection for the creative spirit. In her study of leadership, Patricia Pitcher explores this in the light of teaching itself being an art: "Teaching is a craft; I know because I'm still learning it every day from my colleagues. I have graduated from apprentice to journeyman, but they are still master craftsmen. You cannot *tell* someone how to be a teacher. He or she has to do it under (yes, I said *under*) the patient, tolerant guidance of a master. I have to watch them, listen to them, trust them, follow them."

In the information economy, one would expect the teacher to impart valuable knowledge. This is actually only the initial task. The role of the teacher is to help others learn "a new way of knowing." Sensory-based knowledge only provides a foundation and is inadequate for dealing with paradox. For that we need the higher knowledge of unity, detachment, and intuition. Mary Parker Follett and Peter Senge explain that the most constructive learning is achieved through tension — the conflict between seemingly irreconcilable options or circumstances. Such tension requires that *we* change if we are to change the outcome. Teaching wisdom is therefore not a literal construct with a fixed curriculum. It is a dynamic process, with the learning exchange growing beyond the assembly and accumulation of knowledge to activate a continuous realization of self.

In business, we have heard often the expression "walking the talk." It's not enough to teach. If creating knowledge is what now produces value, then the interaction between teacher and learner can be seen as the new factory. Peter Drucker even suggests in *Managing for the Future* that the best way to improve the productivity of knowledge workers is to have them teach others. The process of passing on what we know requires that the "teacher" go deeper into the realization and understanding of the knowledge being imparted. Teaching, then, is not an act of recalling collected data, but of renewing that knowledge through introspection and personal growth. Drucker adds: "It is often being said that in the information age every enterprise must become a learning institution. It also must become a teaching institution."

At companies such as Microsoft, learning is not a precondition for production — it *is* production. William Bridges explains: "Within each team, individuals are always given a little more than they can accomplish on their own, so there is constant collaboration among team members.

New employees, given important responsibilities from day one, are assigned a 'buddy/mentor' to help them learn the ropes." Teaching is integral to doing, which, of course, is the only way to innovate and learn continuously.

Organizations that are not in the knowledge-intensive industries of communications and software are still in a business in which knowledge confirms competitiveness. Home Depot sells the types of things we associate with the industrial economy. Yet its growth, reputation among customers, and fiscal results have made it as much a prototype for the new economy as Microsoft. One unique characteristic is that the founders of the company, who are now its president and CEO, continue to lead the training and development sessions for staff. CEO Bernard Marcus notes that "nobody else does training this way. It's time consuming; it's hard work." This again is where patience achieves payout. The skills for managing complex customer relationships require mentoring, not memorization.

As a company that rejected training, CIBC does not discount the value of such teaching. Employees are encouraged to seek a mentor within the company to help with skills they want to develop. These interactions again take time, but the investment yields not only knowledge, but also more facility for cross-functional teamwork.

Every company will need to find its own tools for encoding and nurturing wisdom. Whether or not training is involved, it is important to remember that training and teaching are not the same thing. Training involves skill development. Teaching, as it applies to wisdom, involves human development. While skill is obviously important, productivity is achieved when the full creativity, intelligence, and acuity of the individual worker is brought to that task. Training imparts functional expertise; teaching adds common sense.

The principles of teaching provide an organization with very different authority structures than traditional management. Truth is given more importance than power. Inner confidence and creativity are seen as integral aspects of productivity. And learning becomes the job description regardless of role, position, or title. New ideas are important for renewal, but companies for whom teaching is an ethic usually create their own models, as well as their own meaning. The value, as always, is that which lies within.

Those who are wise, who have earned their own mastery, tend to teach from certain principles that provide guidance for creating "teaching" organizations.

1. *Preach what has been practiced.* Christ provoked his followers and contemporaries with actions as well as words. He taught compassion and charity, using stories like that of the "Good Samaritan," but he also dined with those whom society perceived as "impure" (including tax collectors), he cleansed lepers, defended adulterers, and suffered ignomy for his beliefs.

2. *Explain by example.* What is obvious to the wise is often incoherent to the average person. The koans used by Zen masters, the stories illustrating the truths of Confucius, and the parables spoken by Christ all challenge those who hear them to see their reality in a new way.

3. *Stretch with accessibility.* Metaphors and aphorisms work (think of the information superhighway) because they make complex, unpredictable, and ambiguous situations decipherable to the majority. Like a joke, they require that the listener make a leap and use their own imagination to construct a new reality map.

4. *Practice truth.* Truth resonates. The passion for truth gives wise teachers their fundamental authority.

5. *Ritualize the process and the progress.* In the late 1930s during a major labor strike in Ahmedabad, Gandhi printed a daily newsletter for locked-out workers that sought to give their sacrifice some wider context. As described in Erik Erikson's biography, the great pacifist leader also created a ritual for his teaching. "Every afternoon Gandhi would arrive with his co-workers in a 1915 Overland roadster, over the only then available bridge down river. They would be awaited by a crowd of workers, rarely numbering less than 5,000, and sometimes closer to 10,000, some having walked two or three miles, now seated to watch the little man in the loincloth speak — for very few could hear him. What he said, they knew, would only enlarge on the content of the leaflets which the few literate workers had read aloud in various quarters of the city."

Teaching is a personal activity. While technology greatly increases the information available to us, it has not spawned a commensurate degree of wisdom. For that we still need human beings, physical contact, personal exposure, and a sense of communion.

A Breather at the Bottom

Real progress, as in anything else of value in life, requires effort, concentration, and mastery. Wisdom is rare precisely because it is so difficult to fathom and so demanding to achieve. Although I have defined ten steps, this is not another ten- or twelve-step program. Despite our facility with information, and desire for readily implementable process, wisdom does not lend itself to sound bites. Growth at this level requires patience and persistence. We can only work at it, reflect, integrate, and grow wise by doing wise things.

However, not all is drudgery. As with craftsmanship and creativity, there is great pleasure in the effort, and great satisfaction in the doing. Leo Lefebure, in his study of the similarities between Buddhism and Christianity, writes: "To suffer is not enough. We must also be in touch with the wonders of life." Growing wise is as rewarding as being wise.

Aristotle wrote in his *Ethics* that "wisdom must be the most finished form of knowledge." This provides a useful context for the modern business world buzzing with so many facts. If information is more valuable than data, then knowledge is more valuable than information. And if understanding is more valuable than knowledge, then wisdom, as the highest form of understanding, is the most valuable of all. This is why Aristotle saw wisdom as a completion. And this is why wisdom indeed represents the ultimate value in the new economy.

Nine

The Wisdom Index

Some accounting companies and industry associations are already struggling for standards to audit, weigh, and report the asset value of knowledge and creativity. Formulating a methodology for consistent and comparable valuations of what is essentially a product of judgment is a very complicated undertaking. Still, there is urgency in proceeding. The hard asset values of the industrial economy are proving to be as impermanent and liable to mistakes of judgment as the soft assets of knowledge, artistry, and relationship.

An Audit of Ten Dimensions

The previous chapters expanded a topology for wisdom that carries many of the characteristics (and ambiguities) of this shifting economy. To help with the process of personal exploration, and to set some benchmarks for measurement, I have created this "Wisdom Index." I do not presume for these questions to preempt the need for comprehensive accounting standards. These questions allow individuals and companies to work through the principles of the previous section in order to customize its lessons, determine relevance, and reflect on needs and progress.

The Index provides ten questions for each of the ten dimensions of wisdom. Designed as a series of "yes" and "no" questions, the Index is a general guide for determining development within a single aspect of wisdom. The questions are not a test, but a mirror — the opportunity to look frankly at the longer-term issues that often get submerged by the urgent pressures of the day-to-day.

I know from my own experience in running a company that learning is internalized in degrees. Rarely do people derive the full benefit of what they learn. In fact, the glow of new insight seems to recede in only a few days after someone has come back from a seminar or workshop. People are not lazy about learning. It is just that even the most compelling ideas have a way of being eroded by the unrelenting priorities of the everyday.

Questions force us to see issues more clearly, to define implications for ourselves, and to envision how we can resolve them. Importantly, the questions also give us a measure of how much we already know — how much progress we have already made. Our common sense is often buried under project and operating pressures, but it is still there. We all have more wisdom than we think. So the Index is very much about uncovering and celebrating "assets" as well as identifying "liabilities."

Since wisdom is not an achievement but a continuum, the Index exercise can be repeated over time. As a regular audit it may help show progress on certain dimensions. Such mileposts are particularly useful when an organization is experiencing significant change — either during a restructuring, merger, competitive threat, or management identity crisis. It helps foster a mindfulness for wisdom at a time when it is usually in short supply. Finally, the Index can be a type of test for plans, structures, strategies, personnel policies, and new product development. Scan the questions to see what fits, or to suggest other questions that need to be asked.

The Index is designed from a company's point of view. However, because the practice of wisdom is only a human capability, the majority of questions have relevance to the self-employed as well. My goal has been to encourage people to acknowledge, respect, and develop their own potential in whatever circumstances they work.

As well as providing a measurement and perspective, the Index may be used in conjunction with other training and development programs to raise the internal appreciation for wisdom. This may form the basis of a stand-alone workshop. Individuals can use it as part of a performance measurement process, evaluating themselves, or even peers, teammates, subordinates, or superiors, their department, division, or company.

Beyond its internal applications, the Index may also provide a useful discipline for taking stock of competitors, industry leaders, or potential partners and strategic allies. Some may even use it as a benchmarking exercise with clients, customers, consumers, and suppliers. In such external use, the Index provides not only a calibration of performance, but an opportunity for dialogue and interchange.

TIMELESSNESS

1. Can you retell a story from your company's history that defines one of its principal competencies, strengths, or skills?

2. Is this story known and fully understood by the majority of employees?

3. Do you have a formal and regularly practiced program for orienting new workers and reorienting current workers on the key lessons of the company's history?

4. Is there a measurement taken annually other than financial to audit the unique capabilities, skills, knowledge resources, and development needs of the company?

5. Are you aware of using or leveraging a unique company strength in the day-to-day implementation of projects and operations?

6. During any restructuring or rationalizing, has your company introduced any formal steps for protecting the historical understanding of itself and its people?

7. Would a customer or supplier be able to express the defining character of your company?

8. Have you formally mapped out how a key skill or core competence of your company will provide leverage and success in the future?

9. Are you too busy to think during the typical workday?

10. Do you feel part of a greater continuity — does your work provide the fulfillment of being part of making history?

CLARITY AND FOCUS

1. Do the average employees who work within your company have a better understanding of the organization's strategy and mission than hired consultants and researchers?

2. Has your company recognized that any vertical disintegration will require that information be transmitted in a markedly different way?

3. In reviewing new strategies or mission, is any attention specifically given to how the changes affect the relationship between company and employee?

4. Would your most important supplier rate you as clear in regards to direction, expectation, and overall goals?

5. Is there a formal system in your company for people to ask for more information or clarification on issues of strategy, downsizing, or new plans?

6. Are the internal interpersonal communications skills in your company so developed that people can work on a complex project without direction?

7. Does your company's vision or core strategy "invite" buy-in of employees, providing them with insight and inspiration, as well as direction?

8. Will each employee in the company generally identify the same strengths and weaknesses for the organization?

9. Are the symbols in your company developed so that people can recognize their strategic as well as communications value?

10. In training and development programs, is considerable time also spent on helping individuals with their internal growth?

COMPASSIONATE DETACHMENT

1. Is the function of management in your company recognized to involve manipulation?

2. Is fear consciously avoided as one of the motivators for performance and conformance to company policies and objectives?

3. Does your company give to community causes and charities in a meaningful way (i.e., does it entail genuine sacrifice)?

4. Do the departments, disciplines, and employees in your organization operate to the common good irrespective of territory?

5. Are managers and employees measured and rewarded for behaviors and practices that further interdependency?

6. Do you have a clear, understood, and well-functioning code of ethics?

7. Can two-thirds of your company's employees say what the essential elements of that ethical code are?

8. Is justice explicitly defined as a component of customer, supplier, and employee relationships?

9. Are the virtues or elements that constitute compassion present in any of your company's performance appraisals for either individuals or departments?

10. Have you defined the specific reciprocities that will help solidify your company's relationship with its suppliers and consumers?

TRUTH AND HONESTY

1. Is truth a genuine and understood pursuit within your company or work?

2. Is management as open and receptive to hear surprising bad news as it is for good news?

3. Does information released to employees accurately portray the real issues, problems, and opportunities facing the company?

4. Is there a system for employees to express their views or issues without worry of reprisal from superiors or peers?

5. Are internal communications and announcements written by senior management and issued without the benefit of "spin-doctoring" from public relations specialists?

6. Do senior executives spontaneously sit and meet with employees "just to chat"?

7. Has your company ever candidly admitted to its responsibility for a big mistake, either to staff or to customers?

8. Do senior executives and managers spontaneously meet with consumers in person?

9. Would a key supplier or customer judge your company as emphatically and unequivocally honest?

10. Are people within your organization formally recognized for expressing difficult but honest and important information to management?

JUSTICE

1. Would the majority of employees judge your company to be fair in its dealings with them?

2. Is there a structured mechanism in place for managers as well as employees to voice issues and achieve equitable redress?

3. During restructuring or organizational realignment, have senior management individuals in your company experienced proportionately the same pressures, rollbacks, and cuts as other parts of the enterprise?

4. Is there a policy for consumers or the communities in which your business operates to voice and have redress on issues that affect them?

5. Would you characterize your company as one that follows the spirit as well as the letter of the law?

6. Do the structure and policies at your company accommodate the different time needs of working mothers, single parents, or other workers with special needs?

7. Is interdependence expressed in either the vision, mission, or strategy of your company?

8. Are employees generally highly motivated and do they have good morale?

9. Do suppliers regard your company as fair — to the point of extemporaneously investing in service enhancements or new ideas?

10. Are "fairness" or "justice" established as formal performance measures for executives, managers, and employees?

UNITY AND INTEGRATION

1. Is there a gap in your company between its business objectives and the needs of the customers it intends to serve?

2. Is there a gap between senior management and employees?

3. Is there a gap between your company's plans and strategies, and their implementation and execution?

4. Is there a gap between stated principles and values and actual day-to-day behavior?

5. Are there gaps between different divisions or disciplines within your company?

6. Is there a gap between expected performance of employees and the supports and training they are given?

7. Is there a gap between efficiency and efficacy?

8. Is there a gap between the need for innovation and the resources committed to creativity?

9. Is there a gap between business goals and responsible environmental management?

10. Are such gaps acknowledged and attended to?

INTELLECTUAL AND EMOTIONAL HARMONY

1. Do employees in your firm participate in, and contribute ideas to, substantive "destiny-decisions"?

2. Are the emotional consequences of decisions considered and addressed?

3. Have the training and development programs in your company included recognition of "meaning" and "personal fulfillment" needs?

4. Do mission statements and strategies include consideration of purpose beyond the achievement of business objectives and shareholder value?

5. Is creativity measured and nurtured as a valued skill?

6. Are serious organizational changes explained to workers in a way that acknowledges their need to reconstruct a relevant "meaning map"?

7. Is your work fulfilling at a deep level?

8. Does the concept of "substantial sharing" apply to your firm?

9. Would suppliers and customers characterize your company as one that *surprises* them with relevant innovation or learning?

10. Can employees at your company make a "difference," as well as a living?

EQUANIMITY

1. Would your company be characterized as one that operates with consistency and balance?

2. Are the profit requirements of your company consciously balanced with those of responsibilities to customers and employees?

3. Are the needs of employees for balance in their lives between work and personal interest fully acknowledged and respected?

4. Is consciousness of the long-term strategy and needs of the organization brought to bear on day-to-day decisions?

5. Does your company operate with a working and effective balance between disciplines and departments?

6. Is there a formal system for adjudicating "imbalances"?

7. Is management attention balanced among the needs of the company, customers, and employees?

8. Have reengineering or restructuring exercises specifically attended to the issues and needs relating to balance?

9. Is your organization free of the addictive behavior that would suggest endemic imbalance?

10. Is there an opportunity within your company for individual employees to pursue interests and activities tangential to the company but essential to their sense of purpose and personal development?

SUBSTANTIAL SUBJECTIVITY

1. Do you and your company comfortably balance logical input with intangible and intuitive considerations?

2. In the move to greater efficiency, have you and your organization formally acknowledged a more holistic and subjective decision-making process?

3. Is personal judgment on issues of quality, customer service, and process renewal invited?

4. Have training or development programs encouraged the practice of intuition?

5. Do mistakes receive positive critical attention?

6. Is there a formal or conscious way for learning the lessons of failures and mistakes?

7. Is experience appreciated and honored as an important dynamic of organizational growth and flexibility?

8. Would customers or suppliers characterize you and your company as wise?

9. Is there any discussion in strategy or vision about the pressures of ambiguity or paradox?

10. Do you have occasion and support for "trusting your gut"?

MENTORSHIP

1. Is learning a formally valued and measured dynamic for you and your company?

2. Is teaching recognized as a part of the shared job description throughout the organization?

3. Would customers or suppliers rate your company as one that indeed does practice what it teaches?

4. Are there wise people available within your company to provide counsel to you and others within the organization?

5. Do you have a formal system of mentors for learning the craft skills of management, operations, and personal growth?

6. Do you have the flexibility to engage teachers outside of the organization to provide personal development skills and coaching?

7. Can you identify how what is taught and learned specifically provides value enhancement for products and services to customers?

8. Are you and your company hired for the expertise you can bring to others?

9. Do you or your company teach as part of the shared service and value to customers?

10. Do you have a system for revitalizing what you teach?

III

WISDOM IN PRACTICE

Ten

The Return on
Relationship

Solomon uses very poetic language in his biblical text to evoke the many wonders of wisdom, but he insists that its real beauty is "practicality." Wisdom solves problems. A wise person is fully aware, integrating intelligence and intuition. From this perspective of totality and continuity, problems are not a deviation from normal. They are not bad, nor mistakes. They are just a part of life and work. If anything, problems are the opportunity to be wise.

Robert Grundin observes that creative people, unlike most, "love the problematic." What is perplexing or difficult is what absorbs attention and exercises inventiveness. As long as we run away from problems, or regard them as inconveniences, we deny opportunities for personal growth. Solutions are acts of creation — and solutions are the basic currency of wisdom.

A love of the problematic is especially valuable if one is running a business, managing a project, or developing a career. Problems in business persist despite technology (maybe often because of it) and restructuring. Some are getting more severe, like competitiveness. Others are becoming intractable, like white-collar unemployment.

In my own business, and in my consulting work, I have faced many problems — but they haven't turned me into a pessimist. I believe people and companies are already incredibly wise, just as they are incredibly knowledgeable. The reservoir of problem-solving potential is therefore huge. Two basic factors, however, are impeding progress. First, most people and companies avoid problems, even the ones they are forced to solve. Second, most deny their own wisdom, or even their potential to be wise.

The sections so far have advanced the need for wisdom, my view of its components, and some suggestions for the consciousness-building to attain it. Now we move into the practice of business.

Part III illustrates how companies are advancing on this front of organizational wisdom. Some companies, as we have already seen, are becoming expert at interacting, using intuition as well as knowledge to construct stronger relationships. Others are proving that higher productivity is the result of beliefs and obligations. Some are anticipating the expectations of the market with product and service innovations that show wisdom. This practicality makes getting wise personally rewarding and competitive.

In the Sphere of Relationships

Companies today are engaging in a very different type of economic activity than simply making things: providing added value to customers by interpreting and compressing ever more knowledge, understanding, and meaning into products and services. Charles Hampden-Turner of the Judge Institute of Management Studies at Cambridge University wrote in 1994 that "value adheres and accumulates in the *complex web of relationships.*" This web includes managers and employees, suppliers and strategic partners, as well as retailers, distributors, and even the final customers.

While a company may provide a basic product or unit of knowledge, its value is increasingly created in the interaction or exchange. Assets are therefore not so much owned as realized in the relationship between people. Hampden-Turner explains: "The knowledge revolution and the learning organization which we hear so much about today stores its knowledge not in the head of itinerant globe-trotters, but in the finely woven tapestries of mutualism, of value co-created by a dialogue of equals."

This reverses the accepted orthodoxy of accounting and strategic planning that executives still create equity by investing in physical plant, equipment, machinery, technology, people, and/or training. When value is created by the exchange of knowledge, the equity no longer resides within the confines of a company. Worth becomes a function of the relationship — the meaning and value customers derive from interacting with and committing to the products, services, expertise, and wisdom of the providing enterprise. Now that equity is in the domain of interaction, companies must hone the skills for developing those new value-creating assets, as well as for leveraging and measuring their return.

Earning Trust with Customers

Wisdom is an increasingly valuable asset for companies simply because customers are getting wiser. The consuming culture has been around in its current form for over fifty years. The experience and attitudes toward consumption are therefore mature and middle-aged.

David Morton, president of Quaker Oats Canada, observes that "people are more cynical and, to put it more positively, they're also much smarter." Customers shun disposability, support recycling, and demand enduring products of higher quality. They also expect more from companies than the delivery of a functional product or service. In *The Knowledge-Value Revolution*, Taichi Sakaiyo, an economist and former senior official at Japan's Ministry of International Trade and Industry, writes: "In the new society that is forming, the lifestyle which will earn the most respect will be the one in which the owner's conspicuous consumption of wisdom is displayed."

Research in North America is beginning to suggest that Sakaiyo is correct. Customers today expect good corporate citizenship. This includes creating jobs in the local economy, behaving with responsibility toward the environment, treating employees with respect, and contributing to the causes that are of importance to the community.

And they are not afraid to show their disapproval if companies don't measure up. Earlier I referred to the MarketVision study in which over 25 percent of the 2,000 respondents indicated that they had gone so far as to boycott a company in the last year. This is an amazing statistic. The reasons for such boycotts vary: some consumers avoid tuna from marketers who do not use dolphin-protecting fishing nets; some customers turn away from Japanese cars to try to protect North American jobs; some, such as those boycotting Coke for co-sponsoring a golf tournament with a tobacco company, are using marketplace pressure to advance health causes.

People vote with their purchases. Increasing numbers are now consciously punishing those companies perceived as irresponsible toward employees or the environment. They also avoid those companies whose attitudes or values are out of sync with their own. As the demographic center of the population continues to age, these wisdom-related issues will only become more active.

Consumers understand that in the modern economy, there are layers of interconnections and self-interest. Having seen so many jobs and even white-collar careers displaced, they know that the products they choose directly impact their community. Cadbury learned this lesson in a way that hit hard at its bottom line. After closing a plant in Quebec, the confections maker lost significant market share in that region. Even an impulse purchase as seemingly insignificant as a candy bar is not incidental to a consumer who has information, intelligence, and a conscience.

Wisdom in relation to purchase decisions grows incrementally. But as it emerges, that wisdom shifts the priorities in selling, buying, and using in rather dynamic ways. North Americans bought their cars during the 1980s for their function, quality, and image. These things are still important, but now, because people understand the intricacies of the global economy, they also consider issues like North American content of the vehicle they choose, and the impact of their purchase on jobs. Toyota, whose quality is acknowledged to be at the forefront of automotive manufacturing, has been running an advertising campaign that details the North American content of its cars. It is not so much masking its Japanese heritage as it is seeking to expand its relationship with customers beyond that based on product to one based on mutual interest and benefit.

In expanding the overlap of self-interest between company and customer, executives are recognizing that more than a transaction is at stake. As mentioned earlier, *values* as well as value are being exchanged. Solveig Wikström and Richard Normann explain: "One consequence of this integrative process is thus that the borderlines between the producer-seller and the user break down. A marketing logic is replaced by a logic based on the establishment of long-term customer relations." While a seller of a thing can get away with engineered, mechanistic behavior, a participant in a relationship must bring forth elements of personality, trustworthiness, vision, clarity, surprise, empathy, and selflessness.

In searching for a competitive advantage, companies have good cause to think in terms of relationships. The Royal Bank estimates that it makes about $80 profit per year from each customer it serves. Over a lifetime, a single customer represents over $3,000 in profit value. Banks are now engaged in a marketing war, trying to convince the marketplace that they are not only secure as a source for deposit and loans and dependable as investment choices, but also caring, accessible, and responsive enough to deserve a relationship.

Kathy McMillan, vice-president of marketing at the Bank of Montreal, sets out the thinking behind this new attitude: "The emotional involvement in this product is actually quite high. When some one goes to a bank for a mortgage, it is a terrifying experience for the majority of customers. In essence they are exposing themselves. So you [the company] are either going to receive that information in a supportive manner, or you are going to close that door in a way that no one is ever going to want to open it again."

In the car industry, the lifetime value of a customer — the amount spent for auto purchases, gas, repairs, mufflers, oil, and everything else — is over $300,000. Once complacent, North American manufacturers are now training dealers and devising service programs to attract and hold customers beyond a single car purchase. Similarly, computer companies want to sell service and software in order to move beyond simple transactions for an individual machine.

The attention to relationship is also affecting small, everyday purchases. Packaged goods companies have found their consumers to be less loyal to their brands, more willing to buy low price alternatives or store brands. Having been decimated in many product categories, these companies are now bringing more innovation and value to their products. They are using 1-800 numbers and expanding database collection to heighten responsiveness and earn a long-lasting relationship.

However, much of this personalization and interaction remains just talk. Plans are still written from the perspective of the business, with lots of data on the product and its financial goals, and only a very sketchy understanding of the people doing the actual buying and using. Research is still employed to define the attributes and attitudes people have in relation to the product being sold to them.

In a world seeking more understanding, this research is just too narrow a band of interaction and intelligence. And it was a lesson learned the hard way during a recent new product exercise at Lever Brothers. As Peter Ellwood, president and CEO, says: "We didn't apply our judgment. We researched every last aspect of the product, and its concept and its positioning. Sequentially we tested each step down the decision tree, and ended up three steps back and at the wrong branch. We lost sight of the totality by doing a little bit too much research on the parts."

Even research intended for more personal learning can go awry. Peter Glen, a retail specialist, tells the story of focus groups done for a mall in Maryland to test ideas for attracting more traffic. As is the custom in these sessions, the moderator of the group, after covering all the questions and issues that had been prepared, left for a few moments to confer with colleagues to see if any other probing was warranted. The group had been discussing the usual type of promotions and mall activities. After the moderator left, the people in the group kept talking. The focus group participants were puzzled that after two hours of discussion, there had been no questions about what was really keeping them away from the mall. It was not the lack of glitz and promotion. It was fear. People found the parking lots poorly lit, and therefore threatening. And the roving groups of teens who hung out at the mall made casual shopping and perusing uncomfortable.

Were it not for the video camera recording the focus group, the mall management and researchers would have missed the only relevant issue to their customers.

Business people now *talk* about relationship, but too often their conditioning and perspective still place the needs of the business ahead of those of the customer. Even while trying to listen, the questions are so biased by this conditioning that executives miss the opportunity to learn and serve. Most companies do not have the humility and patience to decipher the real questions of their customers. The urgency "to know" is overriding the capacity to understand.

Max De Pree writes in *Leadership Is an Art*: "The goal of renewal is to be a corporate entity that gives us space to reach our potential as individuals and, through that, as a corporation. Renewal comes through genuine service to others. It cannot come about through a mere process of self-perpetuation. Renewal is an outward orientation of service rather than an inward orientation of maintenance." The goal for efficiency may realize efficiency, but the renewal for stronger relationships with customers comes only from this ethos of service.

Why do so many companies aspiring to greater service end up with customer relationships as soiled as those of airlines, or as fickle as those of cola drinkers? In an article in the *Harvard Business Review*, Richard Normann and Rafael Ramirez analyze the priorities and practices that make IKEA so successful and so respected. They explain that the ethos of connection, and not the tangible product, makes IKEA both unique and attractive to so many customers: "IKEA wants its customers to understand that their role is not to *consume* value but to *create* it."

Most companies have failed to align themselves at a very deep level with the emerging wisdom of customers. As will be explored in the later chapter on marketing, people have generally long ceased viewing themselves as consumers at all. This means that they are appreciating value in new ways, evaluating the service, the responsibility of the provider, and the totality of the choosing-buying-assembling-and-using experience to determine what is important to them.

Most market research and strategic planning define "value" against the obsolete paradigm of consumption. IKEA, in contrast, is smart enough to offer value in the broader, more fulfilling context of "enabling." Normann and Ramirez elaborate: "IKEA offers families more than co-produced furniture, it offers co-produced improvement in family living in everything from interior design to safety information and equipment, insurance, and shopping as a form of entertainment." People react to the company with the familiarity and trust usually reserved for a close friend.

Renewing Faith with Workers/Employees

If relationships with customers are tentative, it is often because the internal relationships within a company are also stressed and suspicious. Very few organizations or individuals have experienced change without dislocation. As we have seen, a natural, although unproductive, reaction to such dislocation is to seek the protection and consolidation of self-interest. This creates conflict in a time when unity is essential. Charles Handy believes that this paradox is what requires a "Chinese Contract" of seeing self-interest in mutual interest. He feels that this mutuality understands "the importance of compromise as a prerequisite of progress. Both sides have to concede to win. [The contract] was about the need for trust and belief in the future. Writ large, it was about sacrifice and the willingness to forego some present good to ward off future evil, or, more positively, it was about investment — spending now in order to gain later."

Most companies have been unable to see beyond self-interest as they have encountered the threats of restructuring. The gods of efficiency and productivity have been served by the endless rounds of cost-cutting and job eliminations, but, for many organizations, the sacrifice has resulted in a deep schism. Executives demand more of their employees; however, their ability to motivate is hamstrung by the constraints of less money for raises, fewer opportunities for promotion and advancement, and no guarantee that even exceptional performers will be protected from the next round of cuts. Employees are grateful for even having a job, while at the same time resenting the threat to their security and the intensification of pressure on them.

Employees may also be tired of change. As discussed in Chapter One, change-fatigue has been mistakenly viewed as employee resistance to new ideas. But when everyone is tired of change, management loses patience with employees, while employees view management with growing skepticism and cynicism. Thus at a time when many organizations face tough external challenges from competitors, they are also suffering from internal disunity and discord.

Daniel Yankelovich, the researcher who pioneered lifestyle studies and who provides public opinion data to numerous corporations, observes that "most managements don't have as firm a handle of the human aspects of restructuring as they do on finance and technology." This indictment speaks directly to the wisdom gap. There may be empathy for those employees who have lost their jobs, but there is usually little time or planning given to those who remain. Most executives agree that their employees are a critically important asset, but overcoming the dislocation and alienation has taken a backseat to finance, structure, and share value. Despite the themes of empowerment, the message from the executive suite seems to be: "These people have jobs. What else do they want?"

The simple answer is that they want, and deserve, much more. Most workers are smart enough to understand the new economy. Having seen the dislocation, they know that the hold on any job, including the CEO's, is tenuous. They are usually willing to adapt, taking on both a bigger workload and more accountability. However, since the stakes have been raised, and the safety net removed, a new bundle of stimuli and motivation needs to be introduced.

What can these be? How can they be activated? For Robert Grundin, the expansion of work and creativity needs purpose. He says that careers, "unless they are leavened by self knowledge, become psychological prisons whose effects grow more damaging as people grow more comfortable in their confines." The task then is to nurture appreciation for self-knowledge for both the individual worker and for the organizational collective.

Change for Good

Some people, and some institutions, seem to change effortlessly. Robin Skynner, a medical doctor and psychotherapist who specializes in group dynamics, has worked with both families and large corporations. Along with British comedian and multimillionaire executive trainer John Cleese, Skynner has written a series of books on change, growth, and quality of life.

Skynner has based his practice on the scientific study of healthy individuals and healthy families. This is an interesting reversal, since most social science research tends to extrapolate what is normal from the study of deviation and dysfunction. Drawing from a famous study of Harvard graduates over a period of fifty years, and from other clinical studies, Skynner observes that one of the defining characteristics of a healthy family or healthy organization is "their remarkable ability to deal with change. These not only seem to be at ease with quite big changes, but even seem to enjoy them, indeed to thrive on them."

The facility with change among healthy human beings and healthy organizational units can be ascribed to what Skynner identifies as three essential stages for adapting.

- First, there is a period of rest, a time to "catch-up with the backlog of readjustment."
- Second, there is a period of intense learning, drawing from the experience of others who have been through similar change to "redraw" what Skynner and Peter Senge call "our mental maps."
- Third, there is unequivocal "emotional support" for dealing with the trauma and opportunity brought on by the change.

In the chaotic pressure of modern business, these three steps seem to be either absurd luxuries or Pollyanna niceties. Companies on the brink of competitive annihilation have little patience, indeed little flexibility, for extending time for reflection and emotional support to confused employees. But the lesson of the many companies that have embarked on several missions of forced change — only to miss achieving the momentum they sought — is that steamrollers eventually run out of steam. Change that is mandated requires constant pressure to activate, and usually only realizes limited, imposed movement.

In my experience, senior executives resist or suspect this notion of "healthy change," even though their own personal process for decision-making has often involved all three of the stages outlined above.

First, the decision to restructure or reengineer usually follows an exhaustive analysis of the current situation. Competitors have been studied and evaluated, the implications of new technology have been weighed, and the changing dynamics in the marketplace have been projected into future trends. Plans and actions for change at the executive level usually only happen once all the implications, conclusions, research, and consultation have been completed. Often, alternative strategic scenarios are explored, as are a variety of tactics and implementation plans. Any radical corporate change without such study, deliberation, and extended use of resources is exceptional, and would sometimes be judged as a violation of an executive's fiduciary responsibility.

Through this analysis, senior managers have the opportunity to work through the second stage, deconstructing existing "mental maps," seeing how established assumptions and operating procedures no longer fit the changing reality of the company. For the "redrawing of mental maps," senior executives often use consultants — anyone from globe-trotting McKinsey staffers to self-employed entrepreneurs like me — to provide an "outside the box" perspective. The "redrawing" for senior managers is done literally, using the elaborate matrices and models the management-change industry uses to help executives reimagine the company, its industry, customers, processes, assets, and liabilities.

In most companies, the concept for the type of needed strategic change takes shape only after (relatively) significant time and resources have been applied to understanding the situation. The managers generating these concepts and making these decisions are supported by the logic of the information they have collected and analyzed. Their confidence in the new approach is also bolstered by the cumulative intelligence, commitment, and experience of all the internal and external experts involved in the final recommendation. This network of collaboration creates the senior level momentum for change, providing the "emotional support" that Skynner identifies as the third critical ingredient in achieving healthy and successful transformation.

What is generally regarded as being prudent and smart for senior management is reversed when it comes time to implement change. Convention suggests moving fast. Fire the redundant. Close the inefficient plant. Replace the obsolete technology. Quick implementation is thought to show decisiveness, to reflect both clarity and conviction. It is even rationalized as being the more merciful thing to do since it alleviates anxiety, telling everyone, whether they stay or go, just where they stand. Abruptly breaking with the past is also believed to make it easier to rally people around the newly envisioned future. A jarring jolt, according to standard management theory, is part of building the momentum for change.

While it does not make sense to prolong the uncertainty surrounding change needlessly, nor to allow ambiguity to erode confidence and trust, few organizations think of applying the wise stages of adaptation that went into the planning at the implementation stage. The basic human need for reflection, "re-mapping," and support are somehow assumed to be dispensable when it comes to the individuals who must actually make the change come to life. This is not necessarily an intentional decision on the part of management. But unconsciousness does not make it any easier to accept or live through. If numb to such fundamental human needs, how can meaningful, trusting relationships ever be activated between management and employees, between company and customer?

Accessing the Latent Wisdom

My consulting work often involves speaking at industry gatherings, association conventions, and company sales meetings. Recently, I was invited to be the keynote speaker at a luncheon attended by several hundred national sales representatives of what used to be called NCR Computers Inc. I had prepared my talk on the agreed-upon topic of "relationship marketing." After spending the morning attending NCR's presentations about general strategy, new products, and new service initiatives, I ended up scuttling my notes and extemporizing.

NCR had made a real breakthrough in reaching out to its customers, releasing to the audience the first wave of a revised customer survey. The expensive tracking research would provide a new, more relevant database for the issues affecting "customer satisfaction" measures. In addition to this external study, NCR for the first time also commissioned research to quantify and track various dimensions of "employee productivity." These investments were already yielding important learning, and were indicative of a growing movement among leading corporations to more enlightened customer service, and smarter, more motivating human resource management.

As I sat through the presentations I was struck by the "company-centeredness" of those measures. Tracking "customer satisfaction" seemed too narrow because it evaluated the relationship in terms of how the customer perceived NCR. Similarly, measuring "employee productivity" put the employees' contribution into a context of value to the company. I was about to talk about "relationship marketing," yet I could not see in either of NCR's well-intentioned research projects the reciprocity and mutuality that are the fundamentals in any relationship. At lunch, I got up and made my observation. I suggested that NCR reverse its tracking methodology, and instead measure "customer *productivity*" and "employee *satisfaction.*"

Making customers more productive would focus NCR's efforts on solving real customer problems. The satisfaction would follow. Similarly, taking the steps to make NCR's employees more satisfied would create the culture that supports genuine service to customers, innovation, and team problem-solving. The productivity would again follow.

As noted earlier, in business, people tend to achieve what is measured. If effects are measured, effects will get the focus. But if causes are measured, then the causes will get the attention and the impact on effects will follow. The benefit of the latter approach is that the change goes much deeper and lasts much longer.

The reception to my criticism and recommendations from NCR was very positive, although it seemed that the salespeople were much more enthusiastic about the juxtaposition than were the executives. As the people responsible for the relationship with the customer, the sales reps understood clearly that they could no longer simply "push" boxes: they had to add value, give service, and create imaginative, performance-enhancing solutions. These people operate in an environment in which creating trust is increasingly the prerequisite for a sale. This trust involves its own reversal, subverting the priorities for making that sale to serve the priorities of the prospect. This is a tricky balance, particularly as companies have imposed bigger sales quotas at the same time that they have also set higher standards for service.

The salespeople I talked to that afternoon generally found the relationship aspect of their job to be rewarding in an unexpected way. They were providing something of value without the immediate linkage to a sale, and this exercise in service was very gratifying. It allowed them to feel as if they were making a contribution to the companies in their territories. This dimension of real service was fulfilling, and it generally created the interaction and environment that also, at the right time, made it easier to realize the commercial needs of their own organization.

While some people still relish the hunt, a growing number of salespeople, like those I talked to at NCR, are thriving and growing by providing knowledge and value to their customers beyond the parameters of the transaction. They seem to be feeling the inner satisfaction derived from what Taichi Sakaiyo calls "the worth or price a society gives to that which the society acknowledges to be creative wisdom."

Salespeople in Saturn dealerships describe a similar, personal joy from doing their work in an environment in which they only serve the information needs of prospects. Saturn has fixed prices, so there is no bartering, no "bait and switch," and no up-selling. Saturn people, including those in sales, are called "customer service representatives." This is not a semantic fudge, but a genuine focus for their job description. These people strike me to be as fulfilled by their job as the customers are by the car, the dealers, and the service.

Common sense suggests that the breakthroughs in service that companies are demanding from their employees require a reconditioning of such expectations. Employees, threatened by continuous cutbacks, may hit productivity targets; however, the extension of a genuine relationship-building service to customers comes only from people who feel challenged, supported, and nurtured by their employers. Their productivity flows as a consequence of this heightened commitment, which, in turn, flows from their heightened satisfaction.

In *Control Your Own Destiny Or Someone Else Will*, Noel Tichy and Stratford Sherman distill the lessons Tichy learned while consulting at General Electric, and teaching in its famous management training school in Crotonville, New York. They write: "The most effective competitors in the 21st century will be the organizations that learn to use shared values to harness the emotional energy of employees. As speed, quality and productivity become ever more important, corporations need people who can instinctively act the right way, without instructions, and who feel inspired to share their best ideas with their employer."

"Emotional energy"; "instinctively act the right way"; "share"; "inspired" — these are the words constituting the new vocabulary of organizational renewal. Business has been learning to cut when the market and the competition are demanding that it give.

This need for generosity should not be surprising. Generosity is *generative*: it creates the conditions for creativity. A generous spirit on the part of an organization will open it to the more substantial exchange of information and values that these more confident and responsive employees deserve and expect. Generosity also means being supportive of the meaning and fulfillment needs that this ever-savvier workforce will be bringing to its assignments. Finally, it means that the company will adopt the precepts of relationship-building from life, "giving to get" rather than just "paying for services received."

Ricardo Semler (see Chapter Seven) has been creating an effective new organizational construct using many of the principles of this new generosity. Semler's group is among the most successful in South America, and an important element in this success is his constant experimentation with the precepts of conventional management. The liberation of managers in Semler's companies is so dramatic that people actually set their own salaries. With such liberation comes added accountability, and Semler's experience is very revealing about how employees reciprocate such generosity.

Generally, Semler's employees work with the enthusiasm of having something to prove. They also collaborate without qualms about title or discipline, and use peer pressure to achieve ever higher productivity, efficiency, and innovation. Surprisingly, the vast majority actually choose a salary that is lower than the national industry average for their job and experience level. In part, people are paying themselves less because of the responsibility entrusted to them. As well, they are also willing to take less because the other elements of their job have become so rewarding.

Such *generosity of spirit* creates conditions of respect, responsibility, and trust. The traditional contractual exchange of money for work is superseded by one that provides meaning, dignity, and the opportunity for growth for both the employer and the employee. The wisdom extended by the company nurtures a wisdom in the employee. Both benefit. Both grow. And both contribute the values that fuel a mutually rewarding renaissance.

Below are some of the emerging meaning influences, contrasted with those being replaced.

OLD MEANING INFLUENCES	NEW MEANING INFLUENCES
• Income and salary increases	• Employability through knowledge
• Promotion opportunities	• Networking and new growth opportunities
• Security	• Creativity and growth
• Job descriptions and expectations	• Context and empathy
• Insulation from unpredictability	• Support for unpredictability
• Compete to succeed	• Cooperate to "win-win"
• Reach the sales target	• Adapt to the unexpected
• Fulfill the company's strategy	• Act with urgency to serve customers
• Develop worth for employer	• Develop self-worth

The acid test for these principles for most companies is sales: this is where the lofty talk about values meets the tough reality of generating volume and share. And for companies driven by sales, the conversion to a new meaning structure is particularly difficult. Xerox is rightly famous for having won its battle with Japanese manufacturers over quality. But Xerox has, in some ways, been fighting an even longer battle with its own customers. The selling culture is so powerful that a prospect has historically been attacked with the same ferocity directed against an enemy to be vanquished.

Xerox's salespeople talk about "slamming boxes," pushing units even when the customer's need may not be served by it. They have been so successful at pressure selling that other companies study and copy Xerox's style, training, and motivation system. But what other companies applaud and seek to emulate, customers have begun to outgrow, dislike, and mistrust. The relentless selling and the unceasing force of self-interest have finally become a liability in a marketplace that offers wide choice and ever increasing service.

Having been caught short by its competition, Xerox has been smart enough to apply its lessons for quality to improving its relationships with customers. Salespeople have been retitled as "relationship managers." This significant reprogramming is based on what David Dorsey, author of *The Force*, calls "a variation of the Golden Rule: Treat your customers as you would treat yourself." Now compensation and bonus structures are being reconfigured to value not only the achievement of sales quotas, but also of different and varied measures of customer satisfaction. Salespeople, driven to install machines, are now learning the skills of also extending "compassion" and "serious, genuine consulting" to customers.

The evolution to such a radically different meaning structure is not easy. The contradictions between sales goals and service delivery persist. And even when the new vocabulary is in place, the gravitational pull of the old meaning structure still exerts its presence. Nevertheless, Xerox is as committed to this renewal of meaning as it was a decade ago to the gospel of quality. As president of U.S. customer operations Richard Barton explains, the company is discovering that, with this new approach, not only are customers more satisfied, but employees are also more fulfilled. Going back to the old adversarial style of selling is therefore unthinkable.

A Lasting Covenant in an Age of Loopholes

Companies have yet to develop the wisdom that in many ways they have already imposed on their employees. Average people have been forced to come to terms with the harsh realities of limitation and uncertainty. Through this pain, many employees have already fashioned their own street smarts. What they now need is for their employers to respect and engage them on this wiser plane.

Wise people learn from experience, and employees who have developed their wisdom in the maelstrom of reorganization look to see whether the company has itself learned its lessons. This is an acid test for companies. Unless they show the guts and honesty to admit the mistakes of the past, building confidence and commitment to the new and improved strategy or structure becomes an exercise in futility. With each wave of change, the depth of wisdom of employees grows, as does their ability to discern the confidence and perspicacity of the executives making those changes.

Sustainability demands sacrifice, and although wisdom is not an elixir for avoiding pain, it provides the intuitive intelligence for understanding and respecting it. With wisdom, change is given context: fears are expressed and valued; action and implications are understood; and the human needs for adjustment are given the time and space the cycle requires. The respect accorded in this interchange does more than simply help people adjust to new organizational structures. By moving the relationship between management and employees to one based on shared wisdom, companies are activating the very asset they need to realize the benefits of the change.

The high-technology industries of Silicon Valley, already adroit at creating value out of knowledge, are at the forefront of matching and responding to the growing wisdom of employees. Companies like Apple and Raychem are not immune to the need for restructuring and streamlining, but they deal with this reality with an understanding that leads to an emergence of corporate wisdom.

Both companies use internal career resource centers to help coach employees on development needs and career planning. Both also engage outside career counselors to ensure that the employees' needs are not compromised by those of the company. Raychem goes even further. The company tries to find development opportunities for employees in vulnerable jobs in other parts of the company. It even interviews departing employees to reinforce to the limited pool of highly talented people that they will be welcomed back.

Such wisdom not only helps in times of displacement, but it also smoothes the implementation of quality and reengineering programs. Robert Waterman has been studying the changing dynamic between employer and employee. He and his consulting partner, Judith Waterman, explain how such wisdom on the part of a company molds self-interest into a benefit for both parties: "Competitiveness — keeping close to customers, staying on top of technology and market trends, and striving to be ever more flexible — becomes every one's responsibility, not that of just a handful of executives. All employees become involved in shaping the company's strategy, in shifting the company's collective eyes from navels to market forces. By looking out for themselves, employees look out for the company."

This new symbiosis is exactly what companies need in order to extract the potential from the changes they are initiating. Managers and employees, often from different divisions and departments, must work together in new ways to effect the desired reengineering. Old job definitions and sequential processes are replaced with simultaneous problem-solving. This is the widely prescribed formula, but what is often ignored is that such organic interchange requires a certain maturity and generosity on the part of all participants. Territory and authority must be surrendered, outcomes must be clear, and the interests of the group must take precedence over those of the individual. Such wise behavior does not happen automatically, especially in those environments in which the culture is overly competitive, overly defensive, or overly optimistic.

Reengineering and quality are in many ways preoccupied with the hardware of companies. Systems and design flows are deconstructed and reassembled to get work done faster, more efficiently, through fewer management layers, and with closer contact to customers. These are all valid rewirings. Nevertheless, people are the essence of companies and somehow, in the orthodoxy of the new management of productivity, they've become the enemy. Efficiency, like war, gets measured in headcount. Managers have become masters of disaggregation, but many have also lost the skill for building and the empathy for motivating.

Wisdom, in contrast, aggregates. It acknowledges the different priorities and pressure points for each constituency, but it also raises appreciation among all involved of the broader stakes. Robert Ozaki writes that "what the humanistic enterprise system offers is an abundance of "organized" freedom . . . [This] refers to the freedom available within the organizational framework of the humanistic firm, for workers to participate fully in managerial decision making and to define and improve their own work rules and environment."

Freedom, because it is based on reciprocity, invites a higher assumption of obligation. This provides a compelling common platform between company and worker, even when sacrifice is demanded. Not all employees are capable of this wisdom, but no company can really be successful without it being imprinted in the corporate genes.

This is one of the major lessons of wisdom. We know from worries about the erosion of democratic principles in North America that the greater the freedom, the greater the responsibility. For companies, the converse is also true. The more responsibility they impose on an individual for performance and results, the greater the need for the freedom to bring the full human scope of talent, expectation, and meaning to work.

Siemens is an industrial giant that is the antithesis of the nimble information type company such as Microsoft. A $60.4 billion company, Siemens is over one hundred years old and famous for its rigid, Germanic bureaucracy. Facing productivity, currency, and share-decline pressures, Siemens undertook what *BusinessWeek* called a "cultural revolution," which is now beginning to realize impressive results. While attending to cost-cutting, the company also began a process of employee education to make workers more aware and sensitized to the customer needs, issues, and complaints. In opening the door for everyone to the customer, Siemens's management lost the authority of final say. Whoever knew the customer best had the responsibility to decide and act.

With this greater responsibility must come more respect. To accelerate product development, "automation manager Klaus Wucher hand-picked a dozen engineers to develop the new system. He rented a house down the road from headquarters, set them loose in jeans, and tapped Kurt Krause, a marathon runner with a competitive spirit, as captain." The team achieved their objective in about half the time Siemens usually allotted for such development, and sales of their "state-of-the-art system boomed." Empowerment for many people has become imprisonment because the greater expectations and accountabilities have not been balanced with more freedom and respect. As Siemens shows, empowerment works not because it saves process steps and money, but because it liberates the incredible potential of the human being.

Work inside and outside companies will continue to carom as individuals and institutions struggle to reach a balance between liberation and responsibility. Companies that have flexed the power of downsizing are now having to learn how to exert a more subtle authority to realize the commitment and contribution of its "out-sourcing" suppliers. At the same time, individuals participating in this more fluid and ambiguous work within and outside conventional companies will need markedly different skills. However, the unforgiving reality of harsh layoffs, the fierce competition and jostling for fewer positions, the politics, and the persistent pressures of a resilient authoritarian model of management make following even the most relevant and workable advice difficult. Struggling with this dislocation, some consultants are now suggesting the concept of "covenant" to describe this changed relationship. This is the right word, because covenant involves a type of wisdom exchange. However, few people have actually defined covenant in its historical and biblical context.

A covenant is an almost sacred agreement. It has two characteristics that go beyond the detailed expectation of a contract. A covenant involves "giving without expectation *more* than is asked for." And it requires "fidelity" — a commitment to persevere, to be honest and faithful to the spirit of the accord as well as to its terms. While it only takes lawyers to construct a contract, it takes wisdom and a reservoir of mutuality to create a covenant. The following grid explores how the interplay of wisdom between employer and employee can create such a covenant.

COMPANY NEED	EMPLOYEE NEED	WISDOM FACTOR
1. Flexibility and productivity for higher performance.	• Expanding skill base to improve personal "marketability" and growth.	• Company investment in training. • Personal commitment to continuous learning.
2. More teamwork, and the sharing of knowledge and accountability.	• Creation of a new meaning system to offset loss of power and reinstate fairness.	• More relevant incentive and reward structures to support culture as well as performance.
3. Innovation and continuous contribution to quality.	• Sense of involvement, an understanding, and voice in strategic and culture formulation.	• Human-based communication, with the company listening, as well as reinforcing messages to staff.
4. Commitment to enhance value and service for customers.	• Support and appreciation from management.	• Consistent application of values so that internal beliefs translate into external action.

Achieving a new covenant requires the ability to see beyond the differences and actually forge commonalties between company and worker. This means not only developing shared interests and values, but also including the needs and capacities of the whole human being in the interchange.

Interestingly, this respect for the totality is what helped Florence, Italy, achieve its great commercial and artistic success in the fifteenth century. The Florentine renaissance was indeed a rebirth, drawing its intellectual inspiration from the Greek and Roman notion of the "complete" human being. Hard work, natural virtue, service to the community, and participation in creative arts were regarded as equal parts of this totality. The Florentines even expanded the medieval notion of a "liberal arts" education from a focus on speech and numbers to include history, poetry, rhetoric, and moral philosophy. They believed that these were the studies that "liberated" human beings to achieve their fullest potential. The modern renewal of commerce is also served by this liberation.

Robert Reich, secretary of labor in the Clinton administration, provides a telling commentary on the employer–worker relationship in an article written when he was a professor at Harvard. Reich contrasts the approaches between U.S. and Japanese car manufacturers: "The Japanese automaker [Toyota] does not rely on automation and technology to replace workers in the plant. In fact, human workers still occupy the most critical jobs — those where judgment and evaluation are essential. Instead, Toyota uses technology to allow workers to focus on those important tasks where choices have to be made. Under this approach, technology gives workers the chance to use their imagination and their insight on behalf of the company."

In a covenant involving wisdom, there is the perspective, clarity, and compassion to nurture and value imagination, as well as efficiency.

Companies that are achieving continuous, constructive renewal are moving toward just such a wholeness, not in the old sense of vertical integration, but in the respectful one of seeking to maximize the latent potential of all the people within the enterprise. This is the crux of the new covenant. In the old management model, companies tended to define themselves by what they sold. This self-definition created self-knowledge about productivity and self-perceptions that were exclusive, protective, and adversarial. In the new economy, companies increasingly only sell what they are. As Dr. Al Kupcis, CEO of Ontario Hydro, puts it, "Success today is a function of character, not just competence."

Wal-Mart calls its employees "associates" because they want them to use their own common sense and good judgment to solve customers' problems and serve their needs. Nike and Microsoft call their corporate head offices a "campus" because success in both industries involves unending learning and interdisciplinary sharing, curiosity, and the youthful energy of new discovery.

Arthur Soler, president of Neilson, flipped the prevailing management logic that views employees as cost: "Everybody else downsized. My attitude was let them. Let them consolidate. But we were not going to downsize for the sake of downsizing because our problem was that we were not growing. So guess what? We added more people. And guess what? We added more money for advertising, business development, and we spent a fortune on training. We raised salaries and even gave people better cars. Now we are attracting and retaining the best people. And guess what? Our top line growth in three years has been over 60 percent."

In a knowledge economy the capacity to imagine and innovate are the most valuable competencies. As Soler suggests, a covenant that elicits such contribution from workers is therefore an investment, not a cost. Chris Argyris, a Harvard professor, writes: "Today, facing competitive pressures an earlier generation could hardly have imagined, managers need employees who think constantly and creatively about the needs of the organization. They need employees with as much intrinsic motivation and as deep a sense of organizational stewardship as any company executive."

A wise company operates with unity between executive and workers, not for the sake of labor peace, but because their needs and goals are essentially intertwined. Such a covenant is created by a mutual respect for the truth. Seeing beyond the agendas that divide management from employees, the truth honors the interdependence. The more committed all parties are to the truth, the less need there will be for the rigidity of the old contract. For example, when BMW and Hewlett-Packard workers in Europe realized the business situation that prompted management's experiment with the four-day work week, most accepted the sacrifice of occasional shift work as the price for securing more jobs.

The truth motivated collaboration, and has borne results of greater productivity for the company, and more personal fulfillment for the individual. Business is still business; volume is still volume; and the bottom line is still the bottom line. However, in forging a covenant based on truth, on a genuine concern for human justice, these companies show that the wisdom of inclusion is not simply complementary but indivisible from smart management. This is the new common sense for an economy in which value ceases to be derived from things and increasingly resides only in relationships.

QUESTIONS OF RELATIONSHIPS

1. CUSTOMER LOYALTY

CUSTOMER WISDOM

- Consumption is a mature framework.

- The demographic center of the North American population is aging and bringing sensibilities of responsibility into their purchase decisions.

- Relationships are earned through reciprocity, continuous refreshment, and a respect for individual value.

- Value is a composite of "quality and price," but also includes human priorities like sustainability, renewal, and regard for the community.

IMPLICATION FOR BUSINESS

- How has the strategy for your company evolved to address the priorities of a post-consumption society?

- What are the "wisdom points" affecting the interaction between your company or brand, and your customer?
- How do you enhance the value of your offering to align with the wisdom needs of your customer?

- What are the dimensions beyond the transaction that give substance to the "relationship" being developed with customers?

- How does your definition of value engage the expansive needs of today's customers?
- What elements make up the "value cluster" of your organization and offering?

2. EMPLOYEE TRUST

Organizations that go through restructuring and waves of change face adjustment cycles. For the companies I've studied, this cycle has had four or five phases:

a. Shock, gratitude, and guilt for having survived the cuts. However, only fear motivates compliance.	b. Tentative commitment gets frayed as the frustrations over new behaviors and systems sap self-confidence and company confidence.	c. Confusion builds cynicism as the gaps in the new strategy create friction and disappointment. *Fear* diminishes as a motivator.	d. A "permission to fail" mentality emerges, as more waves of change suggest management didn't get it right the last time.

• Plot the cycle of change in your own company. What have been the factors either contributing to the experiences outlined above or helping to break through this pattern?

• How has the vulnerability of "survivors" been addressed in your organization during restructurings?

• Has the communication and behavior of the company respected both the rational and emotional needs of employees? How? If not, what can be done to create and sustain this dialogue?

• List the two or three major lessons that have been distilled from past company restructurings. What steps have been taken to incorporate these into the company's reservoir of wisdom? How will this wisdom be applied to the continuous evolution of the organization?

• Define the specific terms of the new or emerging covenant between your company and its employees. What are the terms? How have the various "self-interests" been defined?

   - How have these been valued?

   - How have they been interconnected into a workable "mutuality"?

   - And how have they been communicated to all involved?

3. ADDING MEANING TO ADD VALUE

• How much attention has been paid within your company or group on the issue of "meaning"?

• What were the specific "old" meaning factors?

   - Which of these remain valid?

   - Which have been scuttled?

• How have the "new " meaning factors been designed and incorporated into your company's culture?

   - What are the guiding principles?

   - How are these "new" factors introduced and communicated?

   - How effectively do these contribute to the liberation that feeds renaissance?

• What "meaning" provisions is your organization taking to ensure access to the best people?

• What are the core principles guiding the efforts of the sales group within your operation?

   - How conducive are these to enhancing the productivity and fulfillment of customers?

   - Of employees?

• What are the appropriate elements for developing and formalizing the "generosity in spirit" within your company?

• What are the critical steps for implementing this institutional generosity?

Eleven

Transforming Strategies

As customers grow more proficient in creating their own value, and as companies grow more porous in their boundaries, the roles of strategy, planning, and implementation inevitably change. Where strategy once involved a perspective from above, it now flows in the very details of operation and interaction. Where planning once occupied a position of deliberation and status, it is now much more reflexive, and a more widely shared responsibility. Where implementation once reflected the insight of the strategic plan, it is now very often the strategy itself.

Strategy, like leadership, is no longer the responsibility of an enclave within the upper reaches of a hierarchy. Strategy is everyone's responsibility to understand and contribute to. And creativity and innovation, which have been primarily regarded as the skills of implementation, are themselves of strategic importance. The ability to improvise is no longer tactical but essential.

The Mystery of the Unknown

Many of the companies I work with and provide training to have suffered humiliations of failed strategic plans. Their experience is not unique. One U.S. business magazine published a survey suggesting that over 90 percent of strategies fail or become irrelevant. Tons of research; pages of thoughtful, well-rationalized assumptions; lists of opportunities based on trends; elegantly articulated objectives and strategies; these have done little to protect the companies that practiced even the most accomplished strategic planning.

For example, throughout the 1980s Ontario Hydro continued to develop the mega projects to sustain industry even while information and service companies replaced heavy manufacturing as the drivers for the economy. The company had a sophisticated planning and engineering process in place, yet the gap between the strategy it created and the reality it confronted has saddled this leading public corporation with $36 billion in debt, and a generating capacity that is out of step with the needs of its customers. Hydro's strategic plans, like those of IBM, Sears, American Express, Westinghouse, American Airlines, and countless others were intellectually compelling, but introspective and essentially isolated from reality.

Henry Mintzberg believes strategic planning has failed so many organizations exactly because imagination and intuition have been overrun by reason. He states that "when analysis and intuition do not find a natural balance in an organization, based on mutual appreciation of their respective strengths and weaknesses, supporters of each are drawn into political arguments."

Politics not only defeat synergy, but they also ultimately defeat the totality. Most planning systems are antithetical, or at least impervious, to intuition. They all use intensive data analysis and set formulas for working through the issues. The general operating assumption is: "No fact, then no consideration." They are also based on the belief that when enough "what if" scenarios are advanced, a company can cope with virtually any eventuality.

This system of planning is now being undone by its most fundamental premise. The underpinning of strategic planning is information. And as it exploded in variety and concentrated in density, "what if" options became much more complex and specific. The abundance of this input basically overwhelms the circuitry of strategic planning. In this ever more complex business environment, strategies have become more simplistic, crude, and hopelessly one-dimensional.

The addiction to planning was understandable in a management milieu committed to control. Management was defined as knowing the variables and choosing the course with the most opportunity and least risk. Today, the role of management is by necessity more hands-on than intellectual, more experiential than rational.

As mentioned, Wal-Mart insists that even its most senior executives work in a store at least once a month. This high-priced talent will take turns greeting customers at the door, bagging the purchases for them at check-out, and often walking with customers to help load the car. It is not simply an exercise in goodwill. Nor is it another example of management by "walking around." This is the strategy in action: the opportunity to hear and learn from customers on a one-on-one basis, and to translate that learning into an instantaneous improvement or response.

Wal-Mart's technology is so advanced that head office receives updated sales reports almost as soon as a product leaves the display shelf. This technological advantage is formidable and the timeliness of such data greatly compresses decision-making. But what gives all these light-speed bits and bytes meaning are the human lessons distilled from the frequent personal interchange between Wal-Mart people and Wal-Mart customers.

Today virtually everyone is imitating Wal-Mart, or some other customer-centered success story. I recently conducted an audit of people involved in the marketing activities of three very large organizations. Consistently, managers involved in the process identified their priority as getting "closer to the customer." Even research personnel felt that the understanding of the customer which their studies extracted for strategic planning were somehow less insightful and less actionable than a few short years ago. What few seemed to realize was that the distance they felt from the customer was not a function of poor input but rather of the whole strategy process itself.

An invention for perpetuating the company, strategy has become a way to maintain beliefs and traditions. The more we have invested in those underpinnings of strategy, the more limiting the strategy becomes. Peter Drucker notes that "new opportunities rarely fit the way the industry has always approached the market, defined it, or organized to serve it. Innovators therefore have a good chance of being left alone." Particularly when boundaries are imploding, and needs, attitudes, customers, and processes for value are converging, the parameters of strategy may be more limiting than illuminating.

Strategies are plans that define a positioning for advantage. They include objectives, as well as the tactics or programs for realizing those objectives. The essence of strategies is to maximize leverage and minimize vulnerability. These then are documents of paramount self-interest, in a time when business success requires ever greater mutuality. Most strategic thinking has been so focused on staking out a position of strength relative to the competition that it has lost the context for the very customer the enterprise depends on to survive.

Strategy has tried to be the science of management. In *Fuzzy Logic*, Bart Kosko provides a perspective on the limitations of science from the point of view of a scientist: "The world is gray but science is black and white. We talk in zeros and ones but the truth lies in between. Fuzzy world, non-fuzzy description. The statements of formal logic and computer programming are all true or false, 1 or 0. But statements about the world differ. Statements of fact are not all true or all false. Their truth lies in between total truth and total falsehood."

Strategies often have the pretension of truth, but the reality they seek to control is the fuzzy one in between. The harder we try to tighten strategies, the less relevant they are to a market that is loose and ambiguous.

Most business strategies employ a "this–that" logic: *this* input will deliver *that* consequence. As with Kosko's fuzzy logic, strategies must evolve to the more responsive, less assumptive "if–then": *if* this situation, *then* this option.

"THIS–THAT"	"IF–THEN"
• Strategy reduces risk.	• Strategy is a risk.
• Objective begets result.	• Ambiguity requires flexibility.
• Strategy follows objective.	• Response is the strategy.
• Strategy represents a fixed position.	• Strategy represents a range.
• Strategy defines a plan.	• Strategy requires improvisation.
• Strategy is expressed through tactics.	• Tactics define strategy.
• Results prove validity of the strategy.	• Results continuously refine strategy.
• Strategy precedes activity.	• Activity informs strategy.

For strategy to be meaningful in a business climate of chaos and unpredictability requires changes to both its process and results. The process, now sequential and analytical, must become amorphous and organic. And the result, rather than structured and rigid, must be flexible and interactive. Strategy is too important to be left to planners. In fact, every action expresses strategy (whether consciously or unconsciously). The understanding and insight strategy represents, and the listening and interpretation that go into the formulation of strategy, must be a deeply felt gospel for all the people within an organization.

Gary Hamel and C. K. Prahalad suggest that the whole concept of strategy be reversed: "Senior executives are not the only ones with industry foresight. In fact, their primary role is to capture and exploit the foresight which exists throughout the organization."

Strategy requires wisdom. By seeing beyond the limiting perspective of self-interest, wisdom brings to strategy the dimensions of caring for customers and respecting employees, which are essential for long-term, mutually rewarding business relationships. In the following list, I have summarized the differences between the ineffectual strategic planning paradigm still entrenched in most business organizations, and the emerging one based on the precepts of corporate wisdom.

STRATEGIC MODEL	WISDOM MODEL
1. Strategy is positioning, which leads to a product.	1. Strategy is a process, which leads to a guiding perspective.
2. Strategy is the responsibility of a senior group of specialists.	2. Strategy is a shared value, held and given expression throughout the company.
3. Strategy leads to sustainable self-preservation.	3. Strategy creates compelling and mutually rewarding networks of interdependencies.
4. Strategy is driven by facts and analysis.	4. Strategy balances analysis with intuition and facts with hunches. (If strategy is not taking you into the unknown, then it is not a strategy but a map.)
5. Strategy is fixed, consistent, and immovable.	5. Strategy is flexible, taking into account by learning, experience, and past mistakes.
6. Strategy is unique and proprietary.	6. Strategy nurtures the skills and wisdom that are the source of innovation and competitiveness.
7. Strategy is a sequential process: plans are followed by tactics; implementation by learning.	7. Strategy is simultaneous: learning and doing, reacting and replanning.
8. Strategy follows a set protocol and takes two to four months per year.	8. Strategy is irregular, fast, and formalized for brief review in the cycle that makes most sense for the marketplace.
9. Strategy engenders consistency in all aspects of the business plan.	9. Strategy inspires innovation and the spontaneity to capitalize on unexpected opportunities.
10. Strategy is a discipline of management.	10. Strategy is the stretching of management that yields growth, lessons, and a compounding of the corporate wisdom.

Imagine if Motorola had restricted itself to the strategic model detailed on the left. When it was a dominant provider of radio tubes and components, could it ever have envisioned a future of microchips, cellular phones, and satellite networks? Probably not. The benefit of strategy, however, is not prescience, but openness. Rather than try to predict the unimaginable, strategy should provide the self-knowledge to have context. Rather than simply seek to control the variables, strategy should contain the confidence to be enthralled and stretched by the mystery of the unknown. This necessitates a comfort with ambiguity and a fundamental desire for truth. With inductive strategies and deductive rationales, what we know can get in the way of what can be. With wise context, we *flow* with the unfathomable rather than try to master it.

Motorola, Hewlett-Packard, and Sony have often made product and strategy decisions that are visionary in hindsight, but that at the time seemed unsure, and even unrelated to their core business. (Sony actually introduces a staggering 1,000 new products and variations a year — an average of four a day.) For these companies strategies are more an attitude — curiosity about new advances and confidence to follow through. Similarly, the new products, services, and structures in these companies are not rigid outcomes of a definite and defined plan, but rather have evolved to adapt to the emerging demands of the future.

The differences between strategy assembled step by step and that which flows with wisdom can be seen below.

STEP-BY-STEP VS. WISDOM FLOW

215

The Missing Creativity

Even as companies go through the paroxysm of reengineering, there is a growing realization that productivity gains, no matter how impressive, are not enough to secure competitiveness. "Continuous improvement" may keep a company from falling behind the competition, but only "continuous creativity" can keep it ahead.

Every few years, the opinion leaders of business seem to rediscover the need for creativity. Budgets for Research & Development projects are approved once again, training is reinitiated, and the concept of "creativity" becomes temporarily fashionable. Despite the obvious need for innovation, the creativity that produces it in business continues to be regarded as a discretionary skill, as an expense more than as an asset. When times get tough, the investment in innovation is usually the first to be cut.

The restructuring of the last five years has been so severe because, among other things, many enterprises have largely failed to create earlier the innovations, new products, and opportunities for expansion that would have sustained them in these times. Hamel and Prahalad make the sad observation that "despite excuses about global competition and the impact of productivity enhancing technology, most of the layoffs at large U.S. companies have been the fault of senior managers who fell asleep at the wheel and missed the turn-off for the future."

Ironically, all of the strategic reorganization and downsizing efficiency actually only attacks the result without really addressing the cause. Another painful lesson still to be learned is that reengineering itself is not *regeneration*. Hamel and Prahalad note: "Downsizing attempts to correct the mistakes of the past, not to create the markets for the future."

It is not surprising that creativity is so difficult to manage. Management predicts, it seeks to control and minimize risk, while creativity unravels, seeks to break existing patterns, and thrives on risk. The creative instinct in human beings is almost impossible to understand and measure. It is also often both unpredictable and disruptive. This is hardly what companies, steeped in standardization and consistency, either desire willingly or can accommodate. Management is usually preoccupied with minimizing risk; creativity is risk in action. Overcoming this cultural repellence to creativity is not simply a function of acquiring a new management skill. Companies need to balance the desire to minimize risk with the need to foster creativity. The discontinuities and discord of these polarities confirm the need for a corporate and cultural wisdom.

The psychologist Howard Gardiner explores the characteristics of individuals whose genius and creativity have fashioned much of the thinking and artistic sensibility of this century. From his study we learn that:

1. *Creative people need to fail.* Even the most talented people produce much that is mediocre, with only as little as 10 percent of what they do standing as enduring innovation. Yet the 90 percent is the necessary muddling and experimentation that facilitates the truly remarkable breakthroughs.

2. *Those engaged in creative endeavors need an almost blind support from their immediate network of colleagues and acquaintances.* The process of continuous risk-taking is too daunting and too potentially damaging to the psyche to reserve any energy for deflecting criticism or cynicism.

3. *Creativity itself comes in spurts.* Even for the masters, there are no shortcuts. Creativity requires time for study, synthesis, exploration, and the occasional but invaluable accident.

From Gardiner's analysis, it is clear that a creative person of considerable capability and achievement may have perhaps only a half dozen truly creative breakthroughs. Few companies, however, think on such a humble scale. Few have the tolerance for failure, the commitment to extended support, or the patience to be truly and consistently innovative. As the CEO of an advertising agency, I personally experienced the dichotomy of serving the needs of creativity while also attending to those of managing the business. It was often a difficult struggle, because the two disciplines have their own distinct priorities and pressures.

In most advertising agencies, this duality has been addressed by institutionalizing the split. Employees in "suits" are assigned to plan, budget, and provide the interchange with clients, while the "creatives" are left to roam the halls and perform the alchemy that produces concepts and the occasional big idea.

Despite being rooted in creativity, the business of advertising has actually suffered from its own inflexibility. At a time when companies are seeking more innovation, advertising agencies have lost much of their credibility as sources for creative business solutions. In part, the institutionalized split has prevented them from evolving into the entrepreneurial idea factories that their clients so desperately need.

In other industries, the split between the logic of management and the intuition of creativity is even more pronounced. We are left with companies longing for breakthroughs, strangling their own innovations.

With the overview afforded by wisdom, the logic of business and the intuition of creativity are interwoven. The smartest strategies include a new linkage or insight. And the most compelling creative idea has business impact and gets sales results. Strategy and creativity are therefore circular rather than consecutive. To segment or separate the skills is to compromise the integrity of that circle.

The following list identifies other aspects of the two dimensions. At first glance, they seem to confirm their opposition. But with reflection, it becomes obvious that the two are complementary; that one without the other yields a dangerous blind spot, while the two together create a "completeness."

MANAGEMENT	CREATIVITY
• Logical analysis	• Discontinuity and reconnection
• Accountability for results	• Freedom to risk
• Sequential process	• Simultaneous combustion
• Bias to reason	• Bias to emotion
• Organizational principles	• Organizational values
• Competition	• Cooperation
• Quest for reward	• Quest for achievement
• Appreciation of precedent	• Appreciation of potential
• Assurance of control	• Stimulation of experimentation
• Structures and systems	• Short circuits and shortcuts
• Lessons from mistakes	• Lessons from life

Here again is an example of Schumpeter's "creative destruction." Bureaucracies, even in the smallest companies, tend to be rigidly self-preserving, while innovation tends to be consistently "bureaucracy-bashing." Even the wisest of management teams, even the wisest of organizations, struggle with this paradox. The goal is not so much to effect a compromise between creativity and management, nor is it favoring one form of "intelligence" over the other. Rather, the objective is to instill an overarching unity for the organization, bringing together what is essential, respecting what is essentially different, and eliminating what is merely territorial.

In this constructive tension, wisdom is both expressed and nurtured.

A wise context or culture stimulates and supports an exchange between disciplines and pressures, while respecting the distinct value of each. The dichotomy is not eliminated, but the fundamental dependency is strengthened. A wise sensibility includes clarity of purpose and continuity of self-awareness. This consciousness makes it easier to collaborate constructively, to see creative tension as a value for renewal rather than as a damaging distraction. A wise intelligence also sustains the compassion through which empathy is extended to the creative risk-takers. This provides the support that both Skynner and Gardiner determine to be essential for healthy growth and achievement.

While providing the unity of cause and the harmony between logic and emotion, a wise perspective also exercises the detachment and balance to do what is finally right for the group. In providing confidence and awareness, company wisdom is not just a *factor* in strategic planning and creative implementation. Wisdom is the strategy. And the creativity is wisdom.

QUESTIONS FOR STRATEGY

• What are the available building blocks for nurturing your company's wisdom?
- What are the precepts?
- How are these acknowledged and given value?
- Create your own: Fuse experience with competence, intelligence with driving passion, communication with flexibility, or whichever unique combinations of attributes reflect the strengths of your organization.
• How would you characterize the weighting of "boldness" and "prudence" in your company?
- What are the behavior examples that support your weighting?
- Which of these polarizing assets dominates? And why?
- Which of the two needs reinvigorating? And how?
• What is the boldest move your company made within the last year?
- What problems and benefits resulted from this act of boldness?
- Which lessons have stuck?
• How can the needed active fusion of boldness and prudence be incorporated into your company's strategy and culture?
- What are the steps or plans for realizing this fusion?

STRATEGIC VISION EXERCISE
• Break down your company's mission statement or vision statement into its key components.
- How generic are these?
- What compelling difference or advantage are expressed by them?
- Which elements of human motivation are engaged by them?
- How does the mission reflect and nurture your own, and your own corporate wisdom?
- How does the vision define purpose as well as goals?
• Create a list of interdependencies (management, employees, customers, community, etc.).
- How is vision *leveraging* and *responding* to these interdependencies?
- What "mutuality of self-interest" is being realized by the vision?
• What is the one word or simple phrase that encapsulates your vision?
- Is it inherent? Unique? Meaningful?
- How can it be brought out from within?
- How can it be inclusive of all it affects?

CREATIVITY POINTS

• There is no one way to manage innovation. Each company must create its own system, which suits its heritage, culture, and competencies. However, every company *must* innovate.

• Creativity is hard work. Gardiner's research shows that even the most talented creative people struggled long and hard for their breakthroughs. They immersed themselves in facts. They pursued endless dead ends. If not disciplined in their approach, they were at least very disciplined about working at the problem they were trying to solve. Creativity involves talent, but it *requires* persistence.

• Most companies assume that strategy, because it involves analysis, is more attainable than innovation. In reality, both are rare because both involve the same interplay of analysis and insight. Too many strategies are done to a formula, resulting in mediocrity. And too little innovation is done to strategy, resulting in irrelevance and failure. Some managers are finally realizing that strategy is an act of creation, while creativity is the ultimate expression of good business judgment.

• The "polar dependencies" listed above detail many of the gaps that confound companies and defeat corporate innovation. Which of those polarities apply to you or your company? What strengths can be created through the interconnection and interplay of those polarities? Imagine six initiatives for closing some of those gaps.

• What changes in culture, behavior, and skills need to be made to realize the Florentine ideal of "completeness" for your company?

TWELVE

MARKETING IN THE AGE OF WISDOM

As we have seen, immediately after reorganizing, companies must focus on integration. New assignments, expanded responsibilities, and streamlined processes have to be unified and converted into new operating styles. At this stage, companies tend to be inward-looking. But it is important that they look outside as well — to their customers. This involves an analysis of marketing, the discipline usually entrusted with bridging the needs of the company with those of its customers and prospects.

The New Markets

Marketing is like reengineering: it tries to do the right thing, but it unfortunately has the wrong name. As a concept, marketing had the most relevance in doing what it implied — creating markets. Once those markets matured, marketing also evolved to be the instrument of differentiation and market share growth. In this context, through the shifting mix of product, price, and promotion, companies fight to protect or take away shares of a defined market. Marketers have become more sophisticated in their use of information and research to hone their strategies. However, the basic principles and processes for marketing have remained unchanged since the mid-1950s when the product management structure achieved its formal definition.

Marketing makes sense for markets, but for relating to customers, most of its practices have become obsolete.

First, in a world without boundaries the defining factors for each individual market are blurring. As mentioned earlier, airlines used to compete for travel customers. Telephone companies competed for calling customers. Now both compete against each other and against many other companies for a piece of a much more complex and multidimensional business called "efficiency." Fewer boundaries equate to fewer markets in which to practice conventional marketing.

Second, everything has become marketing to some degree. In a market and society dominated by information, the "sell" is always on, always happening to customers, and (even if unconsciously) always judged by them. Companies are slowly coming to realize that there are no casual or random encounters with customers. Each interaction, whether by a customer service representative, an advertisement, or a logo on an invoice, affects the organization's reputation.

In a time when companies see customers as assets, reputation for a brand is its critical calling card. Where once marketing responsibility belonged to a department, it is now a pervasive concern. A customer-oriented marketing sensibility is being encouraged in manufacturing, operations, service, and sales, and is even regarded by many as the integral aspect of the role of the CEO.

Third, consumers have fundamentally changed. In almost every aspect of modern life, the preoccupations and needs that were once segmented by a defined context are now converging into something else. For example, the wall between work and leisure used to be fixed and pronounced. Now one-third of North American households have a home office with all the interconnective gear of fax, modems, and computers. Activities that were once distinguished by personal geography have merged and blended. People who work at home actually live in their office.

Other dramatic mergers and convergings are occurring. With the personal need for continuous improvement, people are returning to school. Once a preparation for career and work, educational courses are now the ongoing work of career. Many people are undergoing retraining or academic renewal more than once, at different times in their life. The net result is that education has merged with work, and because of software, it is now also often confused with entertainment.

Convergence is a concept we usually associate with technology and industries. The co-mingling of telephone, cable, computer, broadcast, software, and entertainment production has resulted in an instant global information monolith. Convergence is also affecting other industries: banks with software companies; malls with cable TV shopping stations; commercial real-estate buildings with the fax, phone, and PCs that make work from home so easy. In their introspective focus, many companies have failed to see how their own customers have experienced a fundamentally altering convergence of their own.

Throughout these changes, marketing has persisted in imposing definitions that are not there anymore. Companies have struggled in recent years to wring the efficiencies out of marketing programs that reengineering has achieved elsewhere in operations. For the most part, these have not been successful. The declining return on marketing investment has been attributed to consumer apathy. A more accurate view may be that the nonconsumer has simply tired of marketing's irrelevance. But if almost everything is marketing, how can marketing be irrelevant?

The irrelevance comes from exactly this pervasiveness. When everything is a "come-on," the neutralizing defenses are also always on. The apathy of customers goes deeper than their own marketing (or anti-marketing) savvy. While marketers profess an interest in relationship, they keep focusing on the sale. The vast majority of marketing initiatives are biased in favor of positioning, featuring, or communicating on behalf of the product or brand. Even though companies are the principal beneficiaries of a relationship with a customer (they make the sale and the profit), few have yet shown the understanding that this interaction must be *earned*. And fewer still have shown the courage to realize that one must "give to get."

This statement is perhaps the most important principle for revitalizing the practice of marketing. Erik Erikson, the psychologist who did pioneering work in human life cycle study, has explained a concept called "the norm of reciprocity." Simply, if I meet someone for the first time and put out my hand, chances are that the person will reach out and shake it. The key is that the person wanting the contact or relationship is the one who initiates. The receiver, perhaps disinterested, still reciprocates. This is the norm of reciprocity. In the relationship with the customer, the marketer is the initiator and the beneficiary, so the responsibility to reach out and give is continuous. Marketers offer a benefit to a customer for a sale. This is sufficient interchange for a transaction. To elevate this to a relationship requires much greater generosity.

Consumers want more, and companies are coming from behind, trying to deliver more. In the 1980s, competitive advantage was understood to hinge on the quality of products. In the 1990s, competitive advantage clearly depends on the quality of relationships.

It is not that product quality is less important. On the contrary, quality is now expected to such a degree that it has become a "cost of entry." However, as a basic demand, product quality may be the lowest denominator for relationship-building. The more choice customers have, the more success depends on insight into the human dynamic of relationship.

Just as quality required a new ethic, involving all disciplines and departments in its design, measurement, and achievement, so too relationship-building requires for everyone within an organization to become more "marketing-oriented." This does not mean expanding the power of existing marketing structures, but rather spreading the customer intelligence and customer focus to other disciplines.

For example, Saturn provides assembly-line workers with customer satisfaction surveys. In most companies, this research belongs exclusively to the marketing strategists. The logic of having the people who design and make the product as appraised of customer issues as those who sell to them is only now becoming apparent to managers.

The Burnout of Marketing Brands

In a survey on brands issued in the fall of 1994, McKinsey discovered that consumers have much higher expectations of brands today. For example, when customers purchase a new car, only about 30 percent of the decision is based on hard, tangible elements like the style, power, color, interior, braking, price, and engineering. The majority of the decision is based on intangibles, such as reputation of the dealer, image, approval by colleagues, commitment of the company to the local community, and a match of the car's personality with self-perception. That latter element alone, since it is based on values, contains endless subplots such as environmental commitment, job creation, and associations with causes of importance to the individual. McKinsey concludes that companies, even those with the money to invest in big marketing programs, must first "earn the right to brand."

By not concentrating on earning this right, companies are losing their brand power. Studies by DDB Needham Worldwide show that there has been as much as 20 percent drop in the loyalty to national brands in only the last five years. Even more ominous, psychographic researchers at Yankelovich & Associates have learned that consumers believe only about 8 percent of what marketers tell them through their advertising, sampling, packaging, and promotion communication.

The power of branding, and hence the validity of marketing, has been jeopardized by at least five factors:

1. *Customers are smarter about marketing, and much more demanding of quality, value, service, and choice.* After fifty years of having been "sold at," people have by osmosis learned many of the tactics and practices of marketers. They have developed skepticism and often cynicism toward marketers — hardly the ideal attitudes for constructing relationships of reciprocity and loyalty.

The declining relevance of conventional marketing is actually understandable. While marketers think of their users as consumers, the people buying products and services have largely shifted their context. The globalization of the economy, the loss of job security, and the static gains in real disposable income have thwarted the expectations upon which consumption is based. Individuals in society still need products and services, but the confidence and conviction that facilitated consumption are largely gone. Alan Middleton, an author and marketing professor at York University, argues that "consumer" is therefore an empty and misleading designation.

2. *Promotions, discounts, rebates, frequent usage programs, and "price-off" activities — the devices used by marketers to offset declining loyalty — have been shown in numerous studies to actually dilute the value of brands and deplete profitability.* In the struggle to protect market share, companies have resorted to what Professor John Philip Jones of Syracuse University calls "bribes." His research, summarized in an article in the *Harvard Business Review*, shows that such activities only hurt business, even as it increases volume. This is therefore a case of double exposure: marketers have not only disparaged people by regarding them as consumers, they have also depreciated brands by regarding them as a commodity.

3. *Research, the bible for marketers, too often reveals too little understanding about the human beings in the market who actually buy and use brands.* In *Liberation Management*, Tom Peters accuses all marketing research of "discovering the same things." As discussed, research has become a substitute for judgment and a gatekeeper for action. Somehow, the understanding of the human being, fundamental to relationships, has become lost in all the numbers, cross-tabulations, and regression analyses common to the majority of market research.

That all competitors use the same types of research means that everyone is also drawing the same one-dimensional insights from the same limited pool of information.

4. *Retailers have more intimate and ongoing contact with customers, thereby preempting the understanding and connection of national brands.* If national marketers need tangible proof of their declining authority, many need look no further than the resurgence of retailers. Store brands, once the poor-quality, low-cost cousins of the national entries, have become the new badges of street-smart buyers in many product categories. Retailers, like Loblaws in Canada, Sainsbury's in the United Kingdom, and Wal-Mart in the United States, have developed relationships of much greater sensitivity with their customers, in many ways usurping the connection of established brands.

By initiating and innovating within these relationships, retailers not only increased their own relevance, but also effected a fundamental repositioning of national brands. Grant McCracken, a market researcher and anthropologist at Toronto's Royal Ontario Museum, observes that the new store brands have "successfully co-opted the cynicism" that so many people feel toward "marketed" brands. Because they can buy a better product for less, people feel justified in thinking that national brands, with their claims and discounting, were really not all that they claimed to be.

5. *The traditional practice of marketing tends to focus on the issues and priorities of the product at the expense of the customer.* Most companies still have "product managers" to handle marketing decisions. And most marketing plans are structured so that 80 to 90 percent of the information they contain relate to the product or brand. The bias of job description and the overreliance on precedence mean that few companies have been able to adapt to the cloudy convergence affecting their customers. Brand selling is still tied to a "benefits" thinking, which is tied to a "category" context, which just has less and less relevance to customers.

Many marketers use the discipline of matrix analysis (in a form developed by the Boston Consulting Group) to plot the vibrancy of specific brands. If marketing, as it is practiced by the majority of companies, were a product, its life cycle trajectory would appear on the matrix as "mature." In the vernacular of BCG, marketing would be more of a "cash cow" than a "star." Hence the attitude of so many business people that marketing is an activity for "harvesting" rather than "investing."

Interacting by Choice

To reconnect with their more restless and discerning customers, many national brand managers have begun to drop their coins into the promising new video game of relationship marketing. Developing a multidimensional connection with individual consumers is seen as the way to revitalize tired brands. In virtually every product category there have been new programs for listening, service, responding, and following up after sales. These are important initiatives; however, in most cases, the essential basis of marketing is still directed toward a transaction. Plans and objectives continue to focus almost exclusively on the product. Despite the growing use of 1-800 numbers, it seems as if the language and sensibilities of relationships have been co-opted by many marketers only as the latest ruse against a more sophisticated and marketing-hardened target audience.

Human relationship-building cannot work as a tactical embellishment to existing strategies: the very principles, obligations, and processes of marketing must change. As the initiators of this relationship, marketers are seeking to engage customers over their lifetime, offering a combination of hard and soft attributes that encompass performance, value, service, and a broader affinity with values and interests. Interconnecting on this higher plane with individual customers has the potential of creating ever stronger bonds of trust, through what researcher Max Blackston calls "intimacy."

Extending the principles of marketing to this realm of intimacy may increase the opportunity for the mutual exchange between a brand and a buyer. However, it also adds considerable responsibility on to the marketer.

If a product disappoints a consumer on the level of value, the company risks losing a sale. If a trusting relationship disappoints a consumer on the level of values, the company risks losing a customer on the far more damaging basis of disrespect. Relationship marketing cannot be approached as a casual outgrowth of existing practices. The higher stakes for the human beings involved require higher consciousness on the part of the organization.

Relationship standards are already being applied by individuals to virtually all brands, in all price points. And even the most sophisticated of marketers can stumble. Coke, the quintessential multinational, offended many Islamic believers by displaying the Saudi flag in a World Cup promotion, without realizing that this national emblem is inscribed with sacred text from the Koran. Arch-rival Pepsi fell victim to its own religious insensitivity by beaming a laser advertisement for a touring rock show on the bell tower of a medieval church in England.

No harm was meant in either case. Apologies and acts of contrition were quickly delivered. But the question remains: how could companies with so much research available to them, and with so many international resources supporting them, make such disrespectful transgressions?

Part of the answer is a limitation in the often-used concept of positioning. Marketers have used positioning since the mid-1970s to carve a distinct place for their brand within the often jumbled perceptions and understanding of consumers. The focus of positioning has been competitive differentiation, causing brands like Coke and Pepsi to focus so much attention on each other that they occasionally miss talking to their own consumers. The orientation of positioning as a fixed, precise strategy is illustrated by a hypothetical brand on the following spectrum:

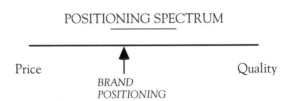

POSITIONING SPECTRUM

Price   *BRAND POSITIONING*   Quality

As competition has intensified, and as consumers have grown more savvy, the rigidity of a fixed position has become more of a liability than an asset. Henry Mintzberg has argued persuasively that a strategic perspective is more relevant and effective than a strategic positioning. Perspective is active and malleable, while positioning is static and inflexible. Perspective reaches out to the buyer, while positioning reacts to the competition.

In a world of relationships in which boundaries among markets have come down, and the issues for individuals have converged, brands must grow in depth of value and wisdom. Participating in a genuine relationship requires not so much a strategic position as a strategic space, as illustrated below.

RELATIONSHIP SPECTRUM

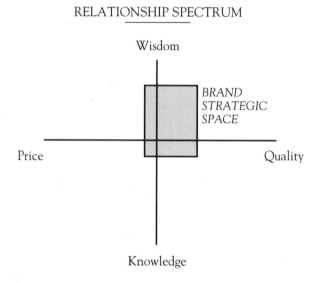

Occupying a strategic space affords a brand the latitude to expand its scope of stimulus. For over thirty years, Dove soap positioned itself as a beauty bar that contains "one-quarter cleansing cream." Each advertisement and communication piece used a visual, now classic, of cream being poured into the shape of a Dove bar. Several years ago, the marketing group at Lever experimented with a new advertising approach — an idea that Canadian President Peter Ellwood admitted was "technically off-strategy." Using a litmus paper demonstration, the brand compared its mildness to other soaps. In a departure from convention, Dove's advertising contained no reference to its historical proposition. Nor did it include any of the traditional shots of cream pouring into the bar.

The public responded immediately. The market share for Dove, which had been static, quickly grew six points. Unexpectedly, the litmus demonstration also effectively repositioned competitive brands, such as Ivory and Neutrogena, that had demonstrated acidity.

In the world of orthodox marketing, any deviation from strategy is believed to risk "confusing consumers" and "diluting brand equity." But the marketers who resist such strategic flexibility are confusing single-minded with simple-minded. Dove's experience shows that buyers, far from being disoriented, are smart enough to process more than one bit of information about a brand. All that is required for this renewing stretch is relevance and respect.

The Interacting Model for Marketing

In recent years, much work has gone into defining what marketers call "brand equity." Companies like RJR Nabisco have been purchased for many times the value of their manufacturing plant, and business people have wanted to get a fix on the real worth of brands — their equity. What is emerging from this investigation is that equity — a brand's fundamental financial value — is actually not owned by the product or the manufacturer. While marketers may engineer a certain value into a brand, the equity is only realized in an interaction with a satisfied and willing buyer.

It is exactly like owning a house. You may spend a lot of money to construct it, but if there is no buyer, the house has no equity. This is a critical realization for modern business people: equity resides outside of the brand, and depends on an interaction with customers for its value. Relationship-building is therefore less an option, but an imperative.

MARKETING MODEL VS. INTERACTING MODEL

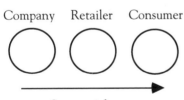

Company   Retailer   Consumer

. Sequential
. Distinct "Self-Interest"
. Adversarial
. Value = Quality + Price

Consumer

Company Retailer

. Simultaneous
. Overlapping "Self-Interests"
. Cooperative
. Value = Quality/Price + "Reciprocities"

To provide a specific context for this new discipline of *interacting*, I have developed a model that builds and extends the original principles of marketing.

PRODUCT MARKETING MODEL	INTERACTING MODEL
1. Focus on the product.	1. Focus on the process for serving customers.
2. Define the target group.	2. Feed and nourish the relationship.
3. Set brand objectives.	3. Respect and value customers.
4. Opportunity comes from analysis.	4. Opportunity comes from synergy.
5. Focus on brand benefit.	5. Develop and refresh relevance.
6. Create strategic advertising.	6. Open the doors for dialogue.
7. Operate against a brand plan.	7. Improvise to sustain the relationship.
8. Driven by a marketing group.	8. Encouraged by a pervasive interdisciplinary attitude.

Such a radical change in the fundamental disciplines and language of marketing is necessary to finally overcome the product bias within most companies. Product strategies remain valuable, but they are not complete. The dimensions suggested in the *interacting* model involve the basic precepts of wisdom: compassion and empathy for others; the commitment to reciprocity; the obligation of interdependence; and the basic need for justice and truth. When equity hinges on interaction, these become essential parts of the enlightened value equation.

The reality of these heightened expectations is already forcing change. What follows are examples of companies that have begun to evolve their brand-centric marketing to focus more on the interaction and exchange required by relationships.

Serving Customers

Product managers focus on products. That's their job. However, "earning the right" to be in a relationship with buyers totally reverses the priorities.

In its old assumptions, marketing was something done to customers and against competitors. Now marketing is a value customers do something with. It may be offering information that goes beyond the particular performance issues of a product and offers advice, insight, or support. It may be providing the degree of accessibility that allows customers of Dell Computers to actually customize their machine with the software and features they want. Or, in its most radical form, it may be giving away the product to establish a totally different reciprocity. In a *BusinessWeek* cover story, "The Technology Paradox," the writers suggest that "with the production cost of hardware and software so low in comparison to the development cost, it actually can make sense to give stuff away in order to establish a market toehold and start a profitable long-term relationship."

Feeding and Nourishing the Relationship

As the McKinsey survey showed, purchase decisions of even the most expensive items involve many more factors than only price or quality.

Chrysler has completed a remarkable turnaround in North America, and now boasts one of the most stylish and exciting model line-ups in the automotive industry. In a recent marketing campaign Chrysler chose to focus not on its cars — products that deserved the attention — but on the jobs its investments were creating in the local community. North Americans are still struggling with the reality of a jobless economic recovery. Job creation and investment in the community are high priorities for many people, so Chrysler's initiative had significance for its relationships, as well as its image.

Respecting and Valuing the Consumer

Objectives are relatively easy to set because they basically define self-interest. But when the focus of the objectives is turned toward the individual, they become much harder to envision.

Gillette has been enjoying considerable profitability since its Sensor brand preempted all the other wet shaving systems with a superior, floating-blade technology. In 1994, Gillette introduced another innovation — rubber fins on each blade, which provided an even smoother shave. Wall Street analysts questioned why the company had invested in yet a greater improvement when users were already so satisfied, and competitors still so far behind. Gillette executives answered that it was their job "to amaze their customers."

Product innovation in most marketing instances is done with the perspective of beating competitors. Self-interest and therefore competitiveness are important. Yet, in the context of relationships, competitiveness seems to be best achieved by focusing respect and diligence on the buyer and prospects. The relevance for the customer enhances the interaction.

Opportunities from Synergy

Marketing is a creature of analysis. Like other aspects of conventional business, it earns credibility by studying increments. However, in the converged reality of the customer, it is much more meaningful to bring things together than to break them apart.

Like other financial institutions, the Bank of Montreal has been trying to break out of the box of impersonality. Instead of pursuing the now expected "we care for you" approach, the company focused on raising the competence of its customers. People realize that issues of financial planning and management are important. While they do not necessarily have the expertise to handle the specifics on their own, they generally do not have the inclination nor patience to ask a large financial company to help.

The Bank of Montreal introduced an information exchange and used real customers to create case histories for others to consider. Different examples of people at different stages of career, income earning, and family growth were developed. The bank did not presume to have all the answers. In the spirit of co-creating value, it simply devised the material infrastructure for an information exchange between customers who had answers and those who had questions. The whole, indeed, emerged as greater than the sum of its parts.

Developing and Refreshing Relevance

Marketing uses a logic of "reach and frequency": get to as many people as possible and repeat one thing so that they will remember it. The old consumer may have needed such mind-numbing tactics, but today's buyer is actually a voracious user of information. *Interacting* requires more than presence. It needs *exchange*, the vital back-and-forth interaction that happens between people.

As suggested previously, Dell revolutionized the computer business by reversing the convention of "reach and frequency" into "access and renew." The company allows over 30,000 customers to reach into the company daily by telephone. Sales and service are interactive. But the telecommunications technology does more than facilitate orders, distribution, and technical assistance. The calls also provide Dell with a window on the issues, concerns, and needs of customers. When problems arise, cross-functional teams deal with the issue within one week.

From this renewing interaction with customers springs the ethic that led Dell to understand clearly its obligations when problems with Pentium first came to light. And in solving such problems, Dell showed the integrity that will expand the interaction and relationship further.

Opening the Doors

Marketing has basically involved a monologue between "seducers" and "resistors." While acceptable for selling, few relationships survive a one-way barrage. *Interacting* requires dialogue.

John Labatt recently put the various disciplines of the conventional marketing mix into a blender and emerged with a lesson in *interacting*. The company actually conducted a national vote in which customers were asked to help choose which of two varieties of a "copper" beer the company would subsequently launch. This was an exercise in which the advertising became the research, the research became the marketing, and the marketing itself became an exercise in listening.

While some saw this as a gimmick (and part of it was certainly a send-up), the point is that customers were invited into the inner sanctum of marketing and asked to play a part in the decision. This again is an example of value that is co-created rather than prepackaged.

Improvising

We have already seen the danger of strategic rigidity. Bill Etherington at IBM provides a concrete example. IBM found itself outflanked by competitors in large part because of the constraints of an overly developed, highly rigid strategic planning system. Etherington compared IBM's old planning approach to a very deliberate and thoughtful chess game. While IBM plotted its next move on the strategic chess board, the marketplace transformed into an entirely different genre, becoming a real-time video game in which the competitors were firing live ammunition. In the urgent struggle for survival there was little time for strategic modeling. The company and its employees were forced to improvise — to do whatever it took to secure customers and rebuild their trust.

Improvisation is a feature of human interaction. It is largely impossible to predict what will happen in the dynamics of a relationship. While strategies attempt to impose guidance on transactions, the only guidance that works in *interacting* is that of ethics and obligation.

Interdisciplinary Attitude

Interacting with customers forces changes on internal operations as well. During the last recession Canadian Airlines International faced bankruptcy. To assure passengers who were watching the company's life-and-death struggle in the business press, CAI developed a unique testimonial advertising campaign that aired interviews with passengers and employees. Interviews made in the morning appeared on television within hours of the footage being shot. The people on camera were real and addressed the issues honestly. The topicality of the dialogue and the self-confidence of the approach impressed upon customers that CAI was not only still flying, but was very clever and resourceful.

Achieving such immediacy required the marketing company, its advertising agency, the production house, and the broadcaster to ignore traditional roles and procedures. Employees and customers served as the creative source, since their words became the message. The producer, who usually oversees details, became the final creative decision-maker. The TV station that aired the advertising also did the editing, a function usually done by the production house. The marketers and strategists who usually have the final decision-making power had to surrender that authority to the crafts people who were putting the whole campaign together.

This was an exercise in confidence and trust-building directed at customers. It required developing confidence and trust between the marketers and their extended team. This suggests another key element of *interacting*: it must be a genuine expression of operating values.

The Renewal of Brands

The idea behind interacting is not to usurp brands, nor to deny companies the opportunity to promote what they do. Brands serve a valuable function. They not only provide the supporting company with a formal presence in the market, but they also clarify expectations and trustworthiness for buyers. With the growing confusion caused by increasing clutter, the importance of branding will only increase. Interacting is a way to make branding truly based on relationship. And it is another expression of wisdom in action.

Brands have considerable potential as containers for corporate wisdom, in large part because they are symbols — they carry meaning. Usually this meaning is only that primitive one of product information. Sometimes brands also carry the meaning of image or culture.

Take, for example, one of the world's most established and valuable brands. The Coke brand represents the information of its secret recipe, as well as the expertise for manufacturing, distributing, and marketing it. This is the base-level information. The brand also contains a code of imagery and meaning that has been ascribed to and associated with Coke for over a century. This information is more abstract, but also more meaningful to customers. It is much harder information to replicate (if even at all possible), and therefore a much greater contributor to the value of Coke.

Brand thinking is not new. Alan Middleton explains that the concept stretches back to antiquity. In fact, many of the brick and clay artifacts uncovered by archeologists in the Middle East bear the markings of their manufacturers. This makes sense because for as long as there has been commerce, there have also been competitors.

Branding is what any seller uses to differentiate themselves from competitors. Today, brands like Crest, Green Giant, Nestlé, and Marlboro have consumer franchises that span the globe. In fact, the trajectory of brand recognition and acceptance follows very closely that of economic development. In Malaysia, Poland, South Africa, and India, the growth of Oil of Olay and Gillette parallels the development of a more prosperous and secure middle class.

While not new, the notion of brands is nevertheless evolving rapidly. Since brands are concentrations of information, the advances in information technology and availability have made brand-building both more essential and much more difficult. Competition is intense, so the information clutter surrounding brands is dense, often desperate. The greater this clutter becomes, the more important it will be to have a strong brand platform to stand on.

Until very recently, the concept of a brand applied almost exclusively to specific products or services. Again as a result of information overload, branding is now stretched to operate both on a much larger as well as more personal level. Think of IBM. Or Tom Peters. Or Sony. Or Steven Spielberg. Whether for a huge, multinational corporation, or for a single person, the recognition, associations, and concentration of knowledge represent values that are essentially those of brands. What we know about these "brands" helps create expectations, set standards for performance, and determine the value that we as customers appreciate and are willing to pay for.

During the last five years we have seen significant upheaval in the world of brands. Market leaders like Coke and Kodak have been usurped by smart, agile, opportunistic upstarts. Researcher Angus Reid, in a composite summary of marketing surveys done for a cross-section of marketers, concludes that this is an age of "unprecedented volatility." Established market leaders have been suddenly dethroned. To defend their franchise, even the most established and highly regarded brands have resorted to price-slashing.

Many business theorists look upon this volatility as confirmation that *branding* is a concept in decline. They believe that customers are more discerning about what they buy. These consumers are also markedly less loyal, and less susceptible to the marketing initiatives that manufacturers have continuously employed to get brands noticed and consumed. Brands are indeed suffering, but it is their content and not validity that should be questioned.

Brands are still largely developed as "fact-carriers." They carry facts about performance, about features, and about pricing and relative value. These facts are often construed to provide a benefit for the customer, but they are usually so slanted in favor of the product that they lack credibility and relevance. As already discussed, facts are actually the units of lowest value on the information chain.

To increase the value of brands means that the knowledge value must grow. That knowledge must add depth and relevance to the relationship, not to the self-interest of that brand. As for people and organizations, the migration up the knowledge scale involves the following basic steps:

1. Bits of data become facts;	2. Facts with experience become knowledge;	3. Knowledge with context grows to understanding;	4. Understanding with reflection creates wisdom.

These steps suggest a process but not the content. How do brands become more effective carriers of knowledge?

Stewart Owen is chairman of Landor & Associates, a U.S. research company that produces an annual poll of the world's most famous brands. In a recent speech, Owen detailed what the company had learned about creating successful and enduring brands. In addition to the important functional elements (such as "be first" or "be best"), Owen observed that the great brands like Mercedes, Disney, Sony, Coke, and Range Rover provided customers and prospects a "package of meaning." Beyond performance and image, these brands spoke in a compelling and honest way to the wider human need. Meaning includes an affinity of values, a pride in having personal dreams, fears, ambitions, and biases not simply reflected but embodied in the brand. This package is not achieved by positioning, but by experience. It is the result of knowledge and understanding, and likely even of a basic wisdom.

Importantly, the brands developed the trust to go with the heightened expectations of customers by consistently delivering superior behavior. They practice what they preach, and tend to give more than they promise. With this base of "meaning," these brands earn the right to a more interactive relationship with customers.

Brands, as the representatives of companies, carry their values and obligations. This is why great brands cannot be constructed by marketing alone — they require the totality of what the company believes and how it operates. The discipline of interacting does not push to make a sale. Instead the customer or prospect is invited to share the quality, value, experience, understanding, and values of the provider. If this seems too soft sell, remember that selling is something only done to buyers. In relationships, the interacting involves giving, sharing, listening, and inviting.

Marketing practitioners have obviously been struggling with the growing demands of customers. For at least a decade, their vocabulary has included the term "value added" to represent features, uses, information, or other alignments that move the worth of the brand beyond its function. Value added may mean including AM–FM stereo cassette players in the base price for cars, or providing a 10 percent free bonus in shampoos.

As competitive pressures have grown, a few marketers have advanced further along this value progression to include an expansion of service. Nissan offering roadside assistance is an example of "service added."

The next progression — from that of service to *interacting* with obligation and values — I have called "wisdom added." The basic elements of this spectrum are shown below.

	CORE VALUE	VALUE ADDED	SERVICE ADDED	WISDOM ADDED
PREMISE	Basic product	Enhanced features	Access and response	Connections beyond the specific transaction
DEMO-GRAPHIC ATTITUDE	Buy what is needed	Buy for convenience	Buy for personal attention	Buy for alignment with broader values
CUSTOMER RESPONSE	I get what I pay for"	"I want higher quality at lower prices"	"I expect respect"	"I want to use my power of choice to make a difference in those things that are important to me"
EXAMPLES	Taste Convenience Core attitude	New package New size/value configurations Promotions Sponsorships	1-800 access Smart recipes After sales support and service	Product affinities (environment/arts/community causes) Corporate responsibilities (jobs/community/support employee relations) Obligations and values

Again, it is important to stress that the more the self-interest between brand and customer is integrated, the greater the responsibility of the company. Meaning must be established; trust must be earned; promises must be kept; and generosity must be extended.

Wisdom-Added Marketing

The brands that have advanced along this information value chain to knowledge and understanding are proving to be the ones with salience and relevance in this increasingly information-fatigued market. Sainsbury's, a successful and trend-setting food retailer in the United Kingdom, has led the way in adding value to its products by putting in knowledge. Several years ago, as the company added new items and lines to its store brand portfolio, the marketing group came to believe that variety and breadth of offering were no longer enough. Products could be copied; prices could be matched. By talking to customers, the marketers realized that people had a different problem than the one Sainsbury's thought it was solving.

Anthony Rees, the vice-president of marketing, explains: "Our customers were interested in the variety of foods we offered, but they were hesitating. On the one hand, they were desperate for a 'Wednesday-night-solution' — something to break the boredom of meals during the week — and on the other, they were unfamiliar with the new foods, and intimidated about making a mistake."

Sainsbury's continued to introduce new items, while shifting its marketing and store promotion activity to solve both the "Wednesday-night boredom" problem and the "intimidation" factor. Using multimedia, Sainsbury's showed interesting foods, while explaining the preparation step by step. Recipe ads have been done before. What made Sainsbury's stand out was its understanding of the customer's dilemma, and its offering of knowledge to help that customer resolve it. One simple initiative increased mozzarella cheese sales in the stores "by a factor of eight," and sales of this cheese grew throughout the United Kingdom by 30 percent.

The commitment to adding value by adding knowledge is such that Sainsbury's has now launched its own magazine. In addition to providing more information about food, recipes, and domestic management, the magazine also covers environmental, social, travel, and well-being issues. It even includes humor. This intentional extension beyond a traditional focus on food is part of how Sainsbury's is expanding its relationship with customers. It not only widens the field of mutual interest, but also affords the company with a more direct channel to the issues of concern to customers. Importantly for customers, food has been transformed by knowledge into a higher competence and a higher confidence.

The evolution of branding from providing performance facts to adding knowledge, and to extending understanding, is necessary to prevent the "genericization" that is eroding differentiation in virtually every product and service category. Clones have made the PC market, once a glamorous technology business, into a black hole of discounting. New technology and speed enhancement are almost instantly matched by low-price imitators. Compaq, a leader in the PC segment, followed the too familiar pattern of other high-tech companies, "crashing and burning" in 1991 when it could no longer sustain a premium price for its premium products.

Compaq had launched the portable computer market in the late 1980s. Making its computers smaller allowed it to charge more. But as Toshiba, IBM, NEC, and others stormed into the laptop segment, the "old" differentiators for Compaq lost their currency with customers. Compaq began a remarkable and far-reaching makeover. In only twelve months, it became the world's most efficient manufacturer, simultaneously pushing ahead with leading-edge technology while also pushing out the boundaries of its business to attract novices, small business, and even the home computer users.

As it added more technology to its machines, and brought less informed and less comfortable customers into its mandate, Compaq faced a growing, potentially undermining, "knowledge gap." It realized that selling machines was no longer simply about providing technology or price, but also required serving the "technophobia" of its growing group of less-sophisticated computer users. The product and the marketing of Compaq now bridge this gap, adding knowledge and understanding to both the selling strategy and the operating systems of its computers. Software is already loaded onto its Presario, as are answering machine and faxing capabilities. Building such knowledge into the machine has facilitated understanding for customers. For the first time, an IBM–compatible PC was indeed "plug and play."

Encoding knowledge into the brand, as well as into the machine, has pushed Compaq to the forefront as a financial performer. Even after dropping prices by over 30 percent, sales volume has almost tripled since 1991, while profits have grown by over 40 percent. New design, manufacturing, and management have played important roles in Compaq's renaissance. But adding knowledge and understanding to its brand has given this company momentum.

The progression from understanding to wisdom is also already becoming apparent in business. Chrysler's Neon, Cadillac's DeVille, and the BMW 3 series are designed and engineered to be 70 to 90 percent recyclable. These are brand benefits that appeal to a deeper consciousness of our times. This evolution has especially strengthened the BMW brand.

The quintessential '80s badge, BMW was overly associated with an image of achievement and conspicuous consumption. With the pragmatism imposed by the recession and the economic deconstruction of the 1990s, most high-end car brands were stuck with an obsolete and irrelevant information code. Porsche and Jaguar sales dropped by more than half; Mercedes sales declined by a third. The luxury car buyers did not stop buying cars, but instead moved their purchase to brands like the Jeep Cherokee and Chrysler Magic Wagon, which inferred the smarter values of pragmatism.

BMW proved to be the luxury car chameleon. It alone among luxury brands held sales and increased market share. This was in part due to its smart focus on the lower priced 3 series, reflecting an understanding and connection with the priorities, concerns, and emerging wisdom of its customers and prospects. While other luxury brands wallowed in outdated and irrelevant imagery, BMW was able to refashion its brand to have currency with the more pragmatic concerns of the 1990s.

These examples show a wider consciousness on the part of those responsible for the interacting between brands and customers. They are still very tentative steps along the progression to wisdom, but they show that many companies are being pulled into "wisdom added" by the values and priorities of customers. To advance fully on this dimension, to lead instead of to follow customers, sometimes requires greater courage and more risk. Molson, Canada's largest brewer, took this leap into the obligations of relating.

Like other large marketing firms, Molson is often approached by interest groups to contribute to various causes. In 1990, the company was asked by a local grassroots organization to "donate some product" (beer) for a small event intending to raise money for AIDS research. As it is prone to do, Molson offered beer, as well as marketing help to produce some promotional posters and tent cards for bar tables. The event was a success, and over time Molson found that more and more local community groups were approaching it for such support in AIDS research fund-raising. The collaboration became more extensive, and in five years the company helped groups in Toronto alone generate over $3.5 million for this cause.

Many companies do good works. What is important about Molson's example is that this activity stands within its basic business operation, instead of as a discretionary add-on. This integration was, in part, serendipitous. Research showed that there had been a major shift in the attitudes among all Canadians, including traditional beer drinkers.

First, the loss of jobs in the restructured economy, and the cuts in social programs, had affected consumers' perceptions of the companies they buy from. They now expected more defined and continuous commitment to the issues, values, and needs of their community. Second, AIDS had become fixed as one of the top five issues for the population in general, as well as for the majority of Molson's franchise.

Charles Fremes, vice-president of public affairs, explains: "AIDS is a mainstream issue, not a marginal one — which is code for gay. We know from our corporate research that our reputation has been enhanced through our involvement in this area. Our consumers like what we're doing."

In fact, in MarketVision's survey, many of those customers expressed their belief that a beer company's support for initiatives like AIDS research is more meaningful and important to them than the usual sports sponsorship.

This turns the orthodoxy of beer marketing on its head. The average beer drinkers, like the majority of people, are aware and concerned about factors beyond their own self-interest. Not only were the broader emotional needs of its consumers unexpectedly engaged by Molson's AIDS work, but employees also show considerable pride and enthusiasm for the company's contribution. Many volunteered personal time to help organize various events. At a time when the corporate culture suffered from several years of cutbacks, this initiative allowed people to step out of the shadow of restructuring, to use their heads as well as their hearts, to begin reshaping the company's values for this more demanding, discerning business reality.

Adding dimensions of wisdom to the equity and meaning of brands becomes even more important as the "baby boomers" move into midlife and beyond. This population segment influences market trends more than any other group. As baby boomers encounter their own mortality, they will increase their sense of obligation and begin to fashion their own wisdom. And they will increasingly seek a connection on these deeper terms from the products they purchase.

Having been so aggressively marketed to for so long, this group will be skeptical. Only companies who are genuine in the values they represent will be accepted. For these savvy customers, the wisdom of interacting is a way for companies to earn a relationship as well as make a sale.

AN EXERCISE FOR INTERACTING

GROWING "WISDOM ADDED"

Using the *Working Wisdom* model, I have prepared a few basic questions for each attribute of wisdom to help give more context to the progression of value.

WORKING WISDOM	IMPLICATION FOR INTERACTING
PERSPECTIVE	
Timelessness	• What values does the brand represent?
	• How can these bring relevance to a future relationship?
	• How do these help earn trust and "the right to brand"?
Clarity and Focus	• What is the meaning represented beyond the function?
Compassionate Detachment	• How is genuine empathy extended to customers?
	• What are the brand's specific obligations?
VALUES	
Truth and Honesty	• Is the brand positioning fundamentally honest?
	• What are the real benefits and advantages?
	• What innovation will afford the most honest leverage?
Justice	• How is broader responsibility to customers and other constituents met?
ACTION	
Unity and Integration	• What are the interconnections among the brand, the company, suppliers, retailers, and community?
	• How are these acknowledged?
	• How is respect tangibly extended to the customer?
Intellectual and Emotional Harmony	• What are the human rewards beyond function that are imbedded in the brand?
Equanimity	• How are the objectives of the brand balanced with the needs of the customer, constituents, and community?

SUPPORT

Substantial Subjectivity

- What are the insights driving the thinking of the brand?
- How do these reflect personal judgment?
- Who is personally responsible for the customer? How is this responsibility given the primacy it deserves?

Mentorship

- How is information encoded in the brand used to help build knowledge-value for customers?
- How is the legacy of the brand managed for continuity and accountability?

THIRTEEN

THE JOB THAT IS
THE SECURITY

In this new economy, most of us must function as stand-alone "brands." We must compete for jobs and assignments by projecting our skills, as well as our reputations, into the marketplace. And it is not just the self-employed who must undergo this form of self-marketing. Traditional jobs are mostly without security, so even the individuals who hold them are having to earn and re-earn their place within their company, project, and team. In 1991, I moved from being a company worker to being self-employed, so I know firsthand the vicissitudes of both career paths.

Career and Other Quandaries

It is quite difficult to retain a personal equilibrium when many of our basic assumptions about security, career, and personal worth are being so drastically redefined. The prospect of a new economic model used to promise people more stability and leisure. In an unsettling reversal, the information economy has created as much anxiety as knowledge. It has also merged the issues and priorities of work and life, of knowledge and value, exacting an ever greater investment of time.

Instantaneous obsolescence used to be the cruel fate of computers and machines. Today, it is people who are vulnerable to advancing knowledge, and therefore most expendable. In *Reinventing the Future*, Gary Hamel and C. K. Prahalad warn: "Intellectual capital steadily depreciates. What you, dear reader, know about your industry is worth less right now than when you started reading this book."

If what we know is worth less, is that bad? Derrick de Kerckhove is the director of the McLuhan Institute at the University of Toronto. A student of McLuhan's, and now a teacher, de Kerckhove offers the same insight but the opposite conclusion. The shelf life of knowledge is indeed shorter. However, expertise keeps renewing itself. The trick in any vocation or position is not to pretend to be current, but to have the skills of instantaneous access. In *The Skin of Culture*, de Kerckhove calls this "just in time psychology."

These are exactly the quandaries that make career and personal growth perplexing. Obsolescence is a threat and a necessity. Independence is an imperative and an impossibility. Structure is eliminated and essential. The only certitude is that security, in its old construct, is gone.

Many are already predicting a radically different landscape for work. People are told to expect to have many careers, jumping not only from company to company but also from project to project, and from role to role. Others envision a wired workforce of self-standing entrepreneurs. Working in their homes, teams of experts throughout the world will be assembled via telecomputer to tackle specific projects. From their "smart desks," these best and brightest will provide the ultimate productivity of ultimate experts supported by ultimate technology. Once the task is done, that "virtual company" will dissolve, with its members forming new teams to take on the next assignment from another client.

The future is already here. The reshaping of the corporate world has already pushed millions into self-employment. The same restructuring has also shifted work from a defined job into more of a spontaneous flow of expertise, invention, and cooperation.

William Bridges, a teacher and consultant, calls this harsh reality "de-jobbing." Where work was once a defined container holding specific expectations and reciprocities, it is now a fluid, unpredictable interchange with few rules, but detailed and great expectations. As mentioned earlier, it is not enough to be an "expert" or a "specialist." In this new way of working, the abilities to interact with other team members, to sell one's skills and expertise, and to manage complex relationships within tight budgets and schedules are as important as the competencies defined by old jobs.

As more and more workers get "de-jobbed," the competition for projects becomes more acute. However, success in those projects requires a great degree of cooperation. How does an individual balance the pressure and urgency of self-interest with the expectations for productive, mutually enhancing collaboration?

While job-hopping and self-employment suggest a greater degree of independence than that enjoyed by current corporate employees, the reality is that interdependence in these new work modes will be even more pronounced.

It is not just those outside the confines of companies who will be experiencing these contradictions. In *Jobshift*, William Bridges explains how the "non-jobs" at Microsoft work: "There are no regular hours; buildings are open to employees twenty-four hours of the day. People work anytime and all the time, with no one keeping track of their hours but with everyone watching their output. They are accountable not to conventional management, but to the project team of which they are a part."

Such a system of work is fraught with painful contradictions. While more democratic, it is also more demanding. While affording more freedom, it also exacts a much deeper commitment. While decreasing authority from "above," it dramatically increases pressure from peers. Although this is in many ways a much more mature way to operate, it also assumes that organizations as well as individuals have the maturity to handle it. Obviously, not all do. Without norms of fairness and reciprocity, such a system can be quickly abused and exploited.

The pain of adjusting to such a system is perhaps not surprising. It seems that every time there is a revolution in how value is created, society needs a period of time to reestablish what is fair. The implicit reciprocities of one system need conscious reconstruction (through trial and error) to take hold in the next. In this period between invention and adjustment, the information economy is sometimes as cruel psychologically as the industrial economy proved to be physically. Obligation, critical to project success, ends abruptly once the assignment is complete. Colleagues in a virtual team, once disbanded, become competitors for the next piece of work.

Expediency is driving teamwork and may burn out the concept of teams. Productivity is the rationale for reciprocity and so will diminish collaboration. Freedom is the latest form of oppression and so will deny for many the joyful potential of new information and technology. While companies struggle for a vision that takes in these paradoxes, and society works through their consequences, many of us must simply get on with making a living. But how do we do that? How do we simultaneously insulate and expose ourselves to this brave old world?

I have three suggestions. First, start within. Self-knowledge, as argued throughout this book, is a personal and competitive imperative. Second, become a brand, using discipline and strategies. Third, respect and nurture personal wisdom.

Looking Inside Ourselves

All of us have the right to live life our own way, on our own terms. The reality, though, is that work and the economy within which livelihood and career are developed are largely out of our control. We can either spend time and energy trying to resist or master what is uncontrollable, or we can define and nurture the essence of who we are as individuals.

Bridges describes the latter option as "integrity" or "wholeness." He explains: "With so much change and fragmentation in the new career world, you need a solid core of self. You have to be true to who you are — to your identity." And the reason for this is that "the integrity/identity frame is capable both of maintaining continuity and continuing change."

Coming to self-knowledge and dealing with the pressures of the workplace is hard work. To manage this tricky process, I have defined three categories of factors that define the current workplace. The first category is the "imposed pressures" affecting us; the second represents the "personal needs" for managing this converging chaos; the third indicates the "opportunities" for the individual (the silver lining in every chaos). In my experience, these factors apply equally to the employed, the managerial, the de-jobbed, and the self-standing value creator. Beside each factor I have identified the specific implication for growth and self-knowledge. These implications are asked as questions to reinforce that each response is individual.

	FACTORS	SELF-KNOWLEDGE IMPLICATIONS
IMPOSED PRESSURES:	FRENZY	POISE
	• No time to think, plan, or reflect. Constant reactivity and fluidity.	• What is your threshold for pressure? • How do you keep cool within that threshold?

• What counterbalance do you need to keep cool after passing that threshold?

COMPETITIVE DRIVE
• Intense competition for projects, resources, capital, and advantage.

SELF-WORTH
• What indeed are your most important strengths?
• How are these focused? Nurtured? Advanced?
• What are your liabilities?
• What is the continuity between your particular strengths and weaknesses?

FALLING BEHIND
• Keeping up with fast-changing business, information, and team priorities.

CURIOSITY
• How do you satisfy your curiosity?
• What core interests most satisfy you?
• How can the lessons or satisfactions of your passions be applied to work?
• What insight has most affected your work?
• How was this learned?

"MORE WITH LESS"
• In productivity, quality, innovation, and benefits, the defining ethic is "more with less."

PROBLEM-SOLVING
• How do you problem-solve?
• What specifically do you like and dislike most about *problems*?
• Which activities most engage your creativity?
• What are the satisfactions you derive from them?
• How strong are your skills of synthesis?

PERSONAL NEEDS:

STAMINA
• The pressures of competition and the convergence of work/learning/leisure require a mental stamina.

PERSEVERANCE
• What are your strengths and weaknesses around patience?
• At what do you persevere? How can this be exercised in both personal growth and career?
• What are the elements converging for you?
• How is this convergence changing your basic assumptions and expectations?

COERCION
• Within companies or as "networkers," individuals must simultaneously collaborate and practice "constructive coercion" to make their contribution.

RESPECT
• How comfortable are you with such give and take?
• What is the particular value beyond functional expertise that you bring to a team?
• How do you value what you do?

251

• How do you extend reciprocity within teams?

• What are your methods for having your contribution accepted and acknowledged by others?

SMART SPEED

• Work happens too fast for full analysis and deliberation. Mistakes are too costly to accept deviation from strategy. Strategic thinking is therefore a sensibility rather than a rationale.

INTUITION

• What is the inner gyroscope that helps you keep your bearings?

• How do you internalize strategy?

• How do you exercise intuition?

• How confident are you in your own "substantial subjectivity"?

• What can you do to develop it more?

SYNERGY

• In a world of fewer boundaries, synergy is less an efficiency than an imperative. The harmonious interaction of many produces results beyond the scope of an individual.

INTERCONNECTIVITY

• What aspects of yourself interconnect comfortably?

• What personal assets are made stronger through such intimate interaction?

• How do you earn trust?

• How do you extend trust to others?

SELF-PROMOTION

• Expertise for individuals is like quality for products. It is now "cost of entry." Workers now need to add value beyond their jobs to earn a place on teams and projects.

STRATEGIC VALUE

• What are the core skills you provide?

• How can you use strengths and interests to achieve "value-added?"

• How do you promote yourself, your skills, and achievements?

• What reputation would be ascribed to you?

PERSONAL GROWTH OPPORTUNITIES:

CREATIVITY

• The removal of barriers, security, and guidelines for traditional career paths in effect reduces the risk for more daring creativity and personal risk-taking.

RISK-RECEPTIVITY

• What are the deeper goals and dreams that would give you the most personal fulfillment?

• What risk(s) have you most regretted not taking? What lessons does this provide?

• How can these interests find expression in your work?

VARIETY

• Jobs and work and careers have little of the old continuity, that opens considerable potential for variety and cross-discipline experience.

EXPERIMENTAL

• What other interests intrigue you?
• How comfortable are you pursuing those? Why?
• How eclectic are you in crossing boundaries?
• What is keeping you or pushing you to pursue new career/job/project/school experience?

EXPOSURE

• The interconnection of individuals in companies and within the larger economy is opening opportunities to form partnerships and associations with a rich mix of creative and capable people.

RECIPROCITY

• From whom have you most learned? How and why?
• With whom would you like to work?
• What were the dynamics of the most constructive partnership or association you've had?
• What do you have that enriches that interaction?
• How does team synergy best use your strengths?

FREEDOM

• A non-regimented work style is more pressured but also affords more freedom in terms of options, time, and network.

CONFIDENCE

• Do you see and relish the freedom?
• What can you do to experience more of it?
• How is the freedom fulfilling? Refreshing?
• How does it restore your balance and creativity?

VOCATION

• Jobs used to be apart from the rest of life. The two now meld, creating the potential of real life work.

MEANING

• What meaning do you derive from work?
• How can this be enriched?
• What brings you joy within work?
• What will you regret not having done?

Certainly, creativity and freedom are real options, but many workers are simply struggling earning a living. Obstacles and pressures are wrenching and disruptive. The next project, particularly when we are unsure of having it, is more important and urgent than the next potential. Time is short. Jobs are few. Personal development can wait.

Can it? Meaning, fulfillment, creativity, and sense of self were once regarded as tangential to one's work life. Now, these are the very attributes essential for earning a role in the economy. Stephen Covey, among a growing number of business teachers, suggests that "core" actually requires this aspect of greater purpose, which he calls "spiritual."

In *The Seven Habits of Highly Effective People*, Covey writes: "Renewing the spiritual dimension provides leadership to your life. The spiritual dimension is your core, your center, your commitment to a value system. It is a very private area of life and supremely important one. It draws upon the sources that inspire and uplift you to the timeless truth of all humanity. And people do it very differently."

As Covey suggests, inner knowledge provides the strength, resiliency, and courage to persist through the change. The habits for success and the values of purpose are now the same.

Viktor Frankl goes even further. In *Man's Search for Meaning*, Frankl explains that inner knowledge is not only what helps people through periods of trial, it is often the very meaning of the suffering: "Not only creativeness and enjoyment are meaningful. If there is a meaning in life, then there must be meaning in suffering. Suffering is an ineradicable part of life, even as fate and death. Without suffering and death human life cannot be complete."

All aspects of life yield opportunities for self-knowledge and growth. As seen in Chapter Two, suffering is not so much a detour on the road to wisdom, as its catalyst. With consciousness, every experience provides insight and learning. In the old economy, each of us earned income from what we *did*. In this new commerce of ideas and relationships, we increasingly earn our livelihood from who we *are*. The more consciousness and depth to that asset, the more valuable it becomes.

Becoming a Brand Apart

As the offerings and operations of various companies assume more human traits like obligation, trustworthiness, and knowledge, human workers will increasingly take on the strategic and value-added qualities of brands.

This may seem like a strange correlation, but it is yet another expression of unexpected convergence. Value is now less a function of doing than of being. Who we are is our "brand" — it is how we provide value. Each individual will have a certain set of functional skills and knowledge to sell; however, his or her value will be set as much by reputation as by competence. Like brands, individuals will forge relationships with customers, seeking to add particular and consistent value in every project or interaction.

Quality is obviously important to reputation: individuals will be required to make the same investment in continuous improvement that is expected of any brand competing for market share. This means individuals must learn — not only on the job, but also in other areas of exploration and discovery. Branding is important for differentiation, so individuals will also need that internal marketing sense to be able to stand apart from others and merchandise their specific expertise.

As uncomfortable as it may seem, self-selling is as important for a self-employed engineer, software writer, or strategic consultant as it is for Tide, Compaq, and Ford. Like product and service brands, individuals will also need to project a whole host of values that are relevant to, and compatible with, those of prospective customers.

This metaphor of personal branding is not meant to dehumanize people, but to bring to consciousness the disciplines for self-management and self-selling. Marketing is the new literacy for a wired world, and branding is its necessity. The key is to learn those disciplines of positioning and leverage, while using the advantages of human awareness and connectedness.

The previous chapter suggests expanding the definition of marketing to include the skills of *interacting*. These include elements that are second nature to us (although often unconscious), as well as those that are strategic.

Essentials for Personal Branding

• *Like a product, individual workers must be clear about the basic value proposition they embody, and how this satisfies their customer's functional criteria.* Comprising knowledge, skills, experience, and expertise, this proposition provides the utility customer-clients are seeking. Specialization, however, risks exactly the compartmentalization that most enterprises want to abolish. The basic task is to deliver the utility in a way that is of greatest service to the client. The ability to empathize with those needs of service are therefore as important as expertise.

Solveig Wikström and Richard Normann warn "of the risks of the fragmentation of knowledge." With acronyms and language of specialization, expertise often makes sense only to the experts, and not to the users. The authors believe that "without any hope of understanding the connections," such knowledge is worthless. The task for the human brand is to enfold the utility of expertise into the empathy that allows connection.

• *What we know is a static value. The task then is to keep evolving value to lead to developments of new opportunity.* The job market is never static, and the needs of those companies and clients that will provide work are never fully met. Just as a brand must continuously invest in R&D to keep its basic offering relevant, so too must workers invest in their own potential.

The goals for this renewal are twofold: to innovate in a specific area that competitors cannot easily duplicate; and to create new competencies that are relevant and of growing value to customers. This is why *interacting* is essential. In the exchange, new skills are developed to match new needs. And new expertise increases appreciation for new value. Both "buyer" and "brand" gain as the interests and passions of the individual provide growth and differentiation.

• *Conceiving and forging a distinct and comfortable strategic space in which to operate.* Successful brands operate inside a defined strategic expectation. This means respecting those qualities that are unique, and not attempting to be "all things to all people."

Strategy has usually been used as a guideline for adherence. In the unbounded and melded world of modern business, strategy must instead serve as a springboard. This means taking developmental steps and creative risks that stretch the basic expertise being offered, but in a way that enhances the relationship with the customer-client.

• *Visibility and self-promotion to telegraph qualities and capabilities.* One of the realities of an environment defined by information is that even non-promotion is a promotion. A brand that does nothing is still affected, even transformed, by those that do (remember the tainting of Ivory by Dove).

Promotion may seem crass, but it is the vehicle for managing reputation. Credentials establish expertise, but only reputation carries the assurance of efficacy. Promotion should not mislead, for anything that risks or destroys trust is truly value-depleting. Promotion is how we interact, before the actual work of project management and team building.

• *Provide a "package of meaning."* Brands encode messages about attitudes, style, and capability, as well as utility. This gestalt confers a certain meaning to the buyer. An Apple computer and a PC clone both operate word-processing programs, but the meaning of the brand speaks differently to the creativity and attitude of the respective users.

Human brands have the same semiotic potential. Customer-clients are themselves changed by the resources they deploy. By interacting, we provide not only a service, but also a meaning about the intention, integrity, and perspective of the organization. Therefore, the values we represent reflect the needs and biases of those who engage us.

Essentials for Interacting

• *Earn trust.* The quality of the exchange between customer-client and service provider is determined by trust. Creating such mutuality is a matter of obligations. In a conventional work structure these are often assumed or taken for granted. In interaction, obligations and their personal accountabilities must be consciously managed. Every word and action either contributes or depletes trust.

• *Keep promises.* Product brands offer benefits. Individuals exchange value on the basis of promises. The difference is more than semantic. Promises provide a personal connection for a more expansive interaction. Both reputation and quality of offering are determined by promises kept.

If value in the new economy is created through trust, then promises are its currency and reputation its capital.

• *Extend generosity.* As the seller, the human brand must initiate the exchange of value. Generosity is not giving something away for free, but it involves giving something with no strings attached as an investment in reputation and trust.

Customer-clients are as inundated with information as anyone. They, too, are bombarded with marketing and selling communication. Knowledge workers can be generous by avoiding piling up more information, and instead providing higher forms of synthesis and understanding. With the expiry date on knowledge moving ever closer, sharing what we know is a way to extend value from a shrinking asset.

Branding is a discipline. Such structure affords more control in the area of career management that has often been only casually attended to. Bill Etherington expressed the new reality for all of us when he said: "We're trying to impress on our employees that IBM is no longer responsible for their careers. We'll provide tools and training, but their careers are now up to them."

In addition to doing business, many individuals must now master the skills for running their own business. Planning, thinking strategically, measuring performance, and formalizing learning are among the disciplines entailed. These, however, are not enough: a business of one shares with a corporation of many the need for a guiding vision.

This is common advice — figure out what you want to do before expending time and reacting to the agenda of others. Few individuals, however, need to go through the strategic gymnastics that most companies consider necessary for vision. Before "vision" was co-opted to stand for "big objective" or "single core competency," it used to imply a spiritual awakening. Oxford defines vision as "something which is apparently seen otherwise than by ordinary sight; an appearance of a prophetic or mystical character, or having the nature of a revelation, supernaturally presented to the mind in sleep, or in an abnormal state."

As a revelation, vision cannot be logically assembled or induced. It must be peeled away layer by layer, with the same determination required for exploring the self. This is where the branding of the personal company and its greater human fulfillment again merge. Self-knowledge is the strategy as well as the payout.

Using Wisdom as Equity

In his 1991 speech "What Is a Company For?," Charles Handy expressed the view that "owning people is wrong. Companies are collections of people these days; they are communities, not properties." Workers in more structured companies may particularly relate to this insight; however, its truth applies equally to those who are self-employed.

While not a community, the self-employed have felt the same pressures that have forced virtually every organization to squeeze out higher productivity. As a result, the self-employed can work their own assets as fiercely as any corporation, often with the same disregard for the long term.

This distortion is understandable. A company of one does not have the base of resources over which to spread pressures. In addition to earning a living, the single worker carries the responsibility for the line of credit, quality control, new business creation, and company pension plan.

When you are your only asset, it is perhaps even easier to make the mistakes characteristic of corporations. Since the buck always and only stops with you, it is natural to expect too much and to sacrifice too much. When you work at home, it is hard not to be "always on." And when you work alone, it is difficult not to be a little anxious about where the next project will come from. Because there is no one else, you, the company brand, have to do what is needed to get the job done. After all, it is your reputation on the line. No wonder anxiety and fatigue dominate the corporate culture of so many single-person enterprises.

Overextended and undernourished, many people are finding that working for themselves can bring out their toughest boss. Balance and compassion toward employees are not automatic impulses just because a company only has one. Consciousness must still be raised; obligations must still be defined; reciprocity must still be applied. Conventional companies need wisdom for renewal; companies of one need it for basic sustainability.

The shape of this balance and context are in some ways unique for the self-employed. From my own experience, and from observing others, I have identified the following issues and considerations.

• **Definition of self:** When we stop working for a company and start working for ourselves, several identity issues come into play. The first is self-perception once the titles, meetings, office trappings, and business cards of a conventional job no longer apply. There is often an uncomfortable adjustment to the removal of the familiar, even when we ourselves have made the decision to go it alone. It only makes sense that when you invest of yourself in a job, you feel some separation when that ends. The second identity issue is the blurring of distinctions between work and personal life. As work and life become life-work, the distinctions that give dimension to the self also get blurred.

It is important to have a sense of purpose for life. This will be different for each individual, but it provides the bearings with which we can go through dramatic change without getting lost.

• **Extremes of productivity:** When self-employed, especially in the early days, there often seem to be pronounced swings between "feast and famine." When work comes, it tends to be urgent and all-consuming. When it stops, the void can be agonizing. This unnerving unpredictability is a feature of work without bounds and pressures without logic.

With no sense of balance, the priorities of work can become abusive. Balance depends on perspective — on a sense for the whole range of activities. This is not easy. The perception is well ingrained that when busy, we are valued. To be unoccupied is therefore an implicit rejection or devaluation. Developing balance is therefore a function of developing new skills, as well as unlearning old attitudes and judgments.

Among the new skills is knowing when to give yourself a break. As we saw in company ethics, compassion toward self is a prerequisite for extending it to others. It will not be easy to collaborate with other virtual workers if you have been practicing dictatorial management on yourself.

• **Confidence:** Just because the old job track has been removed does not mean that human beings have outgrown some of its more basic contents. Mileposts for progress, review, and feedback, and opportunities for growth and development remain important motivators and benchmarks.

As these are shorn away in the unbounding of business, individuals will need to calibrate their own measurements. As the progression in wise growth gains momentum, the source of confidence shifts from being what we do to who we are.

• **A wider perspective:** Companies, through conflict and collaboration, at least make available to workers a perspective wider than their own. The self-employed are not hermits, but they do tend to focus on the expertise that provides them with currency.

Wise people are not all-knowing, but more than average people, they do know more clearly what they don't know. This awareness of not knowing is often sacrificed by experts to the details of specialization. The value of expertise is only enhanced by context, so the challenge in making a living selling what we know is to be humble enough to accept and acknowledge the bigger picture.

• **New business development:** There are two basic types of new business, and both are nurtured by breadth. This first is the business we earn from existing client-customers. The obligations we fulfill, the interconnections we establish, and the trust we develop are investments in a future relationship.

The second type is the new business from a totally new client-customer. As knowledge depreciates and expertise becomes more generic, obligations demonstrate a critical difference. A reputation for mindfulness, accountability, and constructive interaction is an important calling card in a time when the control of structure is dissipating.

• **R&R and R&D:** Any enterprise needs new ideas just to remain current with customers, who are themselves continuously advancing within a changing market. For the self-employed, the priorities of the day are often so consuming that little time is available to revitalize the basic offering. Rest is also overlooked as a necessary creative resource because it is easier to see the productivity in doing. The net result is an exhausted individual with an exhausted asset.

Creative regeneration for a company of one involves developing personal skills and insights. What nourishes the individual renews the commercial enterprise.

The concept of career is changing, bringing as always both problems and potential. The dislocation is real for individual entrepreneurs and for workers in radically transformed companies. The new "network" is often very damaging to self-esteem and confidence. Team members or participants in a virtual company are expected to deliver higher quality at greater efficiency at lower price. This equation means that individuals must give more to stay in the game, without assurance that they will get as much back.

So far, the system of new work runs on a deficit that is being funded by individuals. They are initiating interaction, giving more than they receive, and achieving productivity gains in excess of their out-take. The exchange may become more reciprocal once the network economy is up and running, and its rules and regulations are clear. The issue for workers inside and outside companies is to replenish the "more" that they are being asked to give. With no external sources for this replenishment, there is no alternative but to draw it from within.

This is what will begin to ultimately redress the balance. In the scenario envisioned by Peter Drucker, the independent knowledge workers — and not the companies — will have leverage in the new value exchange. In another of those wisdom paradoxes, the more interdependence is practiced, the more freedom ensues. As companies themselves shed hierarchy and gain wisdom in practicing networked value creation, their generosity will be required to attract the most capable and creative of the solo corporations. Reciprocity is ultimately contagious. At this point the opportunities of the new economy finally overtake its pressures and setbacks.

To participate in this new economy requires the courage of knowing what you want, supported by the conviction of knowing who you are. The possibilities in the new economy have yet to be defined, but their scope and potential are already being cast in what we realize from within.

AN EXERCISE IN CAREER PERSPECTIVE

WORKING WISDOM	IMPLICATION FOR JOB/CAREER
PERSPECTIVE	
Timelessness	• The perspective of what one has in terms of experience fused with the desire for what one seeks.
	• A sense of continuity, drawing from even casual experiences a connection to a wider ambition.
Clarity and Focus	• Self-knowledge, since self is the asset.
	• Clear understanding of needs and goals that fulfill personal as well as professional ambitions.
	• Self-confidence — the capital for the personal company.
Compassionate	• Respect for personal needs.
Detachment	• Empathy for those of others.
	• Understanding for interdependence.
	• Appreciation for sharing gain and sacrifice.
VALUES	
Truth and Honesty	• Deep commitment to truth in all interactions.
	• Honesty in action to build an unimpeachable reputation.
Justice	• Fairness in ideal and in practice: with peers, colleagues, customers.
	• Commitment to reciprocity.
ACTION	
Unity and Integration	• Understanding the interconnections and continuities of the network within which one works.
Intellectual and	• Respect for diversity of inner needs.
Emotional Harmony	• Respect for the totality of human needs of others.
Equanimity	• The inner balance during periods of both sacrifice and success.
SUPPORT	
Substantial Subjectivity	• Development of personal judgment and perspicacity.
	• Using the substance of knowledge and experience to create innovative solutions.
Mentorship	• Sharing knowledge with others.
	• Immersing one's self in a lifetime of learning.

Epilogue

Seeking Truth in a World of Facts

If Solomon was right when he suggested that wisdom comes halfway to those who seek it, how do we close the rest of the gap?

Despite the breadth of knowledge available to us, we seem as bereft of wisdom as any generation that preceded ours. And despite the wiring, technology, and networks, we seem as divided and isolated as ever. Where lies the breakthrough? Saint Bonaventure, the thirteenth-century theologian, writer, and teacher, may have provided counsel for us when he described wisdom as "unlearned ignorance."

Unlearned Ignorance

This definition has three challenging implications. First, ignorance would seem to be the preferred state. Bonaventure was an intellectual who tried to balance the self-absorption needed for learning with his vows of poverty and service. In his view, what we learn often takes us away from our natural state of being wise. The assumption is that every person starts with "ignorance," or a blank slate, which represents the latent potential for wisdom. Peeling away the knowledge that has soiled our ignorance is the unlearning needed to reconnect us to our deeper potential.

Second, the unlearning implies that wisdom is not something that can be consciously accumulated and deposited in the personal capability bank. Wisdom is not an achievement of intellectual rigor, but one of opening. It requires taking down those boundaries, established by what we know, to experience the connection with our deeper humanity. Since we can only unlearn it, we must trust that our beliefs will guide us in discerning and expressing wisdom.

The third implication is instructive: Undo, untangle, unvalue, unlearn the knowledge, facts, attitudes, and perceptions that keep us from our own birthright. To get wise, get going.

Bonaventure is a tough read, but knows of which he speaks. As minister general, he saved the order founded by Saint Francis of Assisi from complete disintegration. Like many organizations, the Franciscans floundered after the death of their inspirational founder. The passionate views and spiritual simplicity of Francis attracted thousands of people from across Europe to join the order. Bonaventure struggled with the issue familiar to many managers: retaining the original vision while imposing enough structural discipline to sustain the organization. He succeeded in melding idealism with practicality, and is regarded as the second founder of the order that revolutionized the Church.

Unlearning is not as easy as learning. Once our beliefs, assumptions, and knowledge are established, it is very hard to overcome their familiarity and bias. Learning is a process of adding on and building up. Unlearning involves shedding. In our business world in particular, information is still generally regarded as power, so unlearning sounds like a distinctly noncompetitive thing to do. Yet there is a basic wisdom to this.

Management renewal so far has followed the conventional learning assumption, trying to add by training new disciplines, approaches, and attitudes. Real progress seems to have escaped most who invested in these initiatives. One reason is that the new learning, however valid, was laid upon old beliefs. This layering of knowledge on bias creates dissonance and eventually undermines progress, renewal, and genuine learning.

Unlearning, however, is not an action of retreat. In fact, it requires considerable confidence and self-awareness. To unlearn means that we know ourselves well enough to identify and release those aspects and attitudes of character that undermine our ability to grow. While learning requires that we look outside of ourselves for new stimulus and information, unlearning starts inside. Instead of adding new knowledge, unlearning involves subtracting tired beliefs and assumptions. Instead of stretching memory with more input, unlearning demands reflective stripping away of dysfunctional and obsolete attitudes and misconceptions.

Unlearning works back from effect to cause. It is the deconstruction of what *we know* to better understand *who we are*.

For all the intelligence applied to business, for all the new thinking that appears in seminars, journals, and books, there remains much to be "unlearned" before companies can fully master the wise "ignorance" for surviving in the new economy. Paradigm shifts are so lethal not because of what we do not know, but for how fervently we persist in adhering to what we do know. What we know often makes us blind to new ideas; it keeps us connected to where we are. What we know often makes us presumptive. So, without unlearning, change remains superficial and renewal continues to be elusive.

Ignorance in this context is not "dumb." It is the absence of the learning that distorts our perspective or dissuades us from pursuing our own wisdom. Ignorance is latent potential. It is the honesty to realize that what we do not know cannot hurt us as much as what we think we know unequivocally. The wise are always more respectful of what they do not know than proud of what they do. Ignorance in Bonaventure's unlearning involves an honest and deep sense of self.

The chart below expands on the implications of unlearned ignorance.

TRADITIONAL LEARNING	UNLEARNED IGNORANCE
• Accumulation of new facts	• Shedding old beliefs
• Outside stimulus stretches horizons	• Inside reflection creates depth
• Development of memory	• Development of consciousness
• Facts paint a picture	• Room to view context
• Driven by curiosity to know	• Driven by need for meaning
• Goal is knowledge	• Goal is process
• Makes sense of outer reality	• Makes sense of inner reality

Where Do We Go from Here?

For companies that have stumbled in implementing something as basic as quality management, it would seem to be a hopeless challenge to seek improvements on all the dimensions that describe wisdom.

How can an individual or company be simultaneously just, truthful, and compassionate, competitive, subjective, and committed to endless learning?

This despair reflects that undermining impatience: How can I do all of that right away, or fast enough to get the best results?

Wisdom is something that accrues only over time. It has great potential for reward but at the price of its own, deliberate pace. In fact, it seems that if we rush wisdom, we spoil it. King David, the resplendent ruler of ancient Israel, was precociously wise. But although he had the insight and perspective of wisdom, he was unable to contain his own arrogance because of his immaturity, so he suffered the ignominy of losing his throne.

While it has biblical connotations, wisdom is of immediate and practical benefit. For business, its deliberate consciousness is already being embraced by necessity. After studying more than one hundred companies undergoing transformation, John Kotter concluded that "the most general lesson to be learned from the more successful cases is that the change process goes through a series of phases that, in total, usually require a considerable length of time. Skipping steps creates only the illusion of speed and never produces a satisfying result."

Truth takes time to be discovered and understood. Trust takes time to be earned. Justice and compassion take time to demonstrate. Mindfulness takes time to practice. All of the important and highly effective human capabilities that affect real and successful change simply take time to come to fruition.

This does not mean that the payback for wisdom is only long term, delayed until far into the future. On the contrary, the results are instantaneous. Mindfulness provides an immediate shift in consciousness. It will take time to develop all of the proficiencies, but thoughtful behavior and interaction will bear very quick returns.

The fact that companies are even willing to lay out a program for long-term mindfulness starts the process of re-earning the credibility of employees that has been so dissipated by the many "quick-start, fast-stop" management fads. Honesty begets honesty. Clarity begets clarity. Commitment begets commitment. Over time, those returns only become more substantial. The task is to get on with the unlearning.

Each individual and company will have its own ignorance (potential) to realize. Each will have its own unlearning to do. What follows are issues I believe especially warrant the peeling away that is needed for genuine growth and renewal. In my view, we must unlearn the following:

- *What it means to be* self-sufficient *even as we are all forced to more than ever "go it alone."*
Looking after ourselves in an economy of interdependence means looking after the needs of others. When we make the team succeed,

we succeed. When customers are extended more service and value than they expect, they reciprocate with trust. When we plug into project networks, our reputation for collaboration means even more than our expertise. The ultimate self-sufficiency ironically comes from realizing our ultimate dependencies.

• *What it means to be* knowledgeable, *even as information becomes generic and therefore less valuable.*

Getting smarter by keeping up is almost impossible. While we need to renew the information we use, it is the knowledge about our own self, our own capabilities, that makes us more effective in ambiguity. As always, it is not what we know but what we do with it that counts.

• *What it means to exercise* control, *even as ambiguity and unpredictability become the new norms for operating.*

Empowerment has largely fallen down in the cracks between two paradigms. Accountability to customers collided with the construct of organizational power. What we have not yet unlearned is that there can be no empowerment unless power is released and rechanneled. Control, in the sense of responsibility and results, is still important; however its dictates must give way to obligation and mutuality.

• *What it means to be* competitive, *even as differentiation gets harder and global pressure becomes more intense.*

To compete used to mean to "beat." Today, it means continuous interaction with a spectrum of individuals and organizations — sometimes even competitors. Sharing to win and sharing the win have become the hallmarks of the new competitiveness. This requires undoing the behaviors focused on exclusive advantage and adopting those of partnership and collaboration.

• *What it means to be* productive, *even as efficiency becomes the defining benchmark for global competitiveness.*

In a market in which relationship is the goal and interaction the means, efficiency is less important than generosity. What we give of ourselves, our knowledge, creativity, and accountability may include efficiency, but is not defined by it. Rather than valuing the minimum that goes into input (efficiency), we must learn to value the maximum that can be realized in output (relating).

• *What it means to operate with* urgency, *even as innovation and information come on stream ever faster.*

There is no shortcut for unlearning what has been ingrained. Self-development just takes time. The good news is that what we achieve in the process toward wisdom enhances our substantive adaptability and responsiveness. Even just seeking to be wise makes an important and lasting difference.

• *What it means to build* relationships, *even as teams and customer focus assume greater importance for success.*

The priorities of transaction and project are not those of relationship. Trust is more important than either value or expertise. And the common interest is more important than the individual. We need to unlearn "what's in it for me?" because that depends on "what's in it for others?"

• *What it means to invest in* personal development, *even as skills and knowledge suffer the continuous attrition of obsolescence.*

Unlearning devalues what we have mastered to appreciate more fundamentally who we are. This knowledge remains constant and increases in value, even as information ages and expertise is surpassed by invention. Growth is important, and curiosity is its agent. The key is to desire what we really need. Robert Grundin writes: "Without self-knowledge, or at least without the effort to attain it, we exist merely as higher animals, blind to our weakness, unguided in our strength, possessed of temporal power yet subject to the tyranny of instinct and the fictions of pride." This means that it is what we know from within that provides the only certitude, the only security, for what is happening around us.

Unlearning in Action

All of us are charged with renewing our work and often recreating our careers. As never before, we are also responsible for stretching ourselves to absorb the new skills and competencies that keep our value current. This is a disturbing situation for many, but it also affords great opportunity. Because the economy has so abruptly changed the conditions for job security, we as individuals can actually redefine what it means to be secure. Rather than rely on external institutions, we can start creating the more enduring and fulfilling security that comes from within.

To be of value to others, we must first be of value to ourselves. This requires self-knowledge and self-appreciation. As the outer reality of society, the economy, and the job market grow more complex and insecure, inner clarity and meaning are critically important. These are the ballast that keeps us steady during such stormy transitions. From within we also find the balance, the perspective, and the truth giving real purpose and satisfaction to our lives.

Although there is a price to pay in forfeiting gold watches and regular paycheques, the economy of ideas provides people with the opportunity to make a living while also making a difference. In valuing knowledge and creativity, the new economy allows us to explore and achieve a deeper potential as human beings. Like never before, the clarity we earn for ourselves also earns for us a vital place in the exploding business of knowledge and relationships. This is a richer commerce, one fraught with problems and displacements. But it is also one in which human potential provides the ultimate value. We are still learning how to enhance this commerce. And we are still unlearning how to outgrow the old valuation and measurement of hard assets.

To seek wisdom as a way to earn a livelihood, as a means to improve the culture and performance of our enterprises, is an immensely liberating potentiality. Some will argue that this is overly optimistic. And indeed the chances are that we will stumble our way along this path, just as have the majority of humans before us. However, while the distractions and hardships are many, the choice is still ours. Unless we seek wisdom, we have no chance of attaining it. Unless we strive for meaning, we have no right to find it.

To be wise is itself never a complete achievement. There is always more to unlearn, to absorb, to synthesize, and to create. John the Evangelist writes that "the mouth of the just man murmurs wisdom." That is probably the best we can hope for. To seek it; to grow a little wise; and to murmur the occasional insight. This is not a depreciation. Because wisdom is a work in progress, it enriches the everyday. Because it reveals itself in the mundane, the details of work, interaction, relationship, and growth become fulfilling.

A capacity we all share as individuals is now one that also has economic and organizational value. Regardless of our expertise or title, education or income, unlearning is the expansive job description we all share.

Appendix I

Principles for a Working Wisdom

Writing about business involves various presumptions. Companies are complex and ever shifting. One company may be a paragon of a certain behavior, but its motives or processes may not necessarily align with those of the person doing the analysis. Another company may have a different philosophy or approach, but that does not negate the validity of its own corporate wisdom. To take lessons from either is therefore an act of interpretation.

Many business people have been expressing frustration with the "management fad of the month." New ideas tend to be hyped as the ultimate solution. While generally containing valid insights and remedies, the new concepts inevitably involve some disruption and great effort. Their return is often unclear, and many managers lose hope and seek the next remedy.

Idea mavens push their "big solutions" because business people are looking for the "big idea." The willingness of the customer to see their problems in monochrome allows the provider to promise the single solution. However, if we are honest about the difficulties of business, the unpredictability of change, and the deeper needs of people, we will realize that any shortcut on the path to renewal only cuts us short. Change is too important to assume that it can be measured out in the precise teaspoonfuls of a recipe.

Before writing this book I established some principles to help guide my progression through analysis and recommendation. These principles reflect the human complexity of business and may provide readers with some guidance in using the ideas and concepts of *Working Wisdom*.

1. *Individuals must chart their own course for wisdom*. The bravado of many management doctrines for renewal is to assume that an idea can apply across a wide spectrum of circumstances. In reality, businesses are too different, with diverse needs and pressures, for generalized models.

In fostering individual and organizational wisdom, the differences that frustrate off-the-rack solutions are the very ones that can serve customization and the sharpening of truly competitive competencies. Therefore, the ideas in this book are not prescriptions; they serve as catalysts for reflecting and questioning within ourselves to bring out the most distinctive and effective solutions.

2. *Since there is no definitive "how to" for this process, every one must work toward his or her own realization*. There are no degrees in wisdom. There are no certifications to define its standards, nor associations to regulate its practice. While each of us will realize some wisdom just from the setbacks and surprises of life, very few will attain that level acknowledged and admired as wise.

The discrepancy between a capability that is almost universal and an achievement that is so rare suggests that wisdom is less a gift than a craft. This is a dynamic implied by the title, *Working Wisdom*. Wisdom is indeed a capability that works, advancing our effectiveness as business people. But it also requires *working* — that we invest in the demanding discipline of self-exploration.

3. *The process of developing wisdom is not random, but involves deliberate reflection and conscious practice*. Wisdom is a craft that must be honed; effort and commitment are its principal qualifications. Most human beings are born with sufficient capacity for wisdom to be able to discern it. Many also yearn for it. Yet only a few take on the rigors of rehearsal and practice.

In the frenzy of the current productivity obsession, many of us are seeking solutions to macro problems at the micro level of incremental improvement. Unless we step back and develop a deeper understanding of the changes imposed on us, we risk the ceaseless reactivity that is so tiring and depleting.

4. *While companies may learn some basics about wise behavior from others, the responsibility and deeper learning potential comes from within*. To give context

and relevance to this concept of wisdom it has been necessary to use the device of case histories. Many of the companies used as examples are ones that I have worked with directly; some I have studied and served as a consultant; and others I have read about and analyzed through this prism of wisdom. My exploration taught me much — most importantly, how hard it is to draw definitive and comprehensive lessons from other organizations:

- Even the wisest of companies occasionally do foolish things. The scandal at Kidder Peabody, involving $350 million in false profits, showed that despite its organizational clarity and innovation, General Electric still suffered from all too human blind spots.
- Even the most mistake-ridden organization often contains a formidable reservoir of good judgment. For all the marketing and strategic missteps that plagued IBM, the good judgment and capability of its employees remain a vast and resilient asset.
- No matter how intimately one works with a company, the details of its culture and the depth of its wisdom remain mysterious.

Holding up other companies as models to emulate is therefore not nearly as effective a learning tool as management teaching claims it to be. The key is to view the story and its lessons as *inspiration* — not as a general prescription.

5. *The value of wisdom applies equally to the full range of occupations in both the conventional and virtual economy.* Wisdom is first and foremost an individual capacity, so its value is as compelling for the self-employed consultant as for the corporate careerist. While every job requires greater specialization, knowledge, and know-how, value is only created in an interaction. The more complex and virtual these interactions become, the wiser we need to be to realize their fullest potential.

6. *The language of wisdom is the language of the human spirit, and it warrants as much respect as understanding.* Business has a history of chewing up the language of the human spirit without absorbing its lessons and responsibilities. Out of the "search for excellence," companies scrambled to create moving "mission" statements. As they extended the search to include a winning "culture," companies also adopted the "values" that commit them to the "service" of customers and the "empowerment" of employees. Executives seeking to hone leadership skills followed the renewal pattern, memorizing the principles of "vision" and "ethics." All of this progress in mining the human spirit

for management inspiration, while occasionally successful, has more often than not turned out to be superficial, and in some cases, flatly hypocritical.

Wisdom, while it holds great promise for renewal, requires that a company engage at an even deeper level the human capacity for reason, emotion, and spiritual development. To casually churn this quest for meaning into a momentary management fad risks a far deeper dislocation, and a far more permanent alienation among employees and customers than any previous betrayal of trust.

7. In an economy of knowledge, productivity initiatives hinge on expanding the human potential of an organization. Cost-cutting and reengineering have served companies that have fallen behind and are trying to catch up to a new economic reality. However, business is ultimately about creating value — not just maximizing its efficiency. Such creation is the product of the intelligence, imagination, and intuition of individuals.

While almost every company understands the strategic importance of knowledge, few have come to terms with the resulting shift in power. Without the wisdom to understand and manage this expanding interdependence, the universally admired objectives for "empowered employees" and "enduring customer relationships" risk becoming the latest corporate oxymorons.

Appendix II

Questions of Practicality

The ideas included in *Working Wisdom* have taken shape in my consulting work. With several clients I have "test marketed" the basic expressions of corporate wisdom, as well as some of my models and recommendations. Through this very valuable interchange I was able to refine the basic premise of the book. Importantly, I also heard a consistent chorus of questions about wisdom in business practice. These may reflect some of the concerns or issues of readers, so I have included them, along with a brief discussion, below.

Can organizations be wise?

Yes. As human creations, companies inherit both the foibles and possibilities of people. At their best, companies represent a rush of intelligence and intuition, of imagination and potentiality. Without waiting for the specific guidance of the leader, such companies react and respond to opportunities with the courage and conviction that comes from a collective wisdom.

Once the snub of brutal jokes, British Airlines achieved a remarkable metamorphosis in large part by unleashing the judgment of its own people. Poor service was not a function of old equipment or inadequate systems, but of an attitude. In extending respect to their employees, BA was able to elicit from them the respect toward customers that is fundamental to service. The force of this respect increased passenger volumes and profitability for BA for over a decade.

Respect, because it acknowledges interdependence, is a sign of wider perspective. Still, beyond the issue of reciprocity, is this a real example of corporate wisdom? Here is the progression that shows it.

• All airlines have the obvious data about customer needs, particularly about the requirement of business travelers for punctuality. This is *factual* intelligence.
• Many airlines see the relation between a delay and satisfaction scores. This is *knowledge* intelligence, because data have been created into an insight.
• Some airlines actually empathize with the pressures created by delay, offering extended information about schedules, or, as in the case of Virgin Airlines, providing free limousine service to and from the airport. This is *understanding* intelligence because insight has led to empathy and action.
• Only a very few airlines use the facts, knowledge, and understanding to reverse the power flow within the company so that the customer is served by employees, who themselves are served by management. This is the *wisdom* intelligence that fosters, for example, all SouthWest employees from the CEO to pilots to help accommodate customers at check-in.

Even when the insight is obvious, its practice is demanding. All airlines understand that differentiation and customer satisfaction are realized in those "moments of truth" between staff and traveler, but very few have been able to overcome the paradigm of conflict between management and unions to achieve real and lasting service. The staggering losses of airlines reflect not only the overcapacity of the industry, but the essential disrespect of operators toward employees and customers. The difference between winners like British Airways and SouthWest Airlines and losers like US Air and Alitalia is not airplanes, but humility, respect, and self-confidence.

These are the ingredients of culture. Often talked about, culture is assumed to be the soft part of business, but it is among the hardest of aspects to define and affect to change. Anthropologist C. Turner describes this inculturation in "The Theory and Philosophy of Organizations." He writes: "Culture in work is essentially a creative process, whether the culture maker is a laborer, a machinist or a managing director . . . culture makers are inventors, storytellers, mythologists, makers of possibilities . . . In these aspects of behavior they do not produce outcomes but openings." Culture is that reservoir of self-knowledge that sustains a company in good times and bad.

Although it is critical, culture is not that malleable. Like changing personality, changing culture requires digging away at the apparent habits and behaviors to gain understanding of deeper motives and beliefs. A wise company is culturally attuned to its own purpose, meaning, and obligations. Even companies with productive and successful cultures sometimes continue to struggle with this nurturing of deeper wisdom.

In Donald Katz's book, *Just Do It*, Nike manager and "officer without portfolio," Tinker Hatfield complains: "The matrix [structure] is killing brilliant insights. As enlightened as this company is, a lot of people inside it are not. They will analyze you out of doing something which comes from the gut — even though gut emotions is supposed to be our specialty. I don't see much risk taking."

Culture, as the expression of corporate wisdom, is therefore in constant development. In the push and pull of business, if wisdom is not advancing, it is then retreating. This is why culture requires the constant attention of example and reinforcement.

Teamwork is how a culture builds its muscles. In their important book on high-performance organizations, *The Wisdom of Teams*, Jon Katzenbach and Douglas Smith list five vital components for teamwork:

1. "a set of themes that convey meaning";
2. "enthusiasm";
3. "stories";
4. "personal commitment"; and
5. "performance."

I have taken these dimensions and related them to the wisdom that each encodes and expresses.

- *Meaning* comes from moral purpose, from what Anthony Altos of Harvard and Richard Paschale of Stanford call "superordinate goals." "The underlying beliefs about 'the good' in culture are honored — including such things as honesty and fairness." These goals provide personal fulfillment for individuals, as well as a "compass" for guiding group action.
- *Enthusiasm* comes from confidence and a sense of belonging — of making a difference. This word suggests the energetic involvement of smiles at McDonald's, but, according to Oxford, enthusiasm actually means "to be inspired or possessed by a god — a supernatural inspiration, prophetic or poetic ecstasy." The enthusiastic employee is therefore a conduit as well as contributor to a company's wisdom.
- *Stories* encode the principles, passing on the examples and wisdom of previous performers to shape attitudes and expectations today. Shoshana Zuboff explains the continuing relevance of stories in our technocratic work

environments: "To the extent that skilled practice eludes codification, it provides a living resource for the preservation of oral culture. In each of the workplaces I have discussed, significant dimensions of oral culture have been sustained, drawing their strength in part from the production and reproduction of action-centered skills. In this way, the degree of orality that surrounds a set of practices is also related to the degree of power and autonomy enjoyed by its practitioners."

The wisdom in stories provides more than anecdotal reinforcement of culture. Stories provide the confidence to assume the full responsibility of empowerment.

• *Commitment* comes from obligation, not just "buy-in." While companies have encouraged participation, many confuse the process of involvement with the ethic of commitment. The moral thrust of commitment is clear in Mary Parker Follett's explanation: "Collective responsibility is not something you get by adding up one by one all the different responsibilities. Collective responsibility is not a matter of adding but of interweaving, a matter of reciprocal modification brought about by the interweaving. It is not a matter of aggregation but of integration."

• *Performance*, including profit, is the essential, practical proof that wisdom works. All creative activity seeks a completion, a result, and a profit. The wise do not neglect the result, nor do they underappreciate the importance of the reserve that profit represents. Performance sustains commitment. It is one of the stories and a source for enthusiasm and a part of the meaning. Profit is important, but only as one of several interconnected, equally important influences.

How is company wisdom nurtured?

By example and by consistency. One small step at a time. The upheaval in the economy seems to invite dramatic action against a grand new strategy. In reality, upheaval requires the steadfastness that comes from self-knowledge, self-confidence, and deep character. Exploring this in *Executive Leadership*, Professor Elliott Jaques and consultant Stephen Clement write: "Wisdom can be developed in people. Its development can be reinforced and enhanced, especially by good mentoring by a more senior person." Conscious and deliberate recognition, required for self-knowledge, are also the basis of organizational wisdom.

The companies that thrive in even the most daunting circumstances have been true to themselves first. The deeper the self-knowledge of such organizations, the more adaptable they become. Collins and Porras attribute the consistent innovation, growth, and profitability of leaders like Boeing, Motorola, General Electric, and Wal-Mart to a simple dynamic: "Preserve the core and stimulate progress." In the context of wisdom, because the essentials of character do not change, a company is allowed the most flexibility to change the products, services, and even businesses in order to shift with opportunity.

As already discussed, growing wise on a human basis involves "ascending" to discover new truths and ideals, and then "descending" to practice and apply those insights in the real world. Wise companies also grow through such repeated stretching and applying. These companies start with goals that ennoble the human spirit as well as enrich the bottom line.

Sony's spirit of discovery, Merck's commitment to health and service to humanity, and Apple's goal to revolutionize computers by making them accessible to everyone are a few of the broader pursuits that give companies more impact than their simple commerciality. When such goals are inbred, the traditions and interactions within a company automatically merge the priorities of specific projects with the obligations to the higher purpose. There is no split nor trade-off.

This higher consciousness does not simply sit in strategy meetings, but permeates actions and decisions. The truth in the ideal is taught and learned every day in the practical solutions to problems, in the complex and messy progress on projects, and in genuine gestures of understanding and commitment. With wisdom, there is no separation between "strategy" and "tactic." The act of doing proves the truth, and the truth comes out in the act of doing.

Wise companies draw on the moral precepts and, more importantly, the moral examples of their leaders. Again, this morality is not derived from grand gestures and noble statements, but from example. Reflecting his own deeply held spiritual convictions, Konosuke Matsushita applied such Confucian and Buddhist values as harmony, solidarity, discipline, and dedication to create the largest electronics company in the world.

In *Not for Bread Alone*, Matsushita explains: "We have no way of knowing what is absolutely correct or of judging the truth. It is impossible to teach your employees how to assess a situation correctly. But you can tell them always to remember the importance of sound judgment, and they can learn by experience. The person with a sense of self is aware of his own imperfections and, at the same time he is determined to be accurate in his assessment of a situation. Without those qualities, including the willingness to keep trying, he will not go far in business."

The quest for truth, the honest acknowledgment of limitation, the ability to untangle ego from decisions, and the determination to persist are among the qualities that reflect a working wisdom. The task in seeking wisdom, as it is for improving quality, is to see the great value and importance in even the smallest action.

Buddhist writers explain that all words and actions are interconnected. What I say changes those I speak to. What I do affects not only my life, but those of my family, colleagues, industry associates. In Buddhist logic, there are no casual words or deeds because even the smallest action has a big impact on the collective well-being.

Christ taught that a sin occurred in the thought of sin. The heightened consciousness asked for in these instructions is not to impose a micro-policing on human behavior, but to respect the profound interdependence of work, society, and life. Every worker affects other workers, as well as customers, quality, and profitability. The greater the efficiency an organization achieves, the greater that impact of one individual worker on the whole.

Sogyal Rinpoche calls this consciousness the "wisdom of ordinariness." Setting targets for quality or productivity, many companies have not had the good sense or patience to attend to the "ordinary." Even the talk about cultural change has often failed to respect that this collective energy is not driven by values, but by the thousands of actions, words, meetings, and outcomes reflecting those values.

Organizational structures, even those for flattened, more responsive companies, still use boxes and lines to detail authority and define process. The process for work, as it is for wisdom, is much messier, involving ripples affecting ripples affecting ripples. The ordinary cannot be taken for granted because each word of direction, and each negotiation for agreement, holds the potential for an extraordinary expression of wisdom.

Such progress toward wisdom is difficult. As Konosuke Matsushita suggested, it requires a deeply developed sense of self and an equally developed sense of others. This constant awareness ensures that obligations, as well as opportunities, are being met. With self-awareness and other-awareness, it is possible to do not only one's job, but also the right thing. Although this may sound mechanical, even the most committed firms find it difficult to achieve this consciousness consistently and constantly.

In a recently published study of business ethics, Joseph Badaracco of Harvard and Allen Web of McKinsey observed that the "ethical climate of an organization is extremely fragile." Having clear codes and a committed CEO is not enough to ensure that ethical behavior always wins in the jumbled, pressured, results-driven reality of business. Sometimes consciously, but often unconsciously, managers and employees do the "expedient thing" rather than the "right thing."

The "right thing" operates as the broad inspiration of moral purpose, as well as on the daily scale of interaction and activity. Solomon writes, "Wisdom will not enter a shifty soul, nor make her home in a body that is mortgaged to sin. This discipline will have nothing to do with falsehood; she cannot stay in the presence of unreason, and will throw up her case at the approach of injustice. Wisdom is a spirit devoted to man's good."

Although it makes business sense to pursue wisdom, and it is increasingly a strategic asset, wisdom will grow only where the intent and desire to "do good" — to do the "right thing" — is sincere and genuine. While companies can indeed be wise, this is a renewal model that cannot be fudged. It cannot be implemented halfway and there is no "how-to" program.

How do we reconcile rest and refreshment with the need for urgency?

The great rush by executives to embrace the pressures of change has shown that companies can be as ineffective in operating with urgency and intensity as they have been with old models of rigid process and protocol. Speed does not make up for a lack of substance. For all the entrepreneurial flair and technological imagination in Silicon Valley during the 1980s, very few companies became Apple. And for all the opportunities and low barriers to entry in software in the 1990s, there is only one Microsoft. There have been lots of flashes, but very few enduring businesses. In even the most volatile industries, speed only buys you a chance to succeed.

Rosabeth Moss Kanter, the Harvard professor and author of *When Giants Learn To Dance*, writes in a recent essay: "When I examined the differences between success and failure in change projects or development efforts, I found that one major difference was simply time. Staying with it long enough to make it work." It still takes those old-fashioned virtues of patience and perseverance to keep a company going.

Matthew Fox, a theologian and ecologist who has recently written a book about work and morality, observes that enduring change cannot be achieved through fear but only through "pleasure." Organizations that mandate change without the opportunity for employees to gain context and those that use fear to increase output and efficiency may win a short-term gain, but only at the high price of long-term fatigue.

To contrast the dominant view of corporate change with the wise one, I have developed the following list of attributes and characteristics.

———————

TRADITIONAL CHANGE	CONTINUOUS CHANGE
• Change based on a threat	• Change based on support
• Mandated from the top	• Encouraged through peer interaction
• Fear motivated	• Hope motivated
• Imposed	• Induced
• Corrective	• Restorative
• Reflexive	• Anticipatory
• Big, one-time hits	• Continuous and incremental
• "Surviving" motivated	• "Thriving" motivated
• Diminishing and "downsizing"	• Enriching and growth oriented
• Depleting	• Energizing
• Constraining	• Creative
• Externally driven	• Internally driven

Continuous change, like continuous improvement, operates on principles of reciprocity and shared responsibility. Partnership is more enduring and therefore more effective than subordination. And the inner commitment by all team members achieves greater efficacy than efforts that are mandated.

As with continuous improvement, continuous change takes patience. Frenzied people, of course, do not know how to make time even for important things. Frenzy has become the modern business interpretation of change. But productivity alone is not efficacy, just as quantity is not necessarily quality.

Gary Hamel and C. K. Prahalad explore this speed-success paradox from the perspective of competitiveness: "Yet another way in which competition for the future is different than competition for the present is time frame. Today, speed is of the essence." But innovation is rarely achieved instantaneously. Opportunities take time to come to fruition. This is why so many of the companies scrambling for access to the information superhighway are still unclear about what the business will be that will actually travel on that electronic infrastructure.

Having observed and studied numerous companies and industries, Hamel and Prahalad conclude that "leadership in fundamentally new industries is seldom built in anything less than 10 to 15 years, suggesting that perseverance may be just as important as speed in the battle for the future."

"Perseverance" has yet to make it into the lexicon of change consultants. It is an invisible virtue, rarely included in strategic planning or in discussions of employee performance and corporate culture. Perseverance is neither measured nor nurtured. But as we know from the study of creativity, even when inspiration occurs as a thunderbolt, a breakthrough has always involved consistent, persistent, and sometimes painful diligence. Big ideas are rarely random or casual, just as the quick fix is rarely the enduring one. When asked why his work stood out over those of his peers, composer Igor Stravinski responded that he simply worked harder and longer than any one else he knew.

In our global economy, speed is important. The urgency within companies is not artificial. However, the only way to go faster, to have decisions flow intuitively, and to have empowered, responsive employees make the calls is to take the time to create the necessary support. The deliberate nurturing of the human capacity to interpret a complex situation creatively is what delivers the fastest, most strategically intelligent solution. The more harried the business reality, the deeper the need for thoughtful grounding and wise discernment. Urgency is ultimately served by obligation.

With the advance of information technology, we now operate in a "Just-In-Time" world. What was once an innovation for inventory management in manufacturing is now an ethos. Companies are no longer able to luxuriate in long-term plans — they must devise "Just-In-Time" strategies. To reduce overhead and maximize flexibility, companies are also using more outside resources, assigning temporary, "Just-In-Time" employees to projects.

These changes are realizing improvements in speed, responsiveness, and flexibility. A tactic has again become a strategy. However, Just-In-Time is not simply an exercise in logistics. Achieving the needed cooperation for making this enmeshing of various, autonomous parts work requires a heightened sense of interdependence. The buyer needs the supplier as much as the supplier needs the buyer. Hence, the benefits of Just-In-Time are only fully realized when mutuality, reciprocity, and respect are fully at play. Thoughtful wisdom, rather than slowing things down, is actually the accelerator for achieving the fastest speed and the greatest synergy.

IBM is taking this concept of Just-In-Time to a new, even more complex level. Bill Etherington says it is impossible to determine which technology will achieve the greatest market acceptance. Advances are moving too fast, the competition is too intense, and the innovations too far ranging to be able to predict winners. IBM is therefore proceeding on multiple fronts at the same time, using its own vast resources, plus hundreds of joint ventures, to "put out a lot of product and see what wins."

This is not a reactionary approach. In fact, serving up so many different alternatives is the only smart strategy for satisfying customers who have "so much choice" and "don't know what they want until they see it." Sony and other Japanese companies have been doing this for years because, as Etherington notes, "the Japanese have the great luxury of never having studied market research."

Operating at this level of complexity requires skill and competence throughout the organization. Instantaneous action on so many levels by so many people is only possible with an overriding supra-logic, a collective consciousness from which individual members can derive meaning and direction. Kevin Kelley calls this "the hive mind." Instead of following a linear path to market, organizations with this supra-logic "swarm" to an opening, or zig as a "flock" to a new opportunity.

There is no controlling strategy, although the speed and effectiveness are strategic. Action does not wait for instruction, but flows instead from a group intuition of what the "right thing" is to do. Time is saved because the decision-making path is not just compressed but redistributed. What prevents this ultimate decentralization from degenerating into chaos is that the freedom of action for each unit is balanced by an equally developed sense of obligation.

This enlightened empowerment works because, in Kelley's words, the group is "held together by the conflicting interconnected self-interests of individuals." Fusing expediency with effectiveness allows virtual corporations or, as in the case of IBM, virtual organizations, to work. The self-interest of the individual member of the swarm is best served by the collective good.

Kelley draws from Charles Darwin's study of the natural world to explain the organizational impact for technologically liberated and linked human beings: "There are a variety of swarm topologies, but the only organization that holds a genuine plurality of shapes is the grand mesh. In fact, a plurality of truly divergent components can only remain coherent in a network. No other arrangement — chain, pyramid, tree, circle, hub — can contain true diversity working as a whole. This is why the network is nearly synonymous with democracy or the market."

Wisdom that is encoded in the thinking, interactions, and output of a company allows the member units of a network the most flexibility in pursuing their own priorities and projects. It gives the sense of "other," ensuring that work is complementary rather than contradictory. And it provides the conviction for Just-In-Time urgency on all fronts of an operation.

As in life, the process toward wisdom is never complete. The circular path of ascending to insight and descending to application is continuous. In Japan, Just-In-Time distribution has now become a source of bottlenecks and inefficiency, not because the logic is wrong, but because the consequences of its success were unseen. Around Tokyo and Osaka, there are so many companies using Just-In-Time distribution, that the sheer number of Just-In-Time trucks has created impassable traffic jams. Plants often struggle with parts shortages and work slowdowns because materials arrive "Just-Too-Late."

This is not to suggest that Just-In-Time is not smart or important. What it does show is that our solutions and problems operate in a continuity — each contains the other. Nothing is as easy as it seems. Nothing happens without creating consequences. And nothing is impermanent. Change even overtakes the change agents.

Being fast in adopting new ideas will not necessarily bring the desired response. And if it does, that response itself may be short-lived. It still takes time to think through the implications, to balance trade-offs, and to ensure that the solution is worth the price. The wiser the company, the more comfortable it is in asking these questions and making these judgments. Wisdom therefore carries its own efficiency because the more it is practiced, the faster its insights and prudence will be applied to future problems.

What does wisdom do for shareholder value?

In the years of researching this book and testing its ideas in my consulting practice, I have had very different reactions to the concept of wisdom. These reactions confirm that wisdom is an uncommon business consideration. The CEO of a multinational company responded to the idea from the perspective of popular imagination: "When you say wisdom, I think of an eighty-year-old Tibetan monk."

A group of Generation X product managers at a multinational food company were less romantic and thought that "wisdom is another one of those yuppie things. Older people would worry about that."

One senior vice-president of marketing believed wisdom to be an intellectual exercise, stating that "wisdom is basically an academic issue." Another CEO of a high-tech company felt that what I viewed as wisdom, his organization called "competence or human capital."

My jogging partner, who works on the derivatives desk of a major bank, asked: "So, what does wisdom do for shareholder value?"

Look at the comeback of IBM. Just like many other companies, IBM had been through numerous restructurings. Wisdom was not a conscious objective, just as Louis Gerstner spent little time on articulating vision. The focus has been on action to serve customers. To give momentum to this objective, IBM has used a comprehensive system of benchmarking to establish where it stands relative to best performers throughout industry in key dimensions of performance. Such benchmarking is an act of both "consciousness" and "conscience": it forces attention and clarity on each act, each project, each interface; and it causes a reflective questioning on why some things work, and why others do not.

IBM did not go from smart, to stupid, to smart again. Its newfound wisdom did not arrive magically in the body of one person, or in the form of a specific management group. IBM shed about 25 percent of its workforce, but it effected its impressive rebuilding with largely the same people who were there in the first place. Gerstner did slash costs and shed fat, but he did not depreciate the wisdom latent within his impressive organization. Where others only saw waste and duplication, he also saw unexploited potential.

As results have shown, there is a wise artistry in Gerstner's tough leadership. Michelangelo said that he sculpted by releasing the shape that was already in the marble block. Similarly, the potential that IBM is now showing has been there all along. It only needed the right conditions and inducements from Gerstner and others within IBM for this already present energy to be released.

Seeing the latent wisdom is a tough lesson that such companies as Chrysler and IBM were forced to learn. Others, without waiting to be eighty years old and without crisis, affirm wisdom consciously as a strategic and developmental essential.

Kyocera is a high-tech ceramics company. In addition to being the world's largest supplier of ceramics as a base for microchips and other electronic components, Kyocera also produces "ceramic teeth, ceramic replacements for body parts, ceramic auto engines, ceramic knives, and ceramic bases for solar heating."

Kyocera is very successful and is regarded by graduating students as the best company in Japan to work for — ahead of Sony, Mitsubishi, and Toyota. The company's motto is "Respect Heaven and Love People." Even for Japan, such a statement has only fringe appeal. However, Kyocera does not so much subscribe to the Zen in its motto as practice it every day. Kazuo Inamori, the enigmatic founder and CEO, admits that he "dreams in tiny increments." He sees the potential in every single activity and product, and believes that the largest success is built on such humble, focused attention.

Inamori tells his employees to try to "have a perfect day." The objective is not just to be mistake-proof, but, more importantly, to be fully conscious. With this consciousness, the full questioning, learning, intelligence, and experience of employees are applied to all tasks and interactions.

With such expectations of consciousness, Kyocera is a very demanding place to work. Yet, because its values are so clear and because it works hard to "not separate the abstract from the practical," Kyocera thrives. It attracts people for whom such questioning and consciousness are already important. The company does not so much add wisdom as release that which its employees already have.

Although a driven and difficult company, Kyocera maintains a certain equilibrium by virtue of senior management's enthusiasm for getting their hands dirty. Inamori explains that "we are so good at mixing and baking, because the top people in the company were in front of the kilns all the time."

This is more than the essential practicality of wisdom. Such intimate and deliberate practice ensures that managers never have employees undertake projects or initiatives they do not have personal experience in doing themselves. This is a deeper involvement than the popular practice of "management by walking around." It creates not only accessibility and dialogue, but also the very foundation of justice that is so essential for organizations in constant transition.

As shown by IBM and Kyocera, the practice of wisdom is an everyday occurrence. Whether in response to crisis, or by purposeful design, this wider, deeper context unleashes individuals and companies to work fervently for a cause. It builds trust for greater communication. Such consciousness requires a great commitment from employees, and a deep self-awareness from the company as a whole. As you would expect in a quest for such higher potential, its clarity and focus require disciplined concentration. Programs like "benchmarking" and "management by mixing and baking" represent the hard work of achieving a presence of mind, of recognizing strengths and weaknesses, and of acknowledging and accessing the wisdom already present.

In addition to consciousness, the practice of wisdom also creates conscience. Inamori believes that the responsibility of managers begins with "providing for both the material good and spiritual welfare of my employees." This seems harder and more costly than the normal management pursuits of providing the proper tools and safe environment for productive work. Yet this concern with the broader fulfillment of employees propels performance to a higher level.

Like Hewlett-Packard, Kyocera is a high-tech company whose many innovations are the result of culture and people — not machines or computers. It derives real value, hard competitive advantage, and profits from this wise concern for the integrity and total potentiality of each employee. Conscience, then, is the ultimate pragmatism. And in the practice there is the constant revelation of the ideal.

The hard work of seeking wisdom yields consistent results, but also saves companies from the even more difficult challenge of recovering from folly. The pain of implementing quality is much more pronounced for those companies that have allowed attention to quality to lapse than for those who have persistently and unwaveringly sought it. The creation of a new justice system to fulfill the potential of empowerment is much more difficult for those companies that neglected fairness in the first place. Wisdom requires the investment of conscious-seeking, but it still costs much less than the follies it averts.

A segmented or narrow focus on profit is proven to be less profitable than a wider set of goals. Kyocera grows with its respect for "heaven." Merck and Johnson & Johnson thrive with their driving commitment to human health and well-being. Procter & Gamble continuously renews itself because of its principal dedication to its employees. Hewlett-Packard innovates and establishes new markets because of its defining orientation to the creativity of its engineers. Sony is a world leader because of its determination to unleash the best in each employee.

These are companies that have succeeded remarkably and delivered profits consistently while pursuing higher aims. Collins and Porras compared some of these companies with key competitors and concluded: "Contrary to business school doctrine, we did not find 'maximizing shareholder wealth' or 'profit maximization' as the dominant driving force or primary objective through the history of most of the visionary companies. They have tended to pursue a cluster of objectives, of which making money is only one — and not necessarily the primary one."

Stakeholder value has too often come to mean quarterly result. Shortsightedness is already synonymous with foolishness, and much has already been written about the institutional disadvantage suffered by North American companies as a result of performance myopia.

Norm Simon, executive vice-president of corporate communications at Bell Canada, explains that "survival is no longer simply a function of profit management because profit management can only be achieved by pushing out service and product deliverables." The nature of competition and the value-generating possibility of information mean that the attributes of wisdom now drive performance. Simon believes that to split one from the other "is a semantic failure. Survival demands wisdom as much as price."

Collins and Porras observe: "Profit is like oxygen, food, water and blood for the body; they are not the point of life, but without them, there is no life." Aristotle drew a similar metaphor about wisdom. He wrote: "Wisdom produces happiness, not as medical science produces health, but as health does."

Profit and wisdom are emerging as essential factors in modern business success; however, the difference is that profit is a consequence while wisdom is a condition. Too many of us in business forget that. As shown in the following contrast, to even try to separate the two now represents the height of folly.

CONDITION	CONSEQUENCE
• *Ennobling cause* to provide meaning as well as commercial purpose.	• Guidance for action even when circumstances overtake strategy.
• *Compassion* for needs of employees, customers, and communities.	• Value-added becomes an essential deliverable. Innovation flourishes.

- A commitment to *Justice*.

- Prevailing fusion of *Pragmatic–Idealism*.

- Engenders the reciprocity and personal accountability with which performance and synergy are realized and maximized.

- Performance and profits flow naturally from the attention to immediate detail and the needed investment for long-term success.

How does wisdom affect advantage?

Peter Danielson at the Centre for Applied Ethics at the University of British Columbia has stretched the understanding of the mutual advantage of morality by conducting highly innovative tests with artificially intelligent robots. In various "games," robots programmed to logically maximize advantage for themselves showed that "rationality condemns us to non-optimal outcomes."

As Danielson introduced various degrees of moral constraint (first "conditional co-operation," then "reciprocal co-operation") he showed that "a player capable of responsively constraining herself to pursue outcomes mutually beneficial to itself and other similar players is substantively more rational than a straightforward maximizer. Properly designed moral principles are better means to a player's ends."

There are several reasons for including an experiment from the world of artificial intelligence in this argument.

First, the artificial world, although complicated to program, is still one of very simple choices and motivations. While primitive, this provides a revealing simulation for the much more complicated world of human interaction.

Second, the language and character of business is assuming more and more of the character of the technology it has so ardently adopted. This reminds us that technology is not neutral; it has potential for both exploitation and liberation.

Third, we so respect science that we often accord the behavior of machines more credibility than human beings. That moral robots do better than rationally self-seeking ones will sway some business people to reconsider their biases more than any human argument or case history.

As Norm Simon suggested, we tend to see bottom line as something different from culture, potential, or human values. Even those who acknowledge a relationship between wisdom factors and profit often still separate these two concepts. They are, in fact, increasingly symbiotic. Hamel and Prahalad note that "when the pace of genetic evolution falls behind the pace of environmental change, a species, like the dinosaurs, can get wiped out. The corporate equivalent is wholesale layoffs and massive restructuring. Only with anticipatory unlearning can one hope for a bloodless revolution." The unlearning most needed is that of regarding wisdom and profit as divergent.

Organizations tend to follow the same developmental cycle as human beings. This was the point raised by Philippe de Gaspé Beaubien, the founder and chairman of Telemedia (a global communications company) in a recent speech to Canadian broadcast executives. Beaubien noted that individuals grow "from the dependence of children to the independence of adolescence and young adulthood." This is where identity is defined and personal needs, goals, ambitions, and dreams are set. Beaubien went on to note that as individuals continue their maturation they eventually come to realize that "we are defined even more by our interdependencies" — by our connections to family, community, company, and society.

Interdependence is not the same as dependence. It is not a weakness but a perspective. Through that lens of interdependence, advantage, competitiveness, success, and results are even more important because they carry the weight and obligation for the whole as well as for the self. From this sensitivity to the collective, we learn the following.

1. *Success, productivity, and competitive advantage are not realized by new technology but by people.* Human beings, not the hardware or software, create value. This may be surprising, but it is especially true in the new economics of the information age. While there is a relative abundance of capital and a plethora of technological potential, there remains a limited pool of human talent, creativity, and vision to drive it. Hence the reason Dreamworks SKG attracted $2.5 billion in commitments from corporate behemoths in only three months of operation.

2. *Unity works.* Whether the inspired unity of Kyocera, or the forced entrenchment at IBM — employees and managers united by a purpose produce outstanding results, often in excess of what even the most clever executive could plan for. Bill Etherington explained that the phenomenally successful Thinkpad laptop was "entirely an accident. The scary thing is that it was not planned because we didn't believe we could differentiate the product. Laptops are laptops, right?" But, in the end, an engineer in its research lab created the now famous "pointer," and IBM's laptop became the industry gold standard. After suffering endless embarrassment, IBM's products suddenly assumed the cachet of Nike, becoming so coveted that teens bought Thinkpad carrying cases (without the computer inside) to carry books to school.

3. *Great performance is achieved in the continuous interaction between idealism and pragmatism.* While other ceramic makers saw themselves as a "dirt and dirty" business, Inamori kept asking how his craft-skills could better serve human well-being. Rather than stick to tiles, Kyocera leapt into medical and electronic and

automotive applications, raising the art of ceramic-making to the most demanding specifications of the highest-technology industries. The ideal inspired the practice, but the practice legitimized and gave value to the ideal. Over 120 years ago, Ralph Waldo Emerson wrote: "Raphael paints wisdom, Handel sings it, Phidion carves it, Shakespeare writes it, Wren builds it, Columbus sails it, Luther preaches it, Washington arms it, Watt mechanizes it." Wisdom is not what you think, but what you do as a result of what you think.

4. *Productivity is a function of purpose as well as process.* Restructuring has had a largely defensive rationale. Fix this problem, cut these costs, streamline this process — or go out of business. Survival is certainly important and motivating, but it is a base-level preoccupation. The human spirit seeks to build, to understand, to break through new boundaries into the unknown. This restlessness is not incidental to business. Technology, information, and globalization are destroying many of the existing economic, social, and institutional structures. While cost-cutting serves efficiency in the midst of that destruction, it does not ensure that either the capacity or capability for rebuilding and recreating are brought to the fore. Purpose makes people productive in this more positive reconstruction. It frees people to create new value — not simply stretch the efficiency value that already exists.

5. *Common sense, which provides the enthusiasm for wisdom, is contagious.* Wise leaders do not design and erect wise organizations. Instead, they inspire wise action among the people that follow them. This is the source of sustained competitiveness at companies like Hewlett-Packard and Johnson & Johnson. These organizations understand that the sensibility to do good, to do the right and responsible thing, is latent in people: it is part of our makeup. What is needed is the confidence, imagination, and inspiration to awaken that inherent common sense. Like any other valued asset, it takes disbursement and hard work to grow that sense into wisdom. But, unlike discoveries which can be eventually copied or machinery which eventually wears down, wisdom is a self-generating asset. Once activated, it grows, compounds, accumulates, providing a return far in excess of any investment.

6. *Learning, the currency of the information economy, requires cooperation.* Consider the practice of benchmarking. This has emerged as a pivotal discipline for evaluating, incorporating, and mastering the best practices of the best companies. Benchmarking has been the stick with which Xerox finally beat back its Japanese competitors. It is also the carrot IBM has used to recently resurrect itself.

To learn from the best, companies must often benchmark against their own competitors. In fact, there have been numerous associations and consortia created to facilitate a structured benchmarking exercise, and these often include direct and antagonistic competitors. The Telecommunications Benchmarking Consortium, as an example, includes AT&T, MCI, Bell Atlantic, GTE, and Ameritech. Although the benefits from such collaboration are compelling enough to form the structure, attitudes of antagonism often impede the flow of mutually beneficial learning. In *The Benchmarking Book*, Michael Spendolini writes: "Interestingly, many organizations admit that one of the greatest barriers to this type of benchmarking is themselves. Traditional stereotypes of competitors as untrustworthy or as the enemy get in the way of basic communication among competitors."

This is not an unusual realization. Robert Grundin observes that self-interest defeats virtually any creativity. He writes: "Surprisingly, competitive instincts can impede our powers of discovery. When we compete with our local peers, especially with the purpose of making them realize that we are better than they, we limit ourselves to their models of expertise."

7. Urgency is a reaction, not a cause. There are two types of urgency — that which we control, and that which controls us. The latter is the most common. Urgency that controls us causes us to second-guess what will be and what competitors will do. It is as exhausting as jogging on quicksand.

The urgency that we control is much rarer. It flows from a profound sense of self, and a desire to master something for a larger cause. It anticipates and is enlivened with the energy of leadership and vision. Because all the inner steps, stages, and considerations have been attended to, it flows without panic, without destructive sacrifice.

Taking the time to do it right, with the full benefit of wise development, is usually also the fastest way to complete a project. In "Why Transformation Efforts Fail," John Kotter concludes that many companies did not "anchor changes in the corporation's culture." He argues that change becomes a positive factor for continuous renewal only "when it seeps into the bloodstream of the corporate body." This requires taking the time to use every meeting and every project to reinforce new values, as well as "taking sufficient time to make sure that the next generation of top management really does personify the new approach."

To hurry to an outcome without grounding the needed skills and new attitudes, without nurturing the sustaining wisdom, achieves change that is disruptive without being effective, and tiring without yielding renewal.

Selected Bibliography

Aaker, D. A. and A. L. Biel (eds.) (1993) *Brand Equity and Advertising*. Hillsdale: Lawrence Erlbaum Associates, Inc.

Argyris, C. (1994) "Good Communication That Blocks Learning," *Harvard Business Review*, July–Aug.

Armstrong, K. (1993) *A History of God*. New York: Ballantine Books.

Arnott, N. (1994) "Selling Is Dying," *Sales & Marketing Management*, Aug.

Barnard, C. I. (1990) "The Nature of Executive Responsibility" in A. Campbell and K. Tawadey (eds.) *Mission and Business Philosophy*. Oxford: Butterworth-Heinemann Ltd.

Bartlett, C. A. and S. Ghoshal (1994) "Beyond Strategy to Purpose," *Harvard Business Review*, Nov.–Dec.

Bercholz, S. and S. C. Kohn (1993) *Entering the Stream: An Introduction to Buddha and His Teachings*. Boston: Shambhala.

Berry, T. (1988) *The Dream of the Earth*. San Francisco: Sierra Club Books.

Bohm, D. (1987) *Science, Order and Creativity*. New York: Bantam Books.

Bonaventure, St. *Journey of the Mind to God* (trans. P. Boelmer 1993). Indianapolis: Hackett Publishing Company Ltd.

Borg, M. J. (1994) *Meeting Jesus Again for the First Time*. New York: HarperCollins.

Boyd, J. (1994) "Reengineering . . . Japanese Style," *InformationWeek*, Dec. 5.

Boyett, J. H. and H. P. Conn (1991) *Workplace 2000*. New York: Dutton.

Bridges, W. (1994) *Jobshift: How To Prosper in a Workplace without Jobs*. London: Nicholas Brealey Publishing.

Bstan-'dzin-ryga-mtso, Dalai Lama XIV. (1994) *The Way to Freedom*. New York: HarperCollins.

Buchanan, D. and D. Boddy (1992) *The Expertise of the Change Agent*. Hertfordshire: Prentice Hall International (U.K.).

Campbell, A. and K. Tawadey (eds.) (1990) *Mission and Business Philosophy*. Oxford: Butterworth-Heinemann Ltd.

Carroll, P. (1993) *Big Blues: The Unmaking of IBM*. New York: Crown Publishers.

Clarke, E. G. (1973) *The Wisdom of Solomon*. Cambridge: The University Press.

Cleary, T. (1992) *The Essential Confucius*. New York: HarperCollins.

Cleaver, A. (1993) "Business in a Changing World," *RSA Journal*, Jan.–Feb.

Collins, J. C. and J. I. Porras (1994) *Built to Last: Successful Habits of Visionary Companies*. New York: HarperCollins.

Covey, S. R. (1989) *The Seven Habits of Highly Effective People*. New York: Fireside.

Csikszentmihalyi, M. (1993) *The Evolving Self: A Psychology for the Third Millennium*. New York: HarperCollins.

Dalla Costa, J. (1991) *Meditations on Business*. Scarborough: Prentice Hall.

Danielson, P. (1992) *Artificial Morality: Virtuous Robots for Virtual Games*. London: Routledge.

de Kerckhove, D. (1995) *The Skin of Culture*. Toronto: Somerville House.

De Pree, M. (1987) *Leadership Is an Art*. New York: Doubleday.

Dobyns, L. and C. C. Mason (1994) *Thinking About Quality*. Toronto: Random House.

Dolnick, E. (1995) "Less Is More," *Utne Reader*, May–June.

Dorsey, D. (1994) *The Force*. Toronto: Random House.

Drucker, P. F. (1991) "The Discipline of Innovation" in J. Henry and D. Walker (eds.) *Managing Innovation*. London: Sage Publications.

Drucker, P. F. (1992) *Managing for the Future*. New York: Truman Talley Books.

Drucker, P. F. (1993) *The Post-Capitalist Society*. New York: HarperCollins.

Durlabhji, S. and N. Marks (1993) *Japanese Business: Cultural Perspectives*. Albany: State University of New York Press.

Erikson, E. (1969) *Gandhi's Truth*. New York: W. W. Norton & Company.

Fierman, J. (1994) "The Death and Rebirth of the Salesman," *Fortune*, July 25.

Foster, C. (1995) "Tough Guys Don't Cuss," *Canadian Business*, Feb.

Frankl, V. E. (1959) *Man's Search for Meaning*. New York: Simon & Schuster.

Frye, N. (1991) *The Double Vision: Language and Meaning in Religion*. Toronto: University of Toronto Press.

Gardner, H. (1993) *Creating Minds*. New York: BasicBooks.

Ginzberg, E. (1985) *Beyond Human Scale*. New York: BasicBooks.

Graham, P. (1995) *Mary Parker Follett: Prophet of Management*. Boston: Harvard Business School Press.

Grundin, R. (1990) *The Grace of Great Things: Creativity and Innovation*. Boston: Houghton Mifflin Company.

Halberstam, D. (1991) *The Next Century*. New York: Easton Press.

Hamel, G. and C. K. Prahalad (1994) *Competing for the Future*. Boston: Harvard Business School Press.

Hampden-Turner, C. (1990) *Corporate Culture: From Vicious to Virtuous Circles*. London: Economist Books.

Handy, C. (1991) "What Is a Company For" *RSA Journal*, March.

Handy, C. (1994) *The Age of Paradox*. Boston: Harvard Business School Press.

Handy, C. (1995) "Trust and the Virtual Organization," *Harvard Business Review*, May–June.

Hassard, J. and M. Parker (1993) *Postmodernism and Organizations*. London: Sage Publications.

Henry, J. and D. Walker (eds.) (1991) *Managing Innovation*. London: Sage Publications.

Ingrassia, P. J. and J. B. White (1994) *Comeback: The Fall and Rise of the American Automobile Industry*. New York: Simon & Schuster.

Jacob, R. (1995) "Corporate Reputation," *Fortune*, March 6.

Jaques, E. and S. Clement (1991) *Executive Leadership*. Oxford: Basil Blackwell Ltd.

Jones, J. P. (1990) "The Double Jeopardy of Sales Promotion," *Harvard Business Review*, Sept.–Oct.

Kanter, R. M. (1991) "Change-Master Skills: What It Takes To Be Creative" in J. Henry and D. Walker (eds.) *Managing Innovation*. London: Sage Publications.

Katz, D. (1994) *Just Do It: The Nike Spirit in the Corporate World*. Toronto: Random House.

Katzenbach, J. R. and D. K. Smith (1993) *The Wisdom of Teams*. Boston: Harvard Business School Press.

Kelly, K. (1994) *Out of Control*. Toronto: Addison-Wesley.

Kennedy, N. (1989) *The Industrialization of Intelligence*. Cambridge: Cambridge University Press.

Koselka, R. (1994) "It's My Favorite Statistic," *Forbes*, Sept. 12.

Kosko, B. (1993) *Fuzzy Thinking*. London: HarperCollins.

Kotter, J. P. (1988) *The Leadership Factor*. New York: The Free Press.

Kotter, J. P. (1995) *The New Rules*. New York: The Free Press.

Kung, H. (1989) *Christianity and Chinese Religions*. New York: Doubleday.

LaBier, D. (1986) *Modern Madness*. Reading: Addison-Wesley.

Lancaster, H. (1994) "A New Social Contract To Benefit Employer and Employee," *The Wall Street Journal*, Nov. 29.

Lefebure, L. (1993) *The Buddha and the Christ: Explorations in Buddhist and Christian Dialogue*. Maryknoll: Orbis Books.

Levitt, T. (1986) *The Marketing Imagination*. New York: The Free Press.

Lewis, C. S. (1977) *Mere Christianity*. London: HarperCollins.

Lorenz, K. (1987) *The Waning of Humaneness*. Toronto: Little Brown and Company.

Madsen, P. and J. M. Shafritz (1990) *Essentials of Business Ethics*. New York: Meridian.

Matsushita, K. (1990) "Human Resources and Philosophy" in A. Campbell and K. Tawadey (eds.) *Mission and Business Philosophy*. Oxford: Butterworth-Heinemann Ltd.

Maucher, H. (1994) *Leadership in Action*. New York: ECON Executive Verlags.

McRae, H. (1994) *The World in 2020*. London: HarperCollins.

Mintzberg, H. (1994) *The Rise and Fall of Strategic Planning*. Toronto: Maxwell Macmillan Canada.

Negroponte, N. P. (1995) being digital. New York: Alfred A. Knopf, Inc.

Nhat Hanh, T. (1992) *Touching Peace*. Berkeley: Parallax Press.

Nonaka, I. (1991) "The Knowledge-Creating Company," *Harvard Business Review*, Nov.–Dec.

Normann, R. and R. Ramirez (1993) "From Value Chain to Value Constellation: Designing Interactive Strategy," *Harvard Business Review*, July–Aug.

Ozaki, R. S. (1991) *Human Capitalism*. New York: Viking Penguin.

Pagels, E. (1979) *The Gnostic Gospels*. New York: Random House.

Paschale, R. T. and A. G. Athos (1990) "Great Companies Make Meaning" in A. Campbell and K. Tawadey (eds.) *Mission and Business Philosophy*. Oxford: Butterworth-Heinemann Ltd.

Pitcher, P. C. (1995) *Artists, Craftsmen and Technocrats: The Dreams, Realities and Illusions of Leadership*. Toronto: Stoddart Publishing.

Reich, R. B. (1991) "Entrepreneurship Reconsidered: The Team as Hero" in J. Henry and D. Walker (eds.) *Managing Innovation*. London: Sage Publications.

Reid, P. (1990) *Well Made in America*. New York: McGraw-Hill.

Reid, P. (1991) "If We Can Do It, Any Company Can" in J. Henry and D. Walker (eds.) *Managing Innovation*. London: Sage Publications.

Rheingold, H. (1991) *Virtual Reality*. New York: Touchstone.

Rinpoche, S. (1993) *The Tibetan Book of Living and Dying*. New York: HarperCollins.

Sakaiya, T. (1991) *The Knowledge-Value Revolution*. Tokyo: Kodansha International.

Schumacher, E. F. (1975) *Small Is Beautiful*. London: Abacus.

Sebeok, T. (1994) *Signs: An Introduction to Semiotics*. Toronto: University of Toronto Press.

Sellers, P. (1995) "Now Bounce Back," *Fortune*, May 1.

Selye, H. (1976) *The Stress of Life*. New York: McGraw-Hill Inc.

Semler, R. (1993) *Maverick*. London: Century.

Senge, P. (1990) *The Fifth Discipline*. New York: Doubleday.

Singer, P. (1994) *Ethics*. Oxford: Oxford University Press.

Skynner, R. (1993) *Life and How To Survive It*. Toronto: Reed Books.

Smith, C. (1987) *The Way of Paradox: A Spiritual Life as Taught by Meister Eckhart*. London: Darton, Longman and Todd Ltd.

Smye, M. (1994) *You Don't Change a Company by Memo*. Toronto: Key Porter.

Spendolini, M. (1992) *The Benchmarking Book*. New York: American Management Association.

Sternberg, E. (1994) *Just Business: Business Ethics in Action*. London: Little Brown and Company.

Stewart, T. (1994) "Intellectual Capital," *Fortune*, Oct. 3.

Stewart, T. (1994) "How To Lead a Revolution," *Fortune*, Nov. 28.

Taylor, W. C. (1994) "Control in an Age of Chaos," *Harvard Business Review*, Nov.–Dec.

Telushkin, J. (1994) *Jewish Wisdom*. New York: William Morrow and Company.

The Economist (1995) "The Kindergarten That Will Change the World," March 4.

The Economist (1995) "The Mass Production of Ideas and Other Impossibilities." March 18.Thomson, J. A .K. (trans.) (1953) *The Ethics of Aristotle*. London: Penguin Books.

Tichy, Noel with S. Sherman (1993) *Control Your Own Destiny or Someone Else Will*. New York: Doubleday.

Tillich, P. (1988) *The Spiritual Situation in Our Technical Society*. Macon: Mercer University Press.

Tuchman, B. (1984) *March of Folly*. New York: Alfred A. Knopf, Inc.

Turner, F. (1995) "The Freedom of the Past," *Harpers*, April.

Underhill, E. (1995) *Concerning the Inner Life*. Oxford: Oneworld.

von Daehne, N. (1995) "Database Revolution," *Success*, May.

Warshaw, M. (1995) "Renegades 1995," *Success*, Jan.–Feb.

Waterman, R., J. A. Waterman and B. A. Collard (1994) "Toward a Career-Resilient Workforce," *Harvard Business Review*, July–Aug.

Westley, F. and H. Mintzberg (1991) "Visionary Leadership and Strategic Management" in J. Henry and D. Walker (eds.) *Managing Innovation*. London: Sage Publications.

Wikström, S. and R. Normann (1994) *Knowledge and Value*. London: Routledge.

Wood, C. (1994) *The End of Japan Inc*. New York: Simon & Schuster.

Wurman, R. S. (1989) *Information Anxiety*. New York: Doubleday.

Zemke, R. with D. Schaaf (1989) *The Service Edge*. Toronto: Penguin.

Zuboff, S. (1988) *In the Age of the Smart Machine*. New York: BasicBooks.

Index